Computational and Mathematical Modeling in the Social Sciences

Mathematical models in the social sciences have become increasingly sophisticated and widespread in the last decade. This period also has seen many critiques, most lamenting the sacrifices incurred in pursuit of mathematical rigor. If, as critics argue, our ability to understand the world has not improved during the mathematization of the social sciences, we might want to adopt a different paradigm. This book examines the three main fields of mathematical modeling – game theory, statistics, and computational methods – and proposes a new framework for modeling. Unlike previous treatments that view each field separately, this book provides a framework that spans and incorporates the different methodological approaches. The goal is to arrive at a new vision of modeling that allows researchers to solve more complex problems in the social sciences. Additionally, a special emphasis is placed upon the role of computational modeling in the social sciences.

Scott de Marchi is Assistant Professor of Political Science at Duke University. His work has been funded by the National Science Foundation, and he has published articles in the *American Political Science Review*, *Journal of Politics*, *Journal of Theoretical Politics*, and *Public Choice*. Professor de Marchi was appointed a Fellow-at-Large by the Santa Fe Institute in 1999 and is a faculty member of the Ralph Bunche Summer Institute and the Empirical Implications of Theoretical Models program. His research continues to focus on the field of computational political economy and other mathematical methods, individual decision making, the presidency, and public policy.

Computational and Mathematical Modeling in the Social Sciences

SCOTT DE MARCHI

Duke University

CAMBRIDGE UNIVERSITY PRESS
Cambridge, New York, Melbourne, Madrid, Cape Town, Singapore, São Paulo

Cambridge University Press
40 West 20th Street, New York, NY 10011-4211, USA

www.cambridge.org
Information on this title: www.cambridge.org/9780521853620

© Scott de Marchi 2005

This publication is in copyright. Subject to statutory exception
and to the provisions of relevant collective licensing agreements,
no reproduction of any part may take place without
the written permission of Cambridge University Press.

First published 2005

Printed in the United States of America

A catalog record for this publication is available from the British Library.

Library of Congress Cataloging in Publication Data
De Marchi, Scott.
Computational and mathematical modeling in the social sciences / Scott de Marchi.
p. cm.
Includes bibliographical references and index.
ISBN 0-521-85362-1 (hardback) – ISBN 0-521-61913-0 (pbk.)
1. Social sciences – Mathematical models.   I. Title.
H61.25.D42   2005
300'.1'51 – dc22   2005007051

ISBN-13   978-0-521-85362-0 hardback
ISBN-10   0-521-85362-1 hardback

ISBN-13   978-0-521-61913-4 paperback
ISBN-10   0-521-61913-0 paperback

Cambridge University Press has no responsibility for
the persistence or accuracy of URLs for external or
third-party Internet Web sites referred to in this publication
and does not guarantee that any content on such
Web sites is, or will remain, accurate or appropriate.

For Jim Barefield and Ed Christman

Contents

Acknowledgments	*page*	ix
Prelude		xi
1	Not All Fun and Games: Challenges in Mathematical Modeling	1
2	Looking for Car Keys Without Any Street Lights	34
3	From Curses to Complexity: The Justification for Computational Modeling	78
4	Why Everything *Should* Look Like a Nail: Deriving Parsimonious Encodings for Complex Games	113
5	KKV Redux: Deriving and Testing Logical Implications	144
6	A Short Conclusion	176
References		181
Index		191

Acknowledgments

Without a larger research community, it would have been difficult for me to complete a project of this scope. I am particularly fortunate because an astonishing number of people have read versions of this manuscript and taken the trouble to try to correct the numerous blemishes and mistakes present in my work, some of which remain despite their efforts. I owe a great debt to Jennifer Harrod, Mike Munger, and Lyle Scruggs who (for different reasons) have been forced to talk to me about this project for the last several years. Bob Keohane and I taught a course on qualitative methods in the fall of 2003 at Duke University, and without our weekly conversations and his close reading of the manuscript, I would not have finished. John Aldrich and George Rabinowitz, at numerous coffee breaks and lunch meetings, have both been very influential in how I have approached the issues raised in this book. Ken Kollman, John Miller, and Scott Page are responsible for my interest in applying computational methods to social science, and they offered good advice at every stage of writing this manuscript. My editor Scott Parris at Cambridge has made the final steps of completing this manuscript much easier than I had thought possible.

Some really smart people read the manuscript and sent me comments, including Chris Bond, Jorge Bravo, John Brehm, Russ Denton, Charles Franklin, Chris Gelpi, Hein Goemans, Jeff Grynaviski, Jay Hamilton, Mel Hinich, Jerry Hough, Seth Jolly, Bill Keech, Dean Lacy, Karl Lietzan, Emerson Niou, Brendan Nyhan, Phillip Rehm, Jason Reifler, Tom Scotto, Curt Signorino, Terry Sullivan, Mike Tofias, Camber Warren, and Steven Wilkinson. There are also several groups of people who have helped in indirect ways: the Emerging Solutions Group at PricewaterhouseCoopers, my current poker group (which is just as likely to do Monte Carlo work as not after a game), and the brave souls I have played Diplomacy with over the last two decades. Finally, I'd like to thank the Tooks, Daniel and Jennifer, for everything else.

Prelude

When Aeneas fled from burning Troy, he had some difficult decisions to make. His first priority was to rescue his country gods and relics, but he was covered in gore from combat and did not want to carry these sacred artifacts with his own hands. His solution was novel: Anchises, his father, could carry the artifacts and Aeneas would carry him upon his back. His second priority was to guard the safety of his wife Creusa and his son. With his heavy burden, he "satisficed" by holding the hand of his son and bidding his wife to follow him. Unfortunately, though he succeeded in rescuing the country gods and his son, he lost his wife during his flight from the doomed city.

Earning the appellation "pious" involved some cruel choices for Aeneas, but despite this offense to modern sensibilities (I daresay many of us would have tossed the country gods and told Anchises to walk on his own two feet), it is hard to blame him. Weary from battle, burdened with both his family and the country gods, it would be difficult to pay attention to everything of merit. It is not surprising that he did not even know when or how he had lost his wife.

Graduate school has some similarities. Granted, most students do not have to face a ravaging horde of Greek soldiers, nor are they surrounded by burning buildings. But the press of time is a constant weight, and one is forced to attend to some matters more than others. It is not a coincidence that if you ask students trained in the top research programs in the social sciences what their field is they may answer "mathematical methods" or even something more precise such as "game theory" or "econometrics." Most students spend a large fraction of their time learning these methods, and this comes at the expense of other sorts of work such as history and case studies. Like pious Aeneas, we make choices, and even the most heroic of us are forced to ignore many worthwhile subjects.

The important thing to note is that many of the social sciences, most notably political science and economics, have made a wager. This wager involves both time and space. From graduate students to faculty, we spend our time learning and practicing mathematical methods, in particular game theory and statistical modeling. For the journals and presses, the lion's share of space is devoted to the results generated by mathematical methods. One does not find the best journals customarily publishing case studies of individual countries, firms, or political campaigns. Nor, in the case of the top journals in political science, is much advice (either prescriptive or predictive) given to real-world political actors. Based on the 2002–2003 Report of the Editor of the *American Political Science Review*, 69% of submissions were accounted for by the formal, quantitative, or formal *and* quantitative categories; 63% of accepted articles were in these categories – this during the tenure of an editor striving for diversity.

The presumption of this book will be to examine this epistemological gamble more closely and recommend a set of changes to current practice. It is not as if every scholar has embraced the increasing emphasis on mathematical methods. The last two decades have seen many critiques, most lamenting the sacrifices incurred in pursuit of mathematical rigor. If, as the critics argue, our ability to understand the world has not improved during the mathematization of the social sciences, we might want to adopt a different paradigm. Historiography (or qualitative research) is most often presented as the alternative to the abstractions of mathematical methods. It might, say the critics, be better for the discipline to turn out area-specialists who at least know the history of their cases than to engage in bad modeling that lacks any clear connection to the real world.

I have the good fortune of better than adequate training in history,[1] and I can argue with some fervor that a turn to historiography would not

---

[1] I took undergraduate degrees in computer science and history. Because of latent schizophrenia, I completed the coursework and thesis for a Master's degree in European history at the University of North Carolina–Chapel Hill before switching to the social sciences.

be good for the social sciences. Despite its problems, I remain devoted to mathematical modeling, and the goal of this book is to improve current practice rather than to supplant it. Area-specialization and case studies are necessary prerequisites for the inspiration and understanding implicit in all good models, but in my mind they do not of themselves constitute a coherent methodology for discovering causal relationships.[2]

Required reading for those who wish to supplant mathematical methods with qualitative research should include Peter Novick's *That Noble Dream: The "Objectivity Question" and the American Historical Profession* (1998). From the end of the 19th century to the beginning of the Cold War, history as a discipline was very similar in outlook to modern political science.[3] Novick's book lays out the history of the professionalization project in American history departments over this time period. Much like current social science disciplines, historians believed in their ability to understand causal relationships in the world and sought to give answers to pressing questions about how one prevents war between nation-states or the republican cycle of decay highlighted by political theorists such as Machiavelli.

The problem, after a century of consensus on method, was that historiography foundered upon the shoals of the objectivity question. For Novick, historians who believed in scientific objectivity never adequately answered the fundamental questions of how to tell good research from bad and neutral research from biased. Many historians, spurred on by the emergence of social history and other trends, simply did not believe that the empirical, objectivist tradition produced superior research.[4]

---

[2] There is an enormous literature on qualitative versus quantitative research. For an examination of some of the problems implicit in historical research from a political science perspective, good examples are Lustick (1996) and Goemans (2000).

[3] Although there was not great technical skill present in most historical research, there was a belief in empirical work and the use of history for understanding causality in human affairs. The letters of Henry Adams (at Harvard) to Herbert Baxter Adams (at Johns Hopkins), for example, demonstrate a high level of familiarity and respect for the hard sciences among practicing historians at the end of the 19th century and a belief that scientific objectivity was a worthwhile aspiration for the social sciences.

[4] For an example of an alternative approach to historiography, read Natalie Zemon Davis's *The Return of Martin Guerre* (1983). Davis's work concerns a French tale from the 16th century in which a woman discovers her husband is an imposter and takes him to court. Because the penalty was death by hanging, this was no laughing

One of the more sobering examples Novick uses to illustrate the death of objectivity in the historical profession is the case of David Abraham. The role of German industrialists in the rise of the Nazi Party was a contentious one, and Abraham, a junior faculty member at Princeton in the early 1980s, wrote a manuscript that emphasized the structural relationships in German society that precluded a more moderate outcome to the political turmoil of the Weimar state.

Unfortunately for Abraham, his abstract modeling, which was influenced by Marxist theory, did not endear him to senior researchers in the field. Despite many positive book reviews, Henry Turner at Yale University and Gerald Feldman at the University of California at Berkeley led an assault on Abraham's book. They believed that the footnotes to Abraham's monograph contained serious, willful errors. Misattributed citations, missing or incorrect quotations, and other errors were, in fact, plentiful in Abraham's work. For Turner and Feldman, these mistakes were proof of a malicious agenda that violated norms of historiography. In a book review in *Political Science Quarterly*, Turner wrote:

> Invoking the familiar primacy of economics, Abraham presents a highly reductionist version of the dissolution of the Republic and the rise of Nazism, which he explains in terms of his vastly simplified model of German society.... Unfortunately, Abraham's footnotes do not marshal evidence adequate to support his thesis. Informed readers will also balk at his disparagement or omission of institutions, ideologies, and personalities vital to comprehension of the German calamity. (Turner 1982, 740)

It is hard to convey how contentious this affair became. The journal *Central European History*, for example, featured an exchange between Feldman and Abraham that even included a complete list by Abraham of his errors and whether or not the corrections helped, hurt, or were neutral to his argument. The exchange appeared in press in 1985, but by then Abraham had been driven from the field. For Novick, who was Abraham's advisor, the lesson for historians was that optimism

---

matter. Davis had completed a screenplay on the story and found that her "appetite was whetted" for a more scholarly investigation, despite the lack of an expansive historical record on the story. Her approach to this problem is distinct from previous understandings of historiography: "Watching Gerard Depardieu [the actor] feel his way into the role of the false Martin Guerre gave me new ways to think about the accomplishments of the real imposter, Arnaud du Tilh. I felt I had my own historical laboratory, generating not proofs, but historical possibilities" (Davis 1983, viii).

about the ability to discern causality in history had been replaced by a naïve and defensive empiricism. Other than getting one's footnotes right, there was no other avenue for attacking or defending a model.

There are more modern examples of the continuing crisis in historiography. Michael Bellesiles's book *Arming America: The Origins of a National Gun Culture*, which presented the argument that gun culture in early American society was not as widespread as believed, won the Bancroft Prize when it was released in 2000. Much like Abraham, Bellesiles riled opponents of a different political stripe, and upon scrutiny, it was discovered that much of the data underlying the book's quantitative analysis was either misused (in the case of probate data) or entirely missing from the archives. Despite these glaring problems, the question remained about whether or not his core argument was valid. Ultimately, like Abraham, Bellesiles was forced from the discipline, resigning his post at Emory University under pressure from the trustees at the end of 2002. The Bancroft Prize for his book was rescinded shortly thereafter.[5]

Although I do not believe that Novick has much of a remedy for historiography, I do accept his diagnosis of the problem. If a particular methodological paradigm is to survive, a large majority of practicing scholars has to believe that the costs involved in training and research are merited. Simply put, the output of a methodology has to be superior results, at least compared to existing alternatives. The question economists and political scientists should ask is whether or not Novick's history of the erosion of the belief in objectivity among historians holds any lessons for us.

Despite the enormous successes made possible by the mathematical approach – the Arrow, McKelvey, and Schofield work on social choice is an excellent example – many critics, rightfully, want to know what the last decade has produced. The argument that I will present in this book is that the practice of mathematical modeling is due for a revision. In particular, existing methods are brittle when confronted with complex problems, and there is a genuine lack of correspondence

---

[5] A special issue of the *William and Mary Quarterly* (2002) featured essays by Bellesiles and several other historians that examine the controversy and its implications for historiography.

between deductive models, on the one hand, and empirical tests of these models, on the other.

There are additional problems unique to each of the two major subfields within mathematical methodology. Game theory, for example, has a troubling answer to the question "Is game theory meant to predict what people do, to give them advice, or what?" As Camerer (2003, 5) notes, many game theorists believe that "game theory is none of the above – it is simply 'analytical,' a body of answers to mathematical questions about what players with various degrees of rationality will do. If people don't play the way the theory says, their behavior has not proved the mathematics wrong, any more than finding that cashiers sometimes give the wrong change disproves arithmetic." Although there are examples of formal modelers tackling real-world problems, such as the interesting work of Groseclose, Milyo, and Primo on topics that include the dollar value of a House of Representatives seat, campaign finance, and empirical measures of media bias, many game theorists do not believe that their work needs an empirical referent.[6]

Statistical methodology in the social sciences has its own set of problems that mirrors the opening passage in Dickens's *A Tale of Two Cities*. We have increasingly sophisticated forays into Bayesian and nonparametric techniques. At the same time, replication continues to be problematic, especially as the complexity of statistical methods increases. Recently, the laudable goal of linking formal theory with statistical models has received renewed attention in the research of Signorino and others. Yet, most published research continues to ignore the most basic tenet of statistical work, which requires out-of-sample testing to validate a model.[7] Never before has training in statistical modeling been so widespread in graduate departments around the nation. So, too, has suspicion deepened, as many researchers have adopted Achen's (2003) admonition that a model with more than three independent variables is immediate cause for concern.

---

[6] On the value of a seat, see Groseclose and Milyo (2004a); on campaign finance, see Primo and Milyo (2004); and, on media bias, see Groseclose and Milyo (2004b). Behavioral game theory also tries to put game theory on a more empirical footing – Camerer's book provides a nice introduction to the field. One also might visit Roth's Web site at http://www.economics.harvard.edu/~aroth/alroth.html.

[7] For an excellent statement on statistical modeling that also happens to make this point on the neglect of out-of-sample work, see Good and Hardin (2003).

While some might question whether or not mathematical methodology is in need of revision, it is the case that a sense of unease permeates the social sciences. Those who do not practice these methods are deeply suspicious of the validity of results generated from mathematical models. And those that do practice one field of mathematical methodology are often just as suspicious about the other fields. I will argue that at least some of this suspicion is warranted, and the goal of this book is to provide a set of tools designed to increase transparency and improve modeling. Part of this enterprise involves a constructive critique of existing practice. Despite the widespread belief that the problems that beset mathematical methods are idiosyncratic to each subfield, I will demonstrate that there are a set of underlying problems that span subfields (including analytic, empirical, and qualitative).

Of the problems detailed in this book, the most severe is the curse of dimensionality. In the nonparametric statistics and artificial intelligence literatures, the "curse of dimensionality" is incredibly important, but it is not well known in the social sciences. In brief, the curse states that for any interesting problem, one should count the size of the parameter space needed to model the problem, paying special attention to how large this space becomes as the problem increases in size. If the parameter space implied by a naïve encoding of the problem is huge, one must resort to domain-specific information and a good dose of cleverness to surmount the curse of dimensionality. A brief example will clarify this informal definition.[8]

In the social sciences, preferences are almost always the subject of assumption rather than study. We simplify preferences by imposing *a priori* that for most human decisions, preferences are unidimensional, single-peaked, symmetric, and so on.[9] There is little justification for these assumptions, so why do we make them? Mathematical convenience is the typical answer, but this masks a more serious difficulty. Without simplifying assumptions, many of our models would produce different or unpredictable results.

---

[8] An excellent overview of this problem for statistical models is found in Chapters 4 and 8 of Harrell (2001).

[9] Note that assumptions of this type go well beyond more fundamental (and defensible) axioms such as well-ordered preferences and transitivity.

To be more concrete, imagine you were in an expensive ice cream parlor and had never before tasted ice cream. In addition to the flavors of ice cream, you have the option of adding sprinkles, nuts, syrups, and the like. All told, you have 10 flavors of ice cream and 10 different optional ingredients and want to test every possible flavor so that you could determine a preference ordering. This natural enough desire would probably bankrupt the store (and require you to do some shopping for larger clothes), as $10 \cdot 2^{10}$ possible combinations (recipes) exist. Unless one imposes limiting assumptions on the nature of preferences, there are no shortcuts possible – you would need to test every flavor if you wanted to be certain about your preference ordering. In many cases, you would feel justified in asking for this huge number of samples, because most everyone would agree that although sprinkles and marshmallows taste great singly, in combination they might be too sweet. Recipes are one example where the different dimensions of choice are nonseparable. We do not independently sample each ingredient, arrive at a set of ideal points, and then throw them all together in a pot.

This problem worsens if the ice cream parlor subsequently adds ingredients. Imagine you had just completed the extensive taste tests outlined above and then strawberries were provided as a new option. Would you be able to somehow "save" the results of your previous search, or would you have to begin an entirely new set of tests?[10] Few of us would think that adding strawberries to a hot fudge sundae, for example, would improve the sundae, whatever our preference for strawberries. It is easy to see that as the number of ingredients increases, the size of the resultant parameter space for ice cream recipes expands exponentially – and this is not a good thing![11] In the context of recipes, making the assumption that preferences are always separable would be quite odd, and would likely lead to equally odd results. One should instead depend upon domain-specific knowledge about cooking to simplify matters, but it may not be obvious how to go about this.[12]

---

[10] This exercise is left to readers, especially for those who like ice cream.

[11] I will argue throughout this book that trying to understand a problem like preference formation, without assuming away the complexities of the phenomenon (e.g., nonseparability), is a very important activity despite the ugly combinatorics involved.

[12] Domain-specific knowledge is information about the problem under consideration. Unidimensionality, for example, is appropriate to some contexts and not others – for

Ice cream recipes aside, how ubiquitous is the curse of dimensionality? Some readers will immediately point to statistical work, where the curse of dimensionality appears in a nearly equivalent form. Often, our data are insufficient for testing the huge parameter spaces implied by our independent variables and modeling choices. Like the preferences literature, empirical modelers often resort to limiting assumptions (e.g., linearity of the functional form) to derive results. We rightfully question these results due to their dependence upon atheoretic modeling choices and data mining.

The curse of dimensionality is not, however, limited to statistical work. Game theoretic work falls prey equally often. Assumptions are also parameters, and the structure of game theory comes at the price that results are conditioned upon the values chosen for these assumptions. Additionally, not just any assumptions will do, as formal modelers have to find a way to fit problems into the encoding of game theory (i.e., an extensive or normal form representation of strategies, explicit utility functions, and backwards induction as the solution algorithm). Many "games" do not fit comfortably within this encoding; as a consequence, technical assumptions end up doing a great deal of heavy lifting in many formal models. The intellectual process involved in finding a set of assumptions, choosing an equilibrium concept, and choosing an abstract game to produce an outcome desired *a priori* is not different in kind from the curve fitting of some empirical researchers.

It is important to go beyond criticism, however. The more important objective of this book is to provide both a framework for evaluating models and a set of tools designed to deal with the problems sketched in this prelude. The curse of dimensionality highlights the difficulty of using mathematical models to study complex phenomena. Contributing to this difficulty is the gap between analytic models and empirical tests; it is not a coincidence that as we extend our reach to investigate more complex phenomena, concerns have grown about the quality of our results. One consistent answer to these difficulties is to keep modeling simple, such that one can understand

---

recipes, it would be inappropriate. In all cases, one has to justify assumptions by the final performance of the model, not by appeals to abstract and untested notions about rationality or mathematical simplicity.

and test all the moving parts in a given model. This position is elaborated quite well by Axelrod (1984), but it is not surprising that his advice is largely ignored by scholars attempting to "push the envelope." The main question is how to build more complex models of behavior without sacrificing the ability to subject the results to exacting scrutiny.

Thus, I do not believe that mere ignorance accounts for the existing problems in mathematical modeling in the social sciences. Rather, the complexity inherent in many problems of interest has hampered our ability to generate models with clear empirical referents. In this book, I will integrate computational modeling into existing methods and demonstrate how many classes of problems demand a shared approach that includes computational modeling.[13] Computational methods are poorly understood (and sometimes poorly utilized) in the social sciences, despite an increasing presence in both training and research. Yet, it is my contention that computational modeling offers several advantages over traditional modeling strategies when confronted with a variety of games and decision contexts.

THE BOOK IN A NUTSHELL

There are three components to this book. The first builds a framework for evaluating models. Whatever the methodological orientation of a model, one should ask the following questions:

1) What are the assumptions/parameters of the model? Do the values chosen for the parameters come from qualitative or empirical research, or are they chosen arbitrarily (i.e., for convenience)? More important still, do the assumptions spring from a consideration of the problem itself, or are they unrelated to the main logic of the model?
2) Is there any assurance that the results of the model are immune to small perturbations of the parameters; that is, is there an equivalence class where the model yields the same results for a

---

[13] At the broadest level, computational models are numerical experiments where one uses computers to simulate a problem rather than solve it deductively – Monte Carlo statistical methods are one familiar example.

neighborhood around the chosen parameters? Or, is the model brittle?

3) Do the results of the model map directly to a dependent variable, or is the author of the model making analogies from the model to the empirical referent? Although toy models[14] have their place in developing intuition, they are difficult to falsify, and even more difficult to build on in a cumulative fashion.

4) Are the results of the model verified by out-of-sample tests? In this book, it will be argued that the only appropriate out-of-sample tests for a model are either

   a. a large-N statistical approach that tests the model directly;
   b. a logical implication derived deductively from the model.

5) Is the parameter space of the model too large to span with the available data? This, as noted earlier, is the curse of dimensionality, and one should never neglect the importance of bean counting. To cope with large parameter spaces, did the author of the model derive a domain-specific encoding, provide a feature space,[15] or use theory in other ways to lessen the impact of the curse of dimensionality?

Topics 1–3 are covered in Chapter 1 of this book. In addition, Chapter 1 presents a comprehensive statement on epistemology that justifies the above framework. Topics 4 and 5 are covered in Chapter 2, which also introduces the concept of feature spaces and their role in surmounting large parameter spaces. Examples using currency adoption and the security studies literature on militarized interstate disputes illustrate the main concepts.

While the first two chapters focus on how to assess models, Chapters 3 and 4 focus on the second component of this book: computational

---

[14] Toy models are defined here as a class of simple models without any unique empirical referent. For example, the iterated prisoner's dilemma (IPD) is a simple game that investigates cooperation. It seems unlikely that all of human cooperation is a two-player contest with the exact strategy set of the IPD, and there is enormous difficulty in analogizing from the IPD to actual human behavior with enough precision to do any sort of predictive work.

[15] Feature spaces will be covered in Chapter 2. Feature spaces use domain-specific information (i.e., theory) to reduce the dimensionality/complexity of a problem.

methods and their role in addressing more complex phenomena. The use of computational methods makes it easier to build models that directly map to empirical tests. The main topics are:

1) How do game theoretic and computational models differ? Illustrations will be drawn from the artificial intelligence and combinatorics game theory literatures.
2) How does one "break up" a problem into smaller pieces, thereby overcoming the curse of dimensionality? The concepts of component games and idiosyncratic utility functions are examined in detail.
3) How does one use statistical work or logical implications to verify the results of a computational model (to the degree this is possible)?

In addition to these questions, these chapters provide a gentle introduction to the skills needed for computational modeling. Topics include programming languages, good programming style, and testing computational results.

The final component of the book provides two lengthy illustrations of the main concepts of the previous chapters. Chapter 4 presents the first example, which builds a complete encoding for a complex alliance game. Unlike most game theoretic models, the alliance game presented here has infinite strategies, four or more players, and the possibility of cooperation between different, endogenously created coalitions. Chapter 5 returns to the problem of the ice cream store and nonseparable preferences. Unlike situations in which one has enough high-quality data to do out-of-sample statistical work, studying nonseparable preferences requires the creation of logical implications to leverage existing survey data.

1

Not All Fun and Games

Challenges in Mathematical Modeling

INTRODUCTION

In large part, the inspiration for this book came from three sources, which can be categorized neatly as a failure, a challenge, and an ideal. First, the failure. When I began teaching in the profession, I was immediately assigned to graduate methods coursework. This is the experience of many professors trained in the last decade with a mathematical bent, and I was lucky enough to teach at an institution with an excellent culture. Unlike many other political science departments that exist in a state in which "there is war of every one against every one," Duke's political science department is almost entirely free of disputes about the value of mathematical modeling in the social sciences. Divisions of opinion certainly exist but, more or less, everyone in the department recognizes the virtue of mathematical methods for at least some problems.

Better still, even those who do not practice mathematical modeling believe in good research design. As many prospective faculty members discover during their job talks, "methods questions" and questions about research design are just as likely to come from the theorists of the department as anyone else (though couched in different terminology). Between job talks, faculty brown bags, and informal interactions graduate students have with faculty, it would be hard to finish a Ph.D. at Duke and not try your hand at mathematical modeling.

Despite this positive culture, teaching graduate methods coursework has not been easy. As has been noted in numerous places, the shock most politics students experience on entering graduate school is severe. They expect to talk shop, debate the issues, and deal with "big" questions about the state of the world; instead, their first experience of graduate training at Duke involves a mathematics camp in the dull heat of August. No weighty matters of politics are discussed in this camp, unless one thinks that urns and the different colors of balls one places in them are of great import. Some students take years to get over this shock, essentially repeating much of their methods coursework when they come to a point in their own research where they have a pressing need for it. Others acquire good technical skills but nonetheless have great difficulty finding interesting questions or arriving at "good" models. Clearly, my best efforts were not sufficient and it drove me to think about issues of modeling in the social sciences and how one should attempt to improve matters.

In particular, why were so many bright graduate students, many of whom had good technical skills, unable to make the leap to generating testable theories? Why did many graduate students identify themselves primarily by their choice of method (e.g., game theory) rather than their research question? And, finally, were there any features of mathematical methodology in political science that added to the difficulty of training graduate students? These questions form a thread that continues throughout this book, and, hopefully, the questions offered here will demonstrate that many of the problems in training are related to conceptual problems in our mathematical methodologies.

The second influence on this book concerns a challenge to the discipline raised by Beck, King, and Zheng (hereafter, BKZ). Their paper – "Improving Quantitative Studies of International Conflict: A Conjecture" – appeared in the *American Political Science Review* in 2000. The paper was a broad challenge to empirical work throughout the social sciences, not just in international relations, and turned on the idea of what the proper relationship was between deductive models (usually represented by game theory) and empirical work (applied statistics). Normally, the ideal paper for the mathematical modeling crowd is a well-specified game that reaches some equilibrium outcome, which is then instantiated and tested in an appropriate statistical model. If hiring is any signal of departmental preferences, empirical work or game theoretic work alone is not as desirable as a combination of the two.

The importance of the paper by BKZ is that they argue for an entirely different approach. Instead of modeling the data generating process (DGP), they assume it is complex and interactive, and that prior efforts to model the origin of conflicts using game theory have not amounted to much (at least not anything testable). They conclude that the only reasonable standard for evaluating a statistical model is out-of-sample performance, without regard to the assumptions or specification of the statistical model. Not surprisingly, they adopt a nonparametric approach and use a neural network to generate an empirical model of conflict without regard to any underlying theory. Their article thus challenges the current methodological orientation of the discipline, insofar as they eschew the ideal of mapping a strategic game to an empirical specification.

I was confident that BKZ were wrong on several particulars, most notably whether their model actually outperformed the standard logit model used by many scholars in quantitative international relations. Along with Christopher Gelpi and Jeffrey Grynaviski, I wrote a reply addressing this problem. Additionally, we presented a general framework for comparing models when the goal is maximizing out-of-sample performance.[1] The larger epistemological questions raised by BKZ remained, however, and their challenge cast into doubt the proper relationship between deductive and empirical models. This dispute and how it relates to the broader themes of this book are dealt with starting in the next chapter.

The final source of inspiration that led to this book concerned an ideal of the proper approach to mathematical modeling in the social sciences. This ideal was first advanced in a set of workshops dubbed "Empirical Implications of Theoretical Models" (hereafter, EITM) funded by the National Science Foundation (NSF) in 2002. After these initial meetings, EITM evolved into a joint effort of Harvard, Michigan, Duke, and Berkeley to train advanced graduate students during the summer. Unlike other methods workshops that focus on particular skills (e.g., the Interuniversity Consortium for Political and Social Research's summer courses), EITM has the larger, epistemological goal of helping young researchers to bridge the divide between

---

[1] Our article, plus a response from BKZ, is in the May 2004 issue of the *American Political Science Review*.

deductive and empirical methodology. The goals of EITM were summarized in a 2002 report presented at the NSF:

> Significant scientific progress can be made by a synthesis of formal and empirical modeling. The advancement of this synthesis requires the highest possible levels of communication between the two groups. Formal modelers must subject their theories to closely related tests while, at the same time, empirical modelers must formalize their models before they conduct various statistical tests. The point is not to sacrifice logically coherent and mathematical models. Rather, it is to apply that same rigor to include new developments in bounded rationality, learning, and evolutionary modeling. These breakthroughs in theory will be accomplished with the assistance of empirical models in experimental and non-experimental settings.
>
> How will progress be measured? There are several performance indicators, including the number of articles that use formal and empirical analysis in the major professional journals. Another measurable indicator is the number of NSF grant proposal submissions by faculty and graduate students (doctoral dissertations) that use both approaches. However, the one area that may be the most difficult to measure is improvement in the quality of knowledge. In this regard, the ramifications of merging formal and empirical analysis is a transformation of how researchers think about problems and whether they take intellectual risks in synthesizing the model and testing it. When they do, the primary achievement of EITM will be a better understanding of the political and social world, more accurate predictions, and ultimately the provision of solid information to policymakers whose choices can profoundly affect citizens' quality of life.

Although out-of-sample forecasting is specifically emphasized in the above passage, it is obvious that the EITM founders have in mind something quite different than the nonparametric work of BKZ. Their goal is to rework the discipline so that the chasm between formal modelers and empirical researchers is bridged, with the hopes that this synthesis will lead to better models that have clearly testable empirical hypotheses.

By and large, I was very sympathetic to the goals of EITM, and was lucky enough to be invited to participate as a faculty member in the 2003 session at Michigan. My job seemed easy: take two days and present a framework for accomplishing EITM-style research. In my mind, this meant making an argument for how one might bridge the gap between models (usually deductive) and empirical tests; currently, the clearest statement of the difficulties inherent in this problem is found in two articles by Signorino (1999) and Ramsay and Signorino (2003). After a bit of reflection, the issues involved were more difficult than I at first realized. Many of the arguments presented in this text are a direct result of the questions I faced in formulating my talks for EITM. Chapter 3 lays the groundwork for this investigation, and Chapters 4 and 5 provide a set of tentative answers to how one might implement the EITM statement on methodology.

WHAT THIS BOOK IS NOT

Before proceeding, it is important to say what this book is not. This book, despite appearances in some places, is not a critique of game theory (or formal theory more broadly). Although I am critical of some current practices, it should be obvious that I firmly believe in the aspirations of those who wish to make political science an actual science, complete with predictions and policy advice about events in the real world. My main concern is that game theory has become confused with definitions of human rationality. In this text, I will argue that game theory is a mathematical tool, not a proxy for human rationality where if one departs from game theoretic models one automatically sacrifices any notion of rational agents. As a tool, it is one way to "solve" problems and is better suited to some classes of problems than others. Most of the examples I focus upon concern classes of problems that for a number of reasons are ill-suited for a game theoretic approach, and I propose a set of methods "rational" agents might employ to deal with these complications. The reason for providing tools that expand the class of problems one can deal with analytically is in my mind simple: better models, with more verisimilitude, allow an easier transition to empirical tests. This is the primary goal advanced by EITM.

Game theory also has been confused with pure mathematics, insofar as many practitioners feel no need to connect their models to empirical tests. Much that masquerades under the classification of "theory building" is not worth the appendices, and one should question the usefulness of models that rely upon limiting assumptions to produce whatever narrow result is desired by the researcher.[2] Following Granger (1999),

---

[2] Arrow's impossibility theorem, in contrast, depends upon assumptions that are of substantive interest and produces a result that is extraordinarily broad.

the viewpoint adopted here is that the connection between theoretical models and their empirical referents needs to be direct enough such that we can be satisfied that the tests we conduct are actually dispositive. Dispositive tests distinguish the actual model (or data generating process) from the universe of possible models. This viewpoint is by no means new; rather, it has been the subject of debate in economics for decades.[3] What is perhaps new will be the particular modeling approach adopted here, which combines traditional game theoretic investigations with computational models. The reason for this union hopefully will become clear in subsequent chapters.

This book is also not a critique of empirical work in political science, though, again, one might be confused given that in places I am critical of existing efforts. Just as models without empirical tests are suspect, so, too, are data-driven statistical investigations that fail to make apparent what model is being tested. Good statistical work allows us to distinguish useful models from the universe of irrelevant models; further, it allows us to investigate the generality of a model and the places where assumptions are carrying too much of the load. I will, however, place rather more emphasis on predictive work than is currently the norm within the social sciences, as much of the statistical research that has been conducted in the social sciences aims solely at comparing the in-sample performance (or "explanatory power") of various models.

In-sample comparisons should be seen as innately suspect, as one can easily overfit a statistical model and claim "success" for a theory. More time will thus be spent in this text addressing the curse of dimensionality that has to this point been largely ignored by social scientists.

A Simple Example: Applause, Applause

As is fitting for a book on modeling, let us begin with a simple question. Hopefully, this will introduce most of my essential arguments before we wade into the deep end of the book. The history of this example is

---

[3] See, for example, the October 1993 *Special Issue Anniversary of the American Journal of Agricultural Economics*. Castle (1993) and Leontief (1993) are particularly useful in this issue, insofar as they outline a set of requirements that would help connect deductive models with empirical tests.

a rich one, given that it was used for many years by John Miller and Scott Page at their Computational Economics Workshop at the Santa Fe Institute.[4]

Imagine you are asked to explain or predict the occurrence of standing ovations. You have a performance of some type, where each member of the audience receives a signal from the performance about how good it is (based upon their own internal preferences). Each audience member can then choose to do nothing, applaud, or stand and applaud. They also can sit down again at any point should they decide to stand initially. This is a highly stylized problem but has relevance for social scientists. We often want to understand who stands, or votes, or participates in a riot, and how individual characteristics and social dynamics lead to this behavior.

There are different approaches one might take to this problem, and in social science one can roughly describe the three methodological traditions that could be utilized: empirical, deductive (i.e., game theoretic), and computational. Let us investigate what sorts of answers these traditions, in isolation, might provide to the standing ovation problem.

An empirical researcher would likely start out with questions concerning what measures would be collected for both the dependent and independent variables, and not all of the forms of these measures would be obvious. For example, the dependent variable might be coded as a binary variable measuring whether or not the ovation occurred. If this encoding is adopted, what would the right threshold be for distinguishing an ovation? Would 90% have to stand? More? Less? The choice of scale for the dependent variable is also not obvious; one could change both the temporal and spatial characteristics of the dependent variable. For example, one encoding would measure the length in time of the ovation, but any such measure of time would retain the problem of choosing an appropriate threshold. Alternately, one could measure the likelihood that any given audience member participates in the ovation, thus changing the unit of analysis spatially from the entire audience to each individual member.

---

[4] Past answers to this problem are archived at http://zia.hss.cmu.edu/econ/homework95.html. For the most recent investigation of this problem, see Miller and Page (forthcoming).

Another more insidious problem would involve the nonindependence of observations.[5] Cleary, if subsets of the data set involved repeat performances by the same artist, "buzz" might result in a lack of independent, identically distributed (IID) observations. This problem also would complicate the measure of independent variables. Measures of performance quality and the like could easily be contaminated by interactions either between guests of the same performance (e.g., social pressure) or for members that attend multiple performances across observations in the data set. And members of different audiences are obviously not drawn from identical distributions, as people sometimes choose which performances they attend.

Problems aside, what sorts of questions would the empirical researcher answer? Likely, it would involve establishing relationships between such concepts as "performance quality" (as perceived by the audience), the type of performance, the number of audience members, and so on, and the likelihood or length of an ovation.

A deductive (or formal) modeler would come at this problem from a different angle, where the most important decision would involve specifying the benefits and costs that are present for members of the audience when they decide to ovate or not. Clearly, you do not want to be the only fool in the audience standing and clapping madly; people would stare. Just as clear, you do not want to be the grinch, sitting alone in a sea of excited fans. At some level, though "quality" matters, you only want to reward "good" performances with an ovation, given the effort involved in standing and clapping.

The structure of the game would also involve a set of important considerations on the part of the deductive modeler. How many periods would be included in the game where agents could update their information and make choices? If an ovation occurred, how would people get back to their seats? The same sorts of utility considerations discussed in the preceding paragraph would apply with equal force to agents making choices to sit back down again.

Given these modeling choices, and the input of a few "state of nature variables" such as the quality of the performance, the deductive

---

[5] One also might point out that the observations are not independent spatially – that is, whether or not one member of the audience stands (or later, sits) is likely correlated with the actions of other audience members.

modeler might well reach a good understanding of the individual decisions that work together to produce an ovation. A model might also help worried performance-goers in reaching decisions about whether or not to stand for an ovation in future performances. Ever present, however, would be the worry that the limiting assumptions relied upon to formulate a sufficiently simple model might cut against the usefulness of any insight gained.

The final tradition that might generate a solution for this problem is less well known in the social sciences. A computational (or dynamic systems) researcher, in contrast to the two preceding approaches, would specify a set of rules that governed the behavior of individual audience members, along with a set of contextual variables that described such features as the seating arrangement, the shape of the performance hall, relationships between audience members, and so on. What would these rules look like? On one level, the rules would be functional expressions that would be similar to the utility functions used by a game theorist, though these functions might well be allowed to vary both in time and by the individual type of audience member. On another level, these rules could add substantial verisimilitude to the computational model by incorporating features of the problem that would be difficult to model in a deductive framework (e.g., learning models based upon research in cognitive psychology). One such rule might involve adding vision to the model – given the shape of the performance hall, not all audience members can physically see all other audience members. Any utility function that involved peer pressure should be more sensitive to people within an agent's field of vision than agents outside this field.[6]

Unlike a game theoretic model, it is unlikely that a computational model would produce a set of deductive results. What is far more likely is that the researcher, confronted with the large parameter space generated by the rules used in formulating the computational model, would have to rely upon statistical investigations to understand

---

[6] The outcome of such a rule is that not all audience members are created equal – that is, audience members in the middle rows nearest the stage would have a disproportionate share of influence. One also might consider the type of individual audience members. For example, if a group of Catholics got together to watch a play, it might matter if the Pope were sitting in the audience. I would hazard that if the Pope ovates, so, too, would everyone else.

any "results" of the computational model, much as in the empirical tradition. Statistical relationships between parameters, rules of interest, and the likelihood of an ovation would then be presented, albeit substituting artificial data for real data.

This is a brief sketch of an interesting problem, but it raises questions of importance to all modelers. To begin with, are the approaches complementary or distinct? On the face of it, our three stereotypical methodologists would not have much to say to each other. The empirical researcher is establishing correlations between different measures and the likelihood of ovation; the game theorist provides advice on how rational audience members should select strategies; and the computational modeler incorporates aspects of both of the forgoing approaches to produce a dynamic model that recreates a standing ovation.

All of these models ostensibly explain the same phenomenon, but can one compare or integrate the results? Or, are these simply different answers to different questions? I will argue in the succeeding chapters that it is undesirable to let each type of modeler work in a vacuum; models need to produce results that are directly comparable to competing explanations. Even within each methodological approach, models are often not unique. Different modelers will produce different answers, and the job of social science should be to sort among them by insisting on out-of-sample tests of some kind. If, for example, we are confronted with several different game theoretic models, all explaining standing ovations, how do we decide which one is closest to being right? Unless one of the game theorists makes a deductive mistake, the models will differ because the assumptions differ. Arguing about assumptions is a little like arguing about whether Wolverine is tougher than the Hulk; ultimately, it comes down to taste. This book will argue that a different, integrated approach is required to make sense of these questions.

STRIFE BETWEEN METHODOLOGICAL CAMPS

Currently, there is a sense of mutual distrust between different methodological camps. Let us start with the more forceful critiques of the empirical tradition. As part of the EITM meetings, Christopher Achen argued that one must be suspicious of empirical modeling in the social sciences. Because many models are quite complex, researchers have an abundance of parameter choices that allow them to overfit models, generating any outcome they wish:

Empirical work, the way too many political scientists do it, is relatively easy. Gather the data, run the regression/MLE with the usual list of control variables, report the significance tests, and announce that one's pet variable "passed." This dreary hypothesis-testing framework is sometimes even insisted upon by journal editors. Being purely mechanical, it saves a great deal of thinking and anxiety, and cannot help being popular. But obviously, it has to go. Our best empirical generalizations do not derive from that kind of work. How to stop it? The key point is that no one can know whether regressions and MLEs actually fit the data when there are more than two or three independent variables. These high-dimensional explanatory spaces will wrap themselves around any data set, but typically by distorting what is going on. They find the crudest correlations of course: education increases support for abortion, for example. In the behavioral tradition, that counts as a reliable finding. But no one knows why education is associated with that moral position (higher intellect discovering the truth? mindless adoption of elite tribal norms? correlation with something else entirely?), and that leaves open the possibility that abortion attitudes do not work the way the literature says they do. Getting rid of this cheap sense of "empirical findings" is probably the central task that empirical political research faces....

As an instance of the altered perspective I have in mind, I propose the following simple rule: Any statistical specification with more than three independent variables should be disregarded as meaningless. With more variables than that, no one can do the careful data analysis to be sure that the model specification is what s/he says it is. (Achen in the National Science Foundation EITM Report, 2002, Appendix B)

Or, one might look farther back to Keynes, and his critique of the hapless Professor Tinbergen:

I infer that he considers independence of no importance. But my mind goes back to the days when Mr. Yule sprang a mine under the contraptions of optimistic statisticians by his discovery of spurious correlation. In plain terms, it is evident that if what is really the same factor is appearing in several places under various disguises, a free choice of regression coefficients can lead to strange results. It becomes like those puzzles for children where you write down your age, multiply, add this and that, subtract something else, and eventually end up with the number of the Beast in Revelation....

To the best of my understanding, Prof. Tinbergen is not presented with his time-lags, as he is with his qualitative analysis, by his economist friends, but invents them for himself. This he seems to do by some sort of trial-and-error method. That is to say, he fidgets about until he finds a time-lag which does not fit in too badly with the theory he is testing and with the general presuppositions of his method. No example is given of the process of determining time-lags which appear, when the come, ready-made. But, there is another passage where Prof. Tinbergen seems to agree that the time-lags must be given a priori....

These many doubts are superimposed on the frightful inadequacy of most of the statistics employed, a difficulty so obvious and so inevitable that it is scarcely worth the time to dwell on it. (Keynes 1939)

At root, Achen and Keynes are addressing the same problem in empirical methods. Unbeknown to anyone save the original researcher, choices are made in empirical work. *Lots* of choices. Given the obvious problem of false correlation, it does not seem too much of a stretch to imagine that any empirical modeler, given time, can produce almost any result that is desired. Journals and monographs, by their nature, only report "positive" results and only the "final" model. How much pain or guesswork or outright cheating at the margins that goes into an empirical paper is never seen in print. One way to think of this is to imagine every salient choice made by the empirical modeler as a parameter; results are thus conditional statements made upon the particular set of parameter values chosen. Given how large these implied parameter spaces are, one cannot place much faith in a final report of in-sample performance.

A deductive modeler (typically relying upon game theory) would certainly agree with the forgoing critique of statistical methods/econometrics. Moreover, most formal theorists believe that their methodological approach is immune to the flaws that plague other approaches. Niou and Ordeshook, for example, cite the transparency of formal theory as an enormous advantage over both qualitative and empirical methodologies:

But the rational choice paradigm and formalism are not mushrooms that sprung up in an unattended intellectual forest. They are reactions to a discipline mired in imprecision, vagueness, obscure logic, ill-defined constructs, non-testable hypotheses, and ad hoc argument. They are a reaction to a discipline that in the 1920s proclaimed the Weimar constitution the greatest political-intellectual achievement of its age; a discipline that in the 1960s substituted correlation for cause; a discipline submerged in such conveniently vague and ill-defined ideas as "power," "leadership," "authority," "group," "alliance," "function," "ideology," "culture," "regime," "stability," and "balance." They are reactions to a discipline that substituted the well-turned phrase for concrete constructs, operational measures for theoretical primitives, and the gloss of methodological sophistication for true theory. They are, in short, a reaction to a discipline that did and does precisely what Walt critiques the formal analyst of doing – burying key assumptions in an indecipherable format, although generally that format was a language more to the liking of those who studied French and Plato in college rather than calculus. (Niou and Ordeshook 1999, 87)

In addition, it is obvious that Niou and Ordeshook draw a sharp distinction between the results of formal theory (which are uncontestable; that is, the results follow deductively from the premises) and empirical work that could be rife with spurious correlation. Bueno de Mesquita and Morrow go even further in a defense of formal theory by arguing that of all the virtues one might discover in a social science theory, logical consistency is foremost:

Walt gives three criteria for evaluating social science theories: logical consistency, degree of originality, and empirical validity. We believe that logical consistency takes precedence over the other two criteria; without logical consistency, neither the originality of a theory nor its empirical validity can be judged. Logical consistency is the first test of a theory because consistency is necessary, though not sufficient, for understanding how international politics works.

A basic point in logic drives our view. A theory, in terms of logic, consists of a system of assumptions and conclusions derived from those assumptions. A logical inconsistency exists when two mutually contradictory statements can be derived from the assumptions of a theory. When such a contradiction exists in a theory, then any statement follows logically from the theory. There is, then, no discipline for arguments in a logically inconsistent theory; those using the theory are free to draw any conclusion they wish from the premises of the theory. Logical inconsistencies deny the possibility of a theory having empirical content. Theories derive empirical content by producing falsifiable hypotheses, conclusions that could be contradicted by evidence. A theory gains credence as more of its falsifiable propositions are supported by evidence, although there are no hard and fast rules here. However, because any pattern of evidence can be matched with some conclusion of a logically inconsistent theory, such theories cannot be falsified and so cannot have empirical content. A theory is falsified when an alternative is shown to fit the range of predictions better than the initial theory. Falsification of a theory cannot happen if any evidence can be interpreted as an implication of the theory....

Again, any conclusion can be derived when a logical inconsistency exists, and so the choice of which conclusion to use for policy purposes falls entirely on the tastes or prejudices of the party making the prescription. Indeed, the use of a logically inconsistent theory to justify a policy recommendation is worse than recommendations not supported by any theory....

For these reasons, we believe that logical consistency has pride of place among the criteria for judging social science theories. (Bueno de Mesquita and Morrow 1999, 56–7)

There is, of course, a problem with arguments that attempt to draw a sharp distinction between empirical modeling and formal theory. Although it is the case, as Bueno de Mesquita and Morrow note, that "any pattern of evidence can be matched with some conclusion of a logically inconsistent theory," the exact same statement is true of logically *consistent* theory. As should be obvious (but for some reason is not), one may achieve any outcome one desires with consistent theory; all it takes is the right combination of assumptions, solution concepts, and the like. The chore for formal theory cannot rest solely upon consistency, as *the class of "consistent" games that provide any given result is infinite*.

One can think of this argument in a different way. Imagine a researcher perceives an empirical regularity – for example, that candidates tend to take positions near the middle of a left-right ideological dimension. How many consistent models could the researcher construct that would produce center-seeking candidates? Infinitely many. And only some of the models are "right" in the sense that they are analogous to the real, underlying process. All the other (infinite) models are correlated with the empirical regularity in much the same way that an empirical specification is spuriously correlated with a given sample. Without finding novel data or deriving secondary conclusions, one cannot place much certainty in any single model of center-seeking candidates.[7]

So while one must agree with Bueno de Mesquita and Morrow that consistency is a necessary condition, the more important goal is to choose the "best" theory from the class of consistent theories that produce a desired result. Friedman (1953) sums up the problem created by attributing virtue to consistency alone:

Logical completeness and consistency are relevant but play a subsidiary role; their function is to assure that the hypothesis says what it is intended to say

---

[7] For a similar perspective worth further study, see Lave and March (1975).

and does so alike for all users – they play the same role here as checks for arithmetical accuracy do in statistical computations. One effect of the difficulty of testing substantive economic hypotheses has been to foster a retreat into purely formal or tautological analysis. As already, noted, tautologies have an extremely important place in economics and other sciences as a specialized language or "analytical filing system." Beyond this, formal logic and mathematics, which are both tautologies, are essential aids in checking the correctness of reasoning, discovering the implications of hypotheses, and determining whether supposedly different hypotheses may not really be equivalent or wherein the differences lie.... But economic theory must be more than a structure of tautologies if it is to be able to predict and not merely describe the consequences of action; if it is to be something different from disguised mathematics. And the usefulness of the tautologies themselves ultimately depends, as noted above, on the acceptability of the substantive hypotheses that suggest the particular categories into which they organize the refractory empirical phenomena. (Friedman 1953, 11–12)

Choosing a game that provides a given result (that you want to achieve *a priori*) is thus not at all different than the problem of false correlation in the statistical literature. Not only is this always possible, it is also the case that the mapping of formal theories to results is not a one-to-one correspondence.[8] One might appeal to maxims such as parsimony, or generalizability (or whatever) to discriminate between competing formal theories, but this is very slippery epistemological ground, and places such discrimination firmly in the land of taste rather than science.

Moreover, all choices that go into a particular formal theory that are left to the modeler should be seen as traversing a very large parameter space; again, this problem mirrors the corresponding complaint levied against empirical modelers. As Peltzman (1991) notes, "Game theory has introduced a rigor in the analysis of rational behavior that was missing [but] skepticism about the marginal value of recent theory is warranted [because] conclusions drawn tend to be very sensitive to the way problems are defined and to the assumptions that follow." Game theoretic results are conditional upon these choices, and given

---

[8] Other than trivial examples, it is clear that the mapping of theories X to results Y is a bijection but not an injection. Rather, mapping theories to results is a many-to-one process, and the goal of formal theory should be to sort between the class of possible theories.

the size of these parameter spaces, results must be seen as exceptionally brittle things when the only test is whether or not the formal theory produces an expected outcome. The problems that plague empirical methodologies thus have almost perfect analogues in formal modeling.

One example of the forgoing pathology in formal theory can be found in the dispute between Banks (2000) and Groseclose and Snyder (2000) in the pages of the *American Political Science Review*. Banks, in short, shows that one of the results in Groseclose and Snyder's original paper on creating supermajorities in legislatures is wrong; that is, it fails the consistency condition raised above. The response, however, by Groseclose and Snyder is illuminating, insofar as they simply change an assumption such that the original result holds. As they note, the changed assumption "is crucial for our [Groseclose and Snyder's] results" and "the opposite assumption is crucial for Banks's results" (Groseclose and Snyder 2000, 683).[9] If one perceives that minimal winning coalitions are rare in actual legislatures, this dispute proves that one can certainly arrive at a model that yields that general result, even if one stumbles along the way. Further, it shows that although game theoretic results are in principle transparent, this is not necessarily the case in practice. The Groseclose and Snyder result was in print for four years before the error was found.[10]

Does computational modeling have similar defects? Of course it does. Like the formal theorists, computational modelers often claim that they also have transparent models. Instead of presenting a list of assumptions as a *fait accompli* as formal theorists do, the best computational models typically provide not only the assumptions but also an idea of what happens to the model's results when the assumptions are modified. But, despite this potential advantage, the fact remains that most social scientists cannot be expected to wade through thousands of lines of C++ code to understand the inner workings of a computational model, nor do journals and book editors publish such details. Just as

---

[9] As Groseclose notes (personal communication), empirical work could in principle distinguish between these competing models. Yet, the articles in this debate are entirely absent empirical work, which forces one to argue about assumptions rather than the question at hand (that is, the actual frequency of minimal winning coalitions).

[10] In addition, the normal review process would indicate that three referees also missed the error, as did the dozen or so citations of the article that occurred before Banks's reply (according to the ISS Web of Science).

with empirical and formal models, we are left with a situation in which one can write a computational model (actually, infinitely many) that will (with the right parameter settings, rules, etc.) produce any given result.

The only qualitative differences between computational models and formal theory is that computational models are rather more ecumenical in how they encode problems. Additionally, computational models often possess more verisimilitude at the cost of deductive tractability. One does not "solve" a computational model; one uses it to generate simulated data that one tests with the tools of applied statistics. Computational models are thus related to game theoretic models, except that they usually address more complex problems and lack deductive solutions (but, more on this in Chapter 3).

What sorts of additional problems plague computational models? Take for example the outputs of three models captured in Figure 1.1. Absent any additional information, it is difficult to discern what these slides are showing. All three look very much alike, though there are some differences in the level of clustering apparent in the slides. It may come as a surprise, then, that each of these slides purports to demonstrate a different computational "result," explaining such diverse phenomena as state formation (Cederman 1994), culture dissemination

Figure 1.1. An Example from Computational Modeling

(Axelrod 1997), and collective identity (Lustick 1999).[11] While it is the case that the underpinnings of all of the models are related, this is not a cause for rejoicing – unless one has hopes that social science has stumbled on another iterated prisoner's dilemma. Each model is based upon an Ising model borrowed from physics, where it is used in statistical mechanics. By tweaking parameters (e.g., whether the neighborhood is Von Neumann or Moore), each author produced qualitative output that for whatever reason was suggestive to them. Given how slippery evaluations can be of such visual output, plus the huge parameter space underlying all such models, it is difficult to be any more optimistic about these results than those from any other methodological approach.

The main question is what one does about these difficulties. As we have seen, the problems that haunt the various methodological schools are more similar than they first appear, and the main goal of this book is to propose a solution to these problems. The short answer is that a structured combination of the methodological approaches I have listed is far superior to any approach taken separately. Much of the rest of this book will be spent examining what this "combination" looks like. While this position is at present only sketched, a brief tour of epistemology will help motivate the more detailed proposals that follow.

A SHORT STATEMENT ON EPISTEMOLOGY

From the preceding discussion, I have sketched a few of the problems that complicate the use of mathematical methods in the social sciences. If things are to improve, I would argue that a shift in our underlying epistemology is needed. The argument presented here is very close to the classic statement of Friedman (1953), and it is worth exploring how Friedman's view of epistemology has been critiqued

---

[11] It is important to note that Lustick's model is available for download in a format in which one can easily modify parameter values to test their impact on the results. This is extraordinarily helpful, but falls short of best practice, insofar as what computational modeling needs is a clear result that provides better predictive leverage on a question researchers care about. Like game theory, computational models most often serve as existence proofs.

(and subsequently ignored). As noted by Hausman, Friedman is not a standard instrumentalist:

> Friedman declares, "The ultimate goal of a positive science is the development of a 'theory' or 'hypothesis' that yields valid and meaningful (i.e., not truistic) predictions about phenomena not yet observed" (p. 7). This is the central thesis of instrumentalism. But from a standard instrumentalist perspective, in which all the observable consequences of a theory are significant, it is impossible to defend Friedman's central claim that the realism of assumptions is irrelevant to the assessment of a scientific theory. For the assumptions of economics are testable, and a standard instrumentalist would not dismiss apparent disconfirmations. (Hausman 1984, 217)

What troubles Hausman about Friedman's modification of instrumentalism? In Friedman's words,

> Viewed as a body of substantive hypotheses, theory is to be judged by its predictive power for the *class of phenomena which it is intended to "explain"*. Only factual evidence can show whether it is "right" or "wrong" or, better, tentatively "accepted" as valid or "rejected." As I shall argue at greater length below, the only relevant test of the validity of a hypothesis is comparison of its predictions with experience. The hypothesis is rejected if its predictions are contradicted ("frequently" or more often than predictions from an alternative hypothesis); it is accepted if its predictions are not contradicted; great confidence is attached to it if it has survived many opportunities for contradiction. Factual evidence can never "prove" a hypothesis; it can only fail to disprove it, which is what we generally mean when we say, somewhat inexactly, that the hypothesis has been "confirmed" by experience. (Friedman 1953, 8–9; emphasis added)

The distinction between proving a theory false and confirming a theory by experience is nothing new; most texts on modeling in the social sciences have adopted some version of Popper's work on falsification. What is new is that Freidman, as Hausman points out, limits the investigation or testing of a theory to the particular dependent variable the theory aims to explain. Under this limitation, attacking a rational choice model by "proving" the assumptions are not held by actual human actors is entirely beside the point. Experiments of the sort conducted by Kahneman and Tversky (1979) are useless in critiquing the results of a rational choice model designed to study a particular phenomenon; unless, of course, prospect theory has better predictive ability for the phenomenon in question. Thus, in Friedman's terms, one can only compare theories based upon how well they predict out-of-sample, and the theorist is allowed to pick the dependent variable.

Hausman's problem with this statement is best revealed by his own example:

I suggest that Friedman uses this view that science aims at narrow predictive success as a premise in the following implicit argument:

1. A good hypothesis provides valid and meaningful predictions concerning the class of phenomena it is intended to explain. (premise)
2. The only test of whether an hypothesis is a good hypothesis is whether it provides valid and meaningful predictions concerning the class of phenomena it is intended to explain. (invalidly from 1)
3. Any other facts about an hypothesis, including whether its assumptions are realistic, are irrelevant to its scientific assessment. (trivially from 2).

If (1) the criterion of a good theory is narrow predictive success, then surely (2) the test of a good theory is narrow predictive success, and Friedman's claim that the realism of assumptions is irrelevant follows trivially. This is a tempting and persuasive argument.

But it is fallacious. (2) is not true, and it does not follow from (1). To see why, consider the following analogous argument.

1'. A good used car drives safely, economically and comfortably. (oversimplified premise)
2'. The only test of whether a used car is a good used car is to check whether it drives safely, economically and comfortably. (invalidly from 1')
3'. Anything one discovers by opening the hood and checking the separate components of a used car is irrelevant to its assessment. (trivially from 2')

Presumably nobody believes 3'. What is wrong with the argument? It assumes that a road test is a conclusive test of a car's future performance. (Hausman 1984, 218)

Hausman's example is quite nice: Assume one has a theory that predicts car performance (i.e., does the vehicle drive "safely, economically, and comfortably") based upon a test drive (in which "test drive" is the theory that produces an expectation about the car performance). Further assume that one can take the car to a mechanic, and that the mechanic can open the hood and evaluate (in his mind) the status of various components of the car.

But Hausman makes a logical mistake in the above analysis. The main problem with Hausman's argument concerns his use of the term "only" both in propositions (2) and (2'). Proposition (2) is (in Friedman's terms) correct, but proposition (2') is a misuse of Friedman and contains a logical contradiction. 2' states that the only test of a used car is to see if it drives well, but Friedman certainly does not mean this. Many theories could be proposed other than a test drive to determine the quality of a used car; the only qualification Friedman raises is that all theories have the same empirical referent. If the mechanic in 3' points at a component and states that a component is flawed, one has two choices. Either this theory (i.e., flaws in components imply poor car quality) has an implication for the used car's quality, or else it has no bearing at all on overall quality. If the former is true, Friedman places the implicit theory of 3' on equal footing with the test drive theory; the way one chooses between the two theories is to examine their out-of-sample performance. If the latter is true – a mechanic inspecting components is unwilling to make a statement about the used car's quality – one must agree with Friedman in saying that this statement has little bearing on evaluating our "test drive" theory.

Proposition (2') is thus false, but only because Hausman failed to map his proposition to what Friedman is actually saying. Friedman believes that there is a universe of models, not just one. Thus, the use of the term "only" in reference to the "test drive" theory in proposition (2') is unwarranted:

Additional evidence with which the hypothesis is to be consistent may rule out some of these possibilities; it can never reduce them to a single possibility alone capable of being consistent with the finite evidence. (Friedman 1953, 9–10)

Proposition (2') and (3'), properly restated to be in accord with Friedman, should be:

2'. Testing a used car's quality by seeing if it drives safely, economically and comfortably is one theory of many. One selects from the universe of possible theories by relying upon out-of-sample performance. This selection is also supplemented by consideration of the "fruitfulness" and "simplicity" of a theory.

3′. Anything one discovers by opening the hood and checking the separate components of a used car is irrelevant to its assessment unless one develops a mapping between the mechanic's assessment and the used car's quality.

Of course, what Hausman means to say is that if the mechanic looks at the engine and sees something wrong, we know for a fact that the mechanic is "right" and the test drive is "wrong." But this kind of classification makes no deductive sense, especially if one has ever visited a mechanic or listened to Car Talk on National Public Radio. Real-world mechanics get things wrong all the time, and there is no reason whatsoever to privilege the "mechanic's evaluation" over the "test drive" theory. Friedman's claim that one should treat both of these as competing theories, and adjudicate between them based upon out-of-sample performance, is thus not only logically consistent but far superior to Hausman's classification, which depends upon an unstated and unsupportable leap of faith in the mechanic.

In all of the above, one must distinguish between deductive logic and probabilistic knowledge.[12] If p is a model and q an implication or test of that model, a restatement of Hausman's critique of Friedman seems to be:

i. $p \Leftrightarrow q$
ii. $\sim p \rightarrow \sim q$
iii. Show $\sim p$ to prove that the model is wrong.

Step iii. contains Hausman's argument in a nutshell: showing that p is false – either because the model is inconsistent or because the assumptions are wrong – is all that is required to reject the model. In particular, many within the social sciences advocate scrutinizing the assumptions of a model and are reluctant to accept models that depend upon assumptions known to be false.

This line of attack misses something fundamental about research, however. Models are probabilistic in nature and one often chooses to model a phenomenon at a tractable level of granularity given the precise question asked or the data that are available. Thus, models are

---

[12] I am obliged to John Aldrich for this example.

rarely unique, as the use of "if and only if" in (i) implies. As Nagel notes:

> In any event, physicists show no noticeable compunction in using one theory for dealing with one class of problems and an apparently discordant theory for handling another class... They introduce considerations based on the theory of relativity in applying quantum mechanics to the analysis of the fine structure of spectral lines; they ignore such considerations when quantum theory is exploited for analyzing the nature of chemical bonds. (Nagel 1961, 133–4)

When testing a used car, it is possible that several models all seek to explain the performance of the car and no dispositive test exists to sort between them. Better to adopt Friedman's famous "as if" approach to theories and allow for multiple theories than to decide that some sorts of knowledge (e.g., the mechanic) are privileged.[13]

A better approach than a purely deductive formulation is illustrated by the following graph:

There exists, we would hope, a "true" data generating process that produces the sample q; to our sadness, we will never know what this process is with any accuracy for most phenomena of interest. Our model p, however, may reflect something systematic about the DGP, though it is unlikely it will capture everything systematic about a complex process.[14] A model p that captures something (though not everything) essential of the DGP trumps other models, however, that fail to mirror

---

[13] Compare Friedman's "as if" argument to Nagel's description of physics:

> Everything depends on the problem; there is no inconsistency in regarding the same firm *as if* it were a perfect competitor for one problem, and a monopolist for another, just as there is none in regarding the same chalk mark as a Euclidean line for one problem, a Euclidean surface for a second, and a Euclidean solid for a third. (Friedman 1953, 36; emphasis added)

This argument has caused a good deal of controversy – see footnote 14 in this chapter.

[14] As argued earlier, it is also likely that p is not unique – there are a multitude of models that all reflect different parts of the true DGP – the double arrow between p and the DGP thus reflects Friedman's controversial use of "as if" in his essay.

the DGP. Thus, it is not enough to say that if the assumptions of p are false then the model must be discarded.[15] In the case of statistical models, we accept arguments like this one without question and there is no reason the analogy does not hold for models more generally.

I would thus argue that Friedman's statement on epistemology is more compelling than critics have allowed. I would, however, make two amendments to Friedman's version of instrumentalism.

Amendment 1: Constraints upon Assumptions

On the one hand, I agree that assumptions are often proximate measures for more complicated phenomena, and to the extent they correlate with the real-world process, it is difficult to place much value in criticizing assumptions. As Friedman notes:

> Misunderstanding about this apparently straightforward process centers on the phrase "the class of phenomena the hypothesis is designed to explain." The difficulty in the social sciences of getting new evidence for this class of phenomena and of judging its conformity with the implications of the hypothesis makes it tempting to suppose that other, more readily available, evidence is equally relevant to the validity of the hypothesis-to suppose that hypotheses have not only "implications" but also "assumptions" and that the conformity of these "assumptions" to "reality" is a test of the validity of the hypothesis different from or additional to the test by implications. This widely held view is fundamentally wrong and productive of much mischief.... Truly important and significant hypotheses will be found to have "assumptions" that are wildly inaccurate descriptive representations of reality, and, in general, the more significant the theory, the more unrealistic the assumptions (in this sense). The reason is simple. A hypothesis is important if it "explains" much by little, that is, if it abstracts the common and crucial elements from the mass of complex and detailed circumstances surrounding the phenomena to be explained and permits valid predictions on the basis of them alone. (Friedman 1953, 14)

On the other hand, there is the problem of false correlation. One may always discover a model that predicts a given empirical referent, and it is difficult at times to know whether this discovery constitutes

---

[15] It is always possible that the nonsystematic component of q is what the model actually exploits. One can thus have the appearance of a good model when in fact p only predicts a component of q that is accidental. This is the main reason why one must always compare models based upon out-of-sample tests.

an advance of knowledge. An oft-used example is using the winning conference in the Super Bowl to predict the outcome of the presidential race – whatever theory that is advanced in defense of this result would be met with a great deal of skepticism, no matter how accurately it predicted the presidential race out-of-sample.

Hinich and Munger (1997), in their text on analytic methods, by and large adopt Friedman's perspective on epistemology, with one exception that addresses the forgoing concern about assumptions. They add the criterion that assumptions must be plausible, because opaque assumptions make it difficult to understand how brittle a model's result is:

> We claimed above that a strength of mathematical models is the clarity of the statement of the assumptions. Yet clarity is only a strength if the assumptions themselves are plausible. One cannot tell if an argument works outside its own stylized context by looking only at the argument itself. Consequently, the external application, or "testing," of formal theory is by analogy: The theory is tested by measuring relationships among observable phenomena, in hopes that the observable phenomena are "like" the relationships the model focuses on. Without careful empirical tests, models would just be amusing mathematical exercises. (Hinich and Munger 1997, 5)

Like Friedman, Hinich and Munger also note that empirical failure or falsification is one of the key motive forces in improving models. Why then do Hinich and Munger add the consideration of "plausibility" to Friedman's statement?

While Hinich and Munger do not precisely define a plausibility standard for assumptions, this kind of concept is echoed throughout much of the public choice school, and there is an expectation that assumptions have something to do with the phenomena under investigation. Mueller (2003) and Aldrich (1995, 1997), for example, discuss the idea of adding a constant to models of turnout. As most everyone learns in their first formal theory class, rational voters, knowing that the odds of affecting the outcome of an election (either because their vote decides the election outright or because their vote causes a tie) are negligible, cannot justify turning out to vote because of whatever benefits might accrue due to their preferred candidate winning election. Following Aldrich, if p represents the odds of affecting turnout, B represents the benefit derived from one's preferred candidate winning, c is the cost of voting, and d is the intrinsic benefit of voting (e.g., the expression of citizenship), then when

$$pB - c + d > 0$$

a citizen will vote. Given that p is in most elections arbitrarily close to 0, one has to believe that $d > c$ to avoid universal abstention.

Most models avoid the result of zero turnout by theorizing about the role of d; Mueller points out that although adding the assumption that $d > c$ to models of turnout may seem plausible, it is very difficult to say what the assumption represents. One may claim it stands for civic duty, but just as easily someone else could say the constant stands for the utility of voting as an expressive act. A plausible assumption, then, for Mueller boils down to one's ability to map the assumption to the phenomena in question (i.e., as with Hinich and Munger, the assumption should relate to turnout and decision making). Additionally, the assumption should allow the researcher to distinguish between rival hypotheses.

Here I will settle on a distinction that is broad and builds upon Hinich and Munger's argument that assumptions are related to the phenomena in question and Mueller's additional constraint that assumptions uniquely identify concepts. Assumptions are plausible if three conditions are met:

I. The assumption is related to the phenomena under investigation in a fashion that is not absurd. That is, assumptions may well be gross simplifications of reality. As Friedman notes, the best models are simple, yet nonetheless provide great predictive leverage. "Assume a frictionless surface" is certainly false in many contexts, but it is simple to relate this assumption to models that study motion. As such, it should be preserved without criticism and one should follow Friedman's advice that the way to compare models is to compare out-of-sample performance on the dependent variable selected by the researcher. Arguments that a given model's predictive power is void because actual surfaces are not frictionless would *not* be compelling.

II. The assumption is organically related to logic of the model. For example, one might create a rational investment model that predicts little or no turnout. If one adds an assumption of the sort detailed above that people have a consumption value for voting, this would likely improve the predictive ability of the model, but it fails this condition. The assumption that voting has consumption value and can be represented by the addition of a constant to the turnout calculus is indistinguishable from a universe of other explanations for this constant (e.g., civic virtue). Further, it violates the basic spirit of model, which explicitly focused on investment and not consumption.

III. The assignment of a particular value to an assumption is not, by itself, the dispositive factor in achieving a result. One way to think of this condition is to examine whether or not there is "result convergence" (a continuity condition) when the parameter embodying the assumption is subject to perturbations. As the assumption moves closer and closer to being satisfied, the outcome of the model should move closer and closer to the final result. To the extent there are discontinuities or knife-edge results based upon changing the value of an assumption, one would question the use of the assumption, as the assumption is doing all the work, not the core logic of the model. One example of an assumption that fails to satisfy this condition is the neighborhood metric relied upon in the social science version of the Ising model (see the earlier discussion and Figure 1.1) – slightly different metrics yield dramatically different results. Assumptions are always abstractions from reality, and as such, one would want to believe that results hold within a reasonable neighborhood for each parameter value. If results only hold for a particular value and no other, one would have to defend the choice of this value or else discard the model.[16]

---

[16] One might fault these criteria because they cut against the spirit of Friedman's instrumentalism – if a theory succeeds in out-of-sample tests, why bother with any consideration of the assumptions? The problem, as Nagel (1961, 1963) points out in his discussion of Craig's theorem, is that theoretical statements (whether true or false) have great value in organizing knowledge and in producing new theories. All theories are not equally useful in pursuing these ends, even if they have some empirical success. Moreover, Friedman does not explicitly deal with the problem that theories must include statements (which are themselves theories) on how to map theoretical objects to empirically observable objects. To the extent that this process allows for sleight of hand, insofar as arbitrary or shifting domain restrictions are often embedded in such practices, one should place less confidence in theories that violate the constraints raised here. As a concrete example, imagine N researchers provide N competing theories, all of which are consistent with a data set A, but all of which are wrong. If a new data set B is introduced, by chance alone some subset of the N

Readers will note that one class of assumptions would deserve particular scrutiny under the above conditions: technical assumptions. The name itself should raise a note of caution! To the extent that one finds technical assumptions in a model in which slight perturbations of these assumptions drive the behavior of the model, it is difficult to separate this problem from that of spurious correlation in the world of statistical methodology. At root, when technical assumptions drive results, one has to question how comfortable one is with the idea that an assumption that is unrelated to the phenomenon in question ends up accounting for a model's brittle results. To the extent it is difficult to justify one's choice of such assumptions (or values for them) endogenous to the problem under consideration, this seems exactly the same kind of practice that leads careless empirical researchers to include independent variables in a willy-nilly fashion until an arbitrarily high R^2 is reached.

At this point, many formal theorists may object to the above conditions as overly limiting. Providing a statement along with every deductive model of how changes in the values chosen for the assumptions would impact the results of a model would be quite difficult. Game theory, for example, has no ready-to-hand theory of equivalence classes of games, and it is typically the case that any change in an assumption or parameter value results in an incommensurable game.[17] To demonstrate that results are constant across perturbations in the assumption space would thus be impossible unless one adopts a different approach to modeling.

---

theories may still be seen as valid. There also will be new researchers who produce new and (let us assume) wrong models that comport with (A × B). If there are continual novel datasets, one would hope that at the end of the day, all the prior models are rejected and the difficulty of inventing a new model that comports with (A × B × ...) is progressively more difficult. Whenever data are sparse, however, it seems something else is needed to prevent random chance from usurping good judgment as the final arbiter between competing theories. Keep in mind that journals typically print only positive results, and thus condition III (equivalence classes in parameter space) is particularly useful – else, one cannot know when a model has failed over and again only to be resuscitated at the last moment by a fortuitous selection of parameter values or domain restrictions. In addition to Nagel, Simon (1963), Samuelson (1963), Boland (1979), and Hirsch and de Marchi (1984) represent high points in the lengthy debate over Friedman.

[17] Some of the inspiration for this concept comes from efforts to examine complex models for robustness. In particular, Miller (1998) was particularly influential, as well as the idea of parametric continuity from the optimization literature – see Sundaram (1996) for an overview.

But this is exactly the point. The parameter space generated by assumptions in deductive models should be viewed in exactly the same manner as the parameter spaces underlying statistical models. These "assumption spaces," as noted earlier, are usually quite large, even for simple games. To the extent we are critical of empirical modelers for loading the dice in the myriad of unreported choices they make in formulating a model, so, too, should we be critical of the choices made by formal theorists, especially as it is very difficult to know how crucial a given assumption or parameter value is in generating a result. In this sense, parsimony in parameter spaces is just as valuable in a formal model as it is in an empirical model.

One example of the importance of the concept of assumption spaces is demonstrated in Ramsay and Signorino (2003). Their goal is to derive a statistical model of the divide-the-dollar game directly from the extensive form of the game. The players each have a reservation value that is unobserved. To generate a unique maximum likelihood estimator (MLE), Ramsay and Signorino assign disturbance terms to these reservation values that are IID logistic variables. Their claim is that the MLE estimator they derive depends solely upon the form of the game; further, if one does statistical work using divide-the-dollar games as the data generating process (e.g., through experiments with human subjects), *only* their MLE estimator is appropriate. The problem they point to is important – using an Ordinary Least Squares (OLS) or some other estimator may not be appropriate to the game generating the data. But the fact that their estimator achieves different results than other statistical models should come as no surprise.

The main worry is that their assumption that the disturbance terms for each player's reservation value are IID and logistic violates condition III. For different distributions of the disturbance terms, Ramsay and Signorino would have to derive a unique MLE estimator for the divide-the-dollar game, and there is no logical implication from the structure of the game that one particular distribution is appropriate. Results generated with one assumption concerning the disturbance term would not be the same as results generated with other disturbance terms, even those with similar properties (e.g., a truncated normal bounded by 0 and 1). The fact that Ramsay and Signorino get different results with their method does not of itself cast doubt on prior work that makes different distributional assumptions. To demonstrate their claim that their method is better, Ramsay and Signorino would have to show that the only logical choice of disturbance term was IID and logistic. Given that the subject of study is the divide-the-dollar game across different cultures, this would seem to be a difficult task that seems unrelated to the main problem under consideration (thereby violating condition II as well).[18]

Amendment 2: Logical Implications[19]

Reading this chapter might incline one to the belief that large N studies are the only appropriate way to test models. The main problem with mathematical modeling in the social sciences emphasized throughout is the disconnect between models and empirical tests that have the power to discriminate between competing models.

The reason models need to be clear about their empirical referent (i.e., the dependent variable that will test the model) is that, all too often, we resort to games such as the iterated prisoners' dilemma (IPD) and make broad claims about the results. The IPD purports to study cooperation, and surely it does detail cooperation of a kind. The most celebrated "result" of the IPD demonstrated by Axelrod's (1984) path-breaking tournaments is that tit-for-tat is the right strategy to employ when confronted by an IPD – many articles have taken this as a starting point and the literature on the IPD is vast. Unfortunately, this result is wrong on technical grounds (Binmore 1997), as the success of tit-for-tat depends upon the starting population. Another concern is more fundamental. Axelrod and other scholars use their results from the IPD to arrive at policy recommendations for phenomena ranging from Cold War deterrence strategies to regulatory compliance on the part of firms. Although results from the IPD might help one's intuition in

---

[18] One also should critique the assumption that the errors are IID. In many cultures, it is possible to imagine that the variance of the error term on the reservation value is correlated with the initial offer by player 1. For example, if player 1 makes a high offer (more than 50 cents, which some might label "irrational"), there would likely be very little variance in the error term. And if player 1 offers something close to 0 one would expect little variance. Across cultures, the variety of disturbance terms that might account for the data would be quite large. The logic of condition III would argue that how one's results change based on this choice should be the focus of study rather than a minor technical aside.

[19] This section was derived from conversations with Robert Keohane, during a seminar we jointly taught at Duke University on qualitative research methods in the fall of 2003.

facing the complexities of real-world problems, intuition is difficult to falsify. Once one decides that the IPD and tit-for-tat embody the essence of cooperation, everything looks like an IPD and it is difficult to know when one is in new territory.

Friedman's admonition to do out-of-sample testing curbs this kind of loose analogizing. Large N studies allow for the necessary and *repeated* confrontations with novel data that all modeling requires. There is, however, another approach to model testing that has a long history in the natural sciences as well as the social sciences (for an overview, see King, Keohane, and Verba 1994, section 1.1.3). One can derive logical implications of a model, and see if the implications in fact hold. The example provided by King, Keohane, and Verba concerns the study of dinosaur extinction:

Nevertheless, dinosaur extinction can be studied scientifically: alternative hypotheses can be developed and tested with respect to their observable implications. One hypothesis to account for dinosaur extinction, developed by Luis Alvarez and collaborators at Berkeley in the late 1970s (W. Alvarez 1990), posits a cosmic collision: a meteorite crashed into the earth at about 72,000 kilometers an hour, creating a blast greater than that from a full-scale nuclear war. If this hypothesis is correct, it would have the observable implication that iridium (an element common in meteorites but rare on earth) should be found in the particular layer of the earth's crust that corresponds to sediment laid down sixty-five million years ago; indeed, the discovery of iridium at predicted layers in the earth has been taken as partial confirming evidence for the theory. Although this is an unambiguously unique event, there are many other observable implications. For one example, it should be possible to find the meteorite's crater somewhere on Earth. (King, Keohane, and Verba 1994, 11)

Note that unlike many modeling exercises, the researchers studying extinction did not attempt to fit a model to existing facts.[20] Failure to succeed at this activity is a sign of mathematical ineptitude, rather than a signal of a model's strength. For logical implications to be used as a test, they must be novel and uniquely connected to the logic of the model. This is a harder set of conditions then one might expect; as King, Keohane, and Verba note in a footnote on the same page:

However, an alternative hypothesis, that extinction was caused by volcanic eruptions, is also consistent with the presence of iridium, and seems more

---

[20] For example, if we know that parties converge in a two-party system, producing a model that has this as an implication is trivial.

consistent than the meteorite hypothesis with the finding that all the species extinctions did not occur simultaneously.

We thus have a conundrum. It must be the case that logical implications are able to test theories – the examples of such tests are abundant and important in the history of science. It seems impossible to imagine that anyone would not have been jubilant when Sir Arthur Eddington's expedition verified Einstein's claim that mass curves space, by observing how light bends around stars. When there are other models that (as in the case of iridium deposits) might produce the same logical implication, one has to adopt a betting mentality. The test provided by deriving logical implications matters more when the implications are novel and untested – after one finds, for example, that light bends around stars, future models that "predict" this fact do not gain the same amount of credibility.

Novel implications are thus important in testing models, but one must be careful that the implication follows uniquely from the model in question. Unlike out-of-sample statistical work with large numbers of observations, logical implications, as a kind of test, are of a more qualitative nature. One has to ask how surprising the implication is, and how likely it is that a large class of other models might yield the same result. As noted in King, Keohane, and Verba, one aspect of testing a model via logical implications is shared with statistical work. To the degree possible, one should maximize variance in one's implications thereby enhancing the odds that one might be wrong. For example, instead of merely predicting the presence of iridium, one might derive a specific amount or pattern of sediment around the impact crater, decreasing the odds that other models produce the same implication.

Fortunately, this practice has a long history in natural science and we can stick with Einstein to provide a final example. In a close analogue to the Eddington experiment, the astronomer Sergei Kopeikin measured the displacement of light from a quasar moving around the mass of Jupiter during an eclipse. Because displacement depends upon gravity, he tested whether Einstein's theory that the speed of gravity is equal to the speed of light is true or not (it is – see Whitfield 2003). This test, obviously, is much easier to falsify, as any deviation from the constant for the speed of light would signal disconfirmation. An example of how to derive and test logical implications in the social sciences will be presented in Chapter 5 of this book.

LOOKING AHEAD

One of the core arguments of this text will be that deductive models are most useful in generating intuition about a problem, especially when one investigates limiting cases. But just as important is the process of developing an equivalence class where one has some idea about how changes in assumptions or parameter values change the results of a model.

Computational models supplement game theoretic models by allowing the researcher to investigate explicitly the properties of the assumption space. Computational modeling thus extends purely deductive work by generating equivalence classes of models, thereby increasing the confidence we have in our results. Of course, I agree wholeheartedly with Friedman's original statement of epistemology: Theory without an empirical referent is almost always navel-gazing. To the extent we can all agree on what the salient dependent variables are, thereby avoiding vague mappings from models to empirical referents, so much the better.

The goal of this book will be to provide the tools necessary to develop links between the three methodological traditions in the social sciences and avoid the problems detailed above. As there are already excellent texts on statistical methodology and game theory, much of the focus will be on computational models and out-of-sample forecasting. If the use of out-of-sample empirical tests are the best way to sort between competing theories, computational models naturally lend themselves to drawing out the implications of a purely deductive theory by allowing the researcher to build models with more verisimilitude, thereby decreasing the "gap" between the analytic model and the empirical test.

2

Looking for Car Keys Without Any Street Lights

INTRODUCTION

As we saw in the first chapter, there is a great deal of suspicion in the social sciences about purely empirical research. All too often, one finds models that fit a sample rather too well, demonstrating how modeling choices allow a researcher to discover relationships that are not genuine. Worse still, it is often unclear what is being tested in empirical work when there are ambiguities in the underlying deductive models. In this chapter, I will use the problems that complicate empirical work to highlight more general problems with both deductive and computational modeling. I will focus on empirical modeling initially, however, because these problems appear in a very clear form in empirical models. Moreover, empirical work is more common in the social sciences than either of the other traditions and thus deserves early attention. The goal, however, is not simply to criticize empirical work. Without it, no model stands on very firm ground, so this critique aims at the higher goal of generating a set of standards that would allow empirical work to be tied more closely to testing deductive and computational models. To demonstrate the main points I wish to make, I will draw more from the nonparametric and neural networks literatures than is common in social science. Additionally, research I have conducted with Christopher Gelpi and Jeffrey Grynaviski, and an ensuing debate with Nathaniel Beck, Gary King, and Langche Zheng will provide an example from an ongoing research question in security studies.[1]

---

[1] See de Marchi, Gelpi, and Grynaviski (2004) and the response by Beck, King, and Zeng (2004).

With this in mind, there are two problems I wish to consider in empirical work. The first problem concerns the trade-off between overfitting and underfitting a model. The second problem is named the "curse of dimensionality" in the nonparametric statistics literature, and concerns the size of parameter spaces in models. Both of these problems are underappreciated in social science and so deserve some attention here before progressing to the section on neural networks and security studies. After the section on neural networks, I will conclude with a brief section that outlines how the problems presented in this chapter apply with equal force to deductive and computational modeling – a subject that will be taken up in more detail in Chapter 3 of this book.

CHALLENGES IN BUILDING EMPIRICAL MODELS

Overfitting

We all learn in our first statistical methods class that the data generating process (DGP) is a big part of empirical modeling. It is, after all, the underlying process that we (hopefully) capture in our empirical specification, and to do statistical work we are forced to make assumptions about the nature of the DGP. The more precise we can be in these assumptions and the more accurate our assumptions about the DGP are, the better our statistical work will be – or so the story taught in most seminars goes. Spanos (1986) relates the accepted view of the role between theorizing about the DGP and building a statistical model:

Observed data in econometric modelling are rarely the result of the experiments on some isolated system as projected by a theory. They constitute a sample taken from an on-going real DGP with all its variability and "irrelevant" features (as far as the theory in question is concerned). These, together with the sampling impurities and observational errors, suggest that published data are far from being objective facts against which theories are to be appraised, striking at the very foundation of logical positivism. Clearly the econometrician can do very little to improve the quality of the published data in the short-run apart from suggesting better ways of collecting and processing data. On the other hand, bridging the gap between the isolated system projected by a theory and the actual DGP giving rise to the observed data chosen is the econometrician's responsibility. Hence, in view of this and the multitude of observed data series which can be chosen to correspond to the concepts of theory, a distinction is suggested between a theoretical and an estimable model. A *theoretical model* is simply a mathematical formulation of a theory.... This is to be contrasted with an *estimable model* whose form depends crucially on the nature of the observed data series chosen.... In order to determine the form of the estimable model the econometrician might be required to use auxiliary hypotheses in an attempt to bridge the gap between the theory and the actual DGP. It is, however, important to emphasise that an estimable model is defined in terms of the concepts of the theory and not the observed data chosen. (Spanos, 664; emphases in original)

As with most coins, there is a flip side: data mining. Unfortunately (again, according to seminar wisdom), many researchers engage in data mining, which is a brute force approach of searching through the space of possible models (an infinite set) until one finds a model that "works" for the existing sample. Contrasted with the above approach outlined by Spanos, data mining is empirical work absent any consideration of the underlying DGP. Kmenta (1997) sums up the conventional wisdom neatly:

In current research practice, the availability of well-defined competing models is not that frequent. Economic theory can often indicate which explanatory variables should be included but does not give much guidance with respect to functional form, lags in behavior, inclusion of control variables (e.g., social or demographic), or measurement of variables. Typically a researcher is faced with a list of regressors of which some are clearly to be included in the equation but most are uncertain candidates. The researchers then resort to some ad hoc criteria that enable to them to make a choice.... Probably the most common way of choosing a model in empirical research is by "data mining." A researcher confronted by a list of regressors tries various combinations of variables until satisfactory results (high R^2 "correct" signs of regression coefficients, a reasonable value of the Durbin-Watson test statistic, etc.) are obtained. This is known as "torturing the data until they confess." (Kmenta, 598–9)

Data mining is one example of the more general problem of overfitting. As noted in the first chapter, many researchers distrust empirical results due to the large parameter spaces involved. Often, it is all too easy to "discover" models by leveraging nonsystematic characteristics of a fixed sample. Overfitting is dangerous because it confuses the partially idiosyncratic nature of any fixed sample with genuine characteristics of the data generating process.

A standard example of overfitting can be provided by a very low-tech Monte Carlo experiment. First, generate a standard uniform variable named *normals* for some number of observations.[2] Treat this as your dependent variable. Next, generate a simple index variable x that counts the number of observations (i.e., $x \sim [1..N]$). Obviously, *normals* and x are completely unrelated, but imagine a modeler does not know anything about the DGP that created these variables and is convinced that the two *are* related. The question is, how far wrong could a modeler go in pursuing a relationship between *normals* and x?

If our creative modeler tries a linear regression, disappointment will result. The R^2 is close to 0 and a histogram of the residuals does not look normal for most small samples.[3] Visually, the predicted linear regression line will have a slope close to 0, indicating that no relationship exists. If she turns to a more complex statistical model what might happen? Figure 2.1 shows the results of fitting a lowess regression that depends upon local neighborhoods to fit a function – similar results can be obtained for any neighborhood regression technique[4] (e.g., median splines) or for other techniques that allow dramatic changes in slope (e.g., including several higher order polynomials of x in a linear regression).

The Stata function for lowess allows one to easily change the size of the neighborhood used to fit the estimated function. As the neighborhood gets larger, the results of lowess approach that of the linear

---

[2] In Stata, one has to set the number of observations and then generate the standard normal variable and the index. To accomplish this, use the following commands:
set obs 15
gen normals = invnorm(uniform())
gen x = _n
To graph both the sample and regressions on the sample, use the following command with different parameter values for bwidth:
scatter normals x || lowess normals x, bwidth(.5)

[3] Our creative modeler sees this as evidence that a more complicated relationship is latent in the data. When the sample size exceeds 50 observations, however, the residuals will look normally distributed.

[4] Neighborhood techniques partition the data into different adjacent subsets and fit each subset separately. Imagine a real valued independent variable that ranges from 1 to 100 – dividing this domain into 10 equal intervals and fitting a linear regression to each of them is a crude example of a neighborhood technique. The key parameter is the size of the neighborhoods.

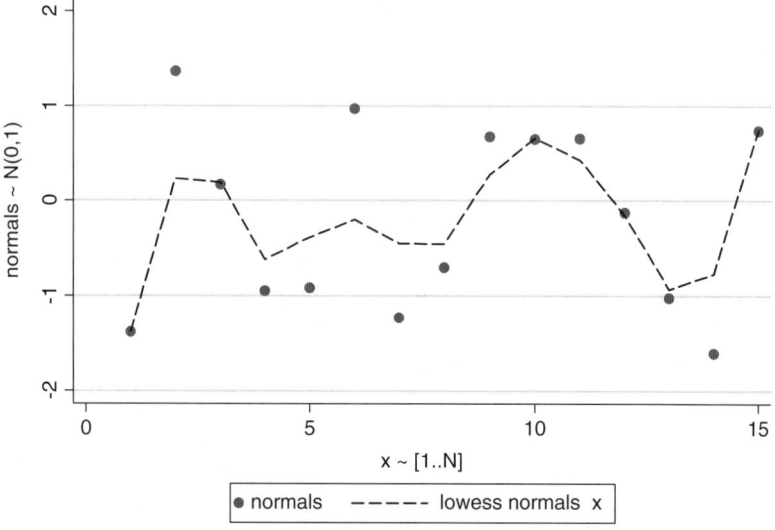

Figure 2.1. Creative Modeling

regression; as the neighborhood gets smaller, the lowess function becomes even more irregular, though better fitted to the sample. Figure 2.1 shows a middle value for the neighborhood size. Absent knowledge of the underlying DGP, a creative modeler will be satisfied with these overfit models (that depend upon small neighborhood values) given how well they conform to the data. In essence, a relationship has been created out of thin air, but visually it is easy to see that overfitting has occurred. The data in Figure 2.1 are evenly distributed around 0 with constant variance, and the lowess function is hopping from one point to another in an unpredictable fashion.

Repeating this experiment for a variety of samples demonstrates that things can go very badly for any modeling technique. Even if one avoids the mistake of using a complex model that overfits the sample, OLS models also can go astray if the sample has a trend (just as this sample has a slight positive slope). It is easy to forget that a sample is exactly that, and there is no direct way to verify that you have not overfit a model.[5]

---

[5] As I have argued in Chapter 1, out-of-sample testing is the only way to avoid the problems raised in this section.

Underfitting

It may not be as obvious that it is also possible to underfit a model, which would mean that one ignores systematic components latent in a sample. Sometimes, underfitting is justified by the researcher on the grounds that self-imposed handcuffs in the estimation process are a necessary safeguard, given the way results are presented in journals. As has been noted in many places, one only publishes the final model, and there is little room in journals for details of the journey that led to those results (or for negative results or replications). If one follows the admonition from Achen quoted in the first chapter, it makes sense to adopt a minimalist strategy, especially if one cares more about overall confirmation for a model than particular point estimates.

But for other research problems, this strategy will not do. In the quantitative literature on the causes of international conflicts, it is clear that better fit models are valuable. Underfitting, when one wishes to predict or assess the possibility of the outbreak of conflict between nations or any other important political event, is every bit as problematic as overfitting. One might imagine that decision makers desire as good a model as possible for use in the allocation of limited diplomatic and military resources for the prevention of war.

An Example: The Currency Game

For most modeling exercises, there is a trade-off between overfitting and underfitting that is difficult for a researcher to detect with any precision. Consider the following example borrowed from Young (2001). N actors in a society must decide on a currency, and there are two possibilities to choose from. Let the first currency be gold and the second silver. Initially, the N actors will be randomly assigned gold or silver with equal probability. Let p_t be the proportion of gold users in the population at time t and $(1 - p_t)$ be the silver users. At each subsequent time period, one actor will be chosen by a uniform draw from the population and will make a new decision according to the following rule:

1. With probability $(1 - \varepsilon)$, if $p_t > 0.5$ (i.e., gold is the dominant currency) the actor chooses gold or remains a gold user if one already; else, if $p_t < 0.5$ (i.e., silver is the dominant currency) the actor choose silver or remains a silver user if one already. If

$p_t = 0.5$ exactly, the actor continues with whatever currency they were using previously.
2. With probability $\varepsilon > 0$ (by assumption) the actor makes a new uniform draw between the two currencies (which means the actor changes currency with a chance of 50%).

Perl code that implements this model is available in the appendix to this chapter.

In this model, a natural dependent variable would be the average number of regime shifts one sees over any given time period; that is, if one allows the above game to go on for 100 iterations, how many times would the currency change from one standard to another? This variable is an integer with a range from [0. .t]. Fortunately, there are not very many parameters that might explain this dependent variable. The two main candidates for independent variables are ε (the mutation rate) and N (the population size). For the sake of this initial example,[6] let us assume that the mutation rate is fixed at 0.5, reducing our investigation to a bivariate regression focusing on the role of N. One would imagine that this setup is straightforward (certainly simpler than a cross-sectional time series study involving multiple nation-states) and that finding a "good" model should be easy.

To look at the issue of overfitting versus underfitting, I created a training set of 500 observations varying N from 10 to 50 (in fact, there are 100 observations for each multiple of 10). Using this sample, I fit three candidate models: a linear, polynomial, and median spline regression. In Figure 2.2, the fit between the three models and a test data set of 500 new observations is presented; the linear, polynomial, and median spline model are graphed against the dependent variable for the number of regime shifts.[7] As is obvious, seemingly trivial

---

[6] We will, however, return to this simple currency game at several points (albeit with some amendment).

[7] Given that the parameter space is small and the model is deterministic, one does not strictly have to go to the trouble to produce a test data set. I have done so here for the sake of good pedagogy (many thanks to Ken Kollman for suggesting this). What may not be obvious to readers that have never done out-of-sample testing before is how easy this is. Simply fit your model(s) to the training set, record the equation, and then generate predicted values using this equation on a new test set. If there is not an actual test set available, one can do this artificially by taking a sample and removing some of the observations with uniform random draws to form the test set.

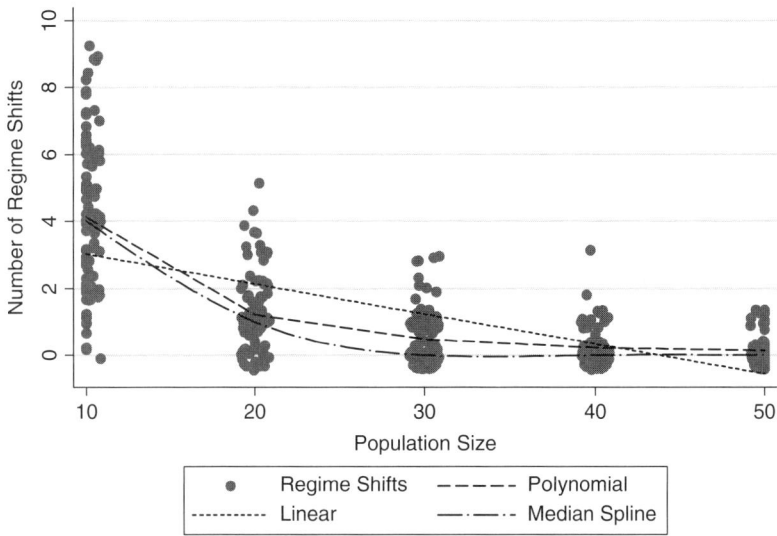

Figure 2.2. Models, Models Everywhere

modeling assumptions result in large differences in model fit, even though each model returns a qualitatively similar set of summary statistics for model performance. The good news in Figure 2.2 is that all three models seem relatively stable; although the linear model underfits the data, it would be difficult to argue that either of the more complex models is overfit or underfit. So as a baseline, one can see that if one is lucky enough to have data generated deterministically in a computational model, the problems of fit are not extreme.

Figure 2.3, however, demonstrates a different lesson. The DGP is the same, except a stochastic term ($\sim N(0,16)$) was added to the measurement of population size. One can imagine that in real-world datasets on currency use the measure for population size is a bit noisy, or there are recording errors, or any number of other problems, though in the data presented here the errors are both relatively small and centered on the true value. As is obvious from Figure 2.3, the addition of a stochastic term to the measurement of population size affects both the linear model and the spline model in unfortunate though different ways. On the one hand, the linear model is clearly underfit, and even within the sample it does fairly poorly at both the low and the high end of the scale for the independent variable. The spline, on the other

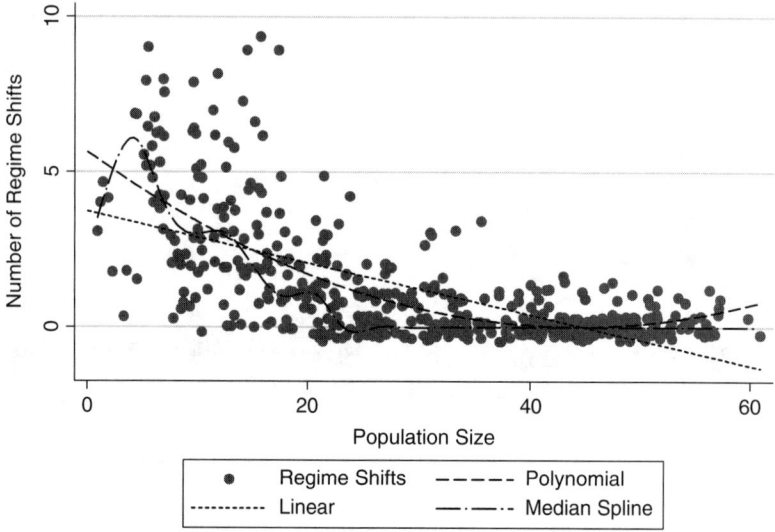

Figure 2.3. Once Again, With Noise

hand, is overfit to the data, with eight internal changes in the sign of the slope.

Only the polynomial model avoids these pathologies, and that is entirely because I limited the order of the highest polynomial term to 2 – allowing the polynomial to add additional terms would have resulted in an overfitted model. If these models were compared using a new test data set, the polynomial model would outperform the others as it is (by construction) less sensitive to idiosyncrasies in the training set. While careful graphical techniques and the availability of out-of-sample test sets can help researchers to select an appropriate model, as I have with the polynomial model, such techniques cannot be relied upon, especially when matters become more complex.[8] Keep in mind that the data in question for this example were generated according to a very simple DGP and that we are only estimating a bivariate

---

[8] Note that the polynomial model has only one parameter (i.e., the order of the highest term) and one independent variable. Thus, one only needs a couple of tries – each requiring a novel out-of-sample set – to arrive at good parameter values. If, however, one has many independent variables and a more complex statistical model, there is never enough data in the world to traverse the parameter space in any systematic fashion.

relationship (which adds simplicity to both the estimation process and any subsequent use of graphical techniques).

There are alternatives to graphical techniques. To deal with more complex modeling situations, a researcher might add a penalty term to summary measures of model fit to reflect the costs of increased model complexity; for example, for polynomial models, a penalty term might be based upon some function of the second derivative of the estimated function, thereby penalizing a model with large changes in slope (see Bishop 1995, sections 1.5, 1.6, and 5.4 for a review of the literature). Penalty terms of this kind essentially smooth the output of a model. "Smoothing" (or regularization) means nothing more than reducing the large slope changes and responsiveness of a model *to the sample*, in the hopes of eliminating the undue influence of outliers or nonsystematic variance in a sample. In Figure 2.3, one can see that flattening out the median spline model would have advantages.

Evaluating theories based upon statistical models is thus a very risky business. As we have seen, the consequences for overfitting or underfitting a model can be disastrous. Even simple decisions are problematic when one is aware of these difficulties. For example, imagine you are considering adding an X^2 term to a regression. Perhaps you have an excellent theoretical reason for doing so, but perhaps not. If the addition of X^2 improves your model, it may just be because you have overfit the sample. By contrast, omitting X^2 might be wrong, causing your model to underfit the sample and denying you vital information about the DGP. Without access to multiple out-of-sample datasets, how would you know which choice was correct?

Parameter Spaces and the Curse of Dimensionality

One way of looking at empirical modeling that may not be obvious is suggested by the above (brief) discussion of smoothing. If one has a model that is overfitted and to the eye appears to have large oscillations, it is natural to look for a way to smooth out these oscillations, thereby producing a better match to the underlying DGP.[9] Modeling

---

[9] And, it should be noted, a concomitantly worse match to the sample. As an example of this point, see Figure 2.1. Imagine a curve that simply connected the dots. This would fit the sample perfectly, but the true DGP in this case is a straight line at 0 on the y-axis. Deviation from this line is noise, and smoothing prevents one's

choices, then, can be thought of as rules for interpolating between different neighborhoods in a sample. Consider the example of a naïve researcher who reads the results of the bivariate regression detailed here on currency adoption. As one could easily imagine, our researcher is dissatisfied with the exclusion of other, possibly relevant, variables, such as culture, government type, urbanization, and the like.[10] He applies for a grant to supplement the above data set of 500 observations with more independent variables; in short, he wants to receive funds to add independent variables to each of the 500 cases in the data set so he can run "better" models that include more aspects of the real world phenomenon. On the face of it, this is a laudable goal, and anyone who has taken a semester or two of statistics in a political science department will have the rule of thumb that so long as the observations are greater than the number of independent variables, everything is fine. Given that 500 observations exist, this seems to be a grant worth funding.

Assume that the naïve researcher wants to collect 10 additional independent variables, and that each variable has a range of 10 possible values (e.g., there are 10 possible values for the culture variable). What size is the resultant parameter space? Sadly, it is 10^{10}, which is impossibly large.[11] One should immediately see that 500 observations will populate this parameter space very, very sparsely, and any results of models incorporating 10 independent variables are automatically suspect. Modeling choices, such as the reliance on OLS regression, are thus a way of forcing a particular method of interpolation on models that must span a given parameter space. In most parameter spaces found in empirical work in the social sciences, the data are quite sparse when one considers the parameter spaces they are asked to populate. OLS, as one type of model, simply imposes the constraint that whenever one finds blank spaces in a parameter space, one continues to draw a line through the voids. Other models, such as a polynomial model,

---

model from fitting the noise. It also should be noted that smoothing represents a bet – you could be wrong (the underlying DGP really could have multiple large changes in slope).

[10] Often, arguments of this sort are made by qualitative researchers who recommend using case studies as a way to investigate the intricacies of a problem.

[11] I am being generous here. One also has to add parameters that are required by the model to any calculation of the complete parameter space.

use more complex functions to interpolate against empty or minimally populated regions of a parameter space.

Since almost any model must interpolate, how does one choose a particular model form? By and large, empirical modelers in the social sciences reason from first principles or by analogy to preexisting problems. For example, when one allows both the population size and the mutation rate to vary in the currency adoption problem, a family of models that works quite well is a maximum likelihood regression using the Poisson distribution for the dependent variable. OLS models, in contrast, fit the data quite poorly (i.e., by underfitting). How would one arrive at the choice of a Poisson model? While some researchers might engage in the naughty practice of graphing a histogram of their dependent variable, one can instead consult a text on distributions and see if the properties of the Poisson distribution match the DGP of the currency adoption game. From Taylor and Karlin (1998) or DeGroot and Schervish (2002), one finds that a Poisson process has the following properties:

i. The number of events (in this case, the number of regime shifts in currency use) in any two disjoint time intervals are independent random variables;
ii. The probability of an event (regime shift) is proportional to the length of the time interval and not to the point in time at which the interval occurs (i.e., the process is stationary);
iii. For short intervals, the probability of two or more events occurring is of a smaller order of magnitude than just one event.

By and large, these properties seem to be a rough approximation of the currency game. Note, however, that (i) is violated, insofar as when a population tips into a different currency regime, it is easier to tip back into the former regime, given that the majority in favor of the new currency has only one extra vote (i.e., only one actor chooses in each time period t). Nevertheless, although the Poisson model is not quite right, it is a better choice than OLS, and probably good enough for most purposes.

There is, however, a quite different tradition for choosing model forms. Nonparametric statistics uses the sample itself to justify the choice of model form, and places much more emphasis on out-of-sample tests to curb tendencies toward overfitting. In order to understand the basic issues involved in nonparametric estimation, it is useful to develop some notation.[12]

Let $Y \in \Re$ be a dependent variable, $X \in \Re^n$ be a vector of n independent variables, and $f(x, y)$ be the joint probability density function (p.d.f.) of X and Y. Our goal is simple: to develop a model $m(X)$ that matches the data generating process of Y as closely as possible. Our first choice thus involves the selection of a loss function.[13] As we have seen earlier in this chapter, the construction of a loss function can be complicated by the addition of penalty terms for model complexity and the like, but a natural first step would be to use mean squared error (MSE): $E[(Y - f(X))^2]$. Clearly, Y and X are given (i.e., they constitute the data), so how does one choose the model $m(\cdot)$?

In one adopts the assumptions of Ordinary Least Squares regression choosing $m(\cdot)$ is straightforward, and almost everyone at some point in their graduate training has derived the normal equations.[14] OLS regression replaces $m(\cdot)$ with X'b and uses calculus to determine the optimal values of the coefficients b. In the case of an arbitrary function $m(\cdot)$, things are not much more complicated:

1. $E[Y - m(X)^2] = \iint (y - m(x))^2 f(y, x) dy dx$; by the definition of expected value.
2. $= \int (y - m(x))^2 f(y \mid x) dy / f(x) dx = E_x E_{Y|X}[(Y - m(X)^2 \mid X]$; by the definition of conditional probability (i.e., $\Pr(A|B) = \Pr(AB)/\Pr(B)$).
3. $m(x) = \arg\min_c E_{Y|X}[(Y - c)^2 \mid X = x]$; at each point X = x, find the optimal value for the model $m(x)$ by minimizing the relevant term in 2 (the other term can be discarded as it includes only X).
4. $\arg\min_c E_{Y|X}[(Y - c)^2 \mid X = x] = E[(Y^2 - 2Yc + c^2) \mid x] \to c = E(Y \mid x)$; using calculus, one can see that the optimal value for the model $m(x)$ is reached when c = Y in the above formula.

---

[12] There are many treatments of the curse of dimensionality and related issues; the notation and development used here is taken from Hastie, Tibshirani, and Friedman (Section 2.4, 2001, section 2.4). One should also look at Bishop (1995, section 6.1.3), DeGroot and Schervish (2002, section 9.6), and Gentle (2002, section 1.3).

[13] A loss function is the measure one uses to penalize models for deviating from the data.

[14] Griffiths, Hill, and Judge (1993) is an excellent introductory text on the subject. The normal equations, in matrix form, are derived by minimizing the residual sum of squares $(Y - Xb)^2 \to X'(Y - Xb) = 0 \to b = (X'X)^{-1}X'Y$.

We thus reach an answer that is hopefully not too surprising: the optimal model, at each point x ∈ X, selects the average of Y for all the observations at that particular point x. And, better still, this choice is optimal, in the sense that the mean squared error is minimized.

This is not, however, what most of us do in practice, though we may not realize how very different our normal practice is. Typically, we replace $m(x)$ with the linear function $X'b$.[15] What is remarkable about this choice is that we have made an incredible assumption. In our use of $X'b$ as a model choice, you will note that we are *pooling* the data to derive our point estimate. Put another way, the entire data set X is used to determine the value of y at every point on the line. Even when there are gaps where no y's exist, we still draw the line to produce a predicted value. As noted earlier, this represents a leap of faith about how to pool data and interpolate across spaces where no (or little) data exist.

The result of equations 1–4, however, are quite different. The optimal choice is $E(Y \mid x)$. Although this looks familiar – it is simply the mean of Y conditional upon x – it presents a very different problem. By not making an assumption that allows us to pool our observations of Y, we must derive our predicted value for Y separately at each point x ∈ X. If we do not have any observations (x,y) at a given point x, then we are out of luck. More disturbing is the implication for the amount of data we need. To be certain of our estimates, we need several observations for each x ∈ X; for even simple modeling exercises, this demands a monstrous amount of data. As noted above, for a model with 10 independent variables, each one taking 10 possible values, we have a parameter space of 10^{10} – to employ the model where $m(x) = E(Y \mid x)$ and we want γ observations for each predicted value y, we would need $\gamma 10^{10}$ observations. This is in contrast to our linear model $X'b$, which is parsimonious in its demand for data because it assumes the relationship between X and Y is the same throughout the entire domain of X.

In the nonparametric modeling literature, the problem involved with estimating $E(Y \mid x)$ is known as the *curse of dimensionality*. As

---

[15] The point raised here is not unique to OLS regression. If one engages in maximum likelihood modeling, as an alternative example, one chooses a different distribution for the model but one is still pooling the data for the estimation of Y in exactly the same way as in OLS.

the parameter space of a model or problem increases, one's confidence in $E(Y \mid x)$ (which, remember, is the *optimal* estimate for minimizing MSE) drops precipitously. Fortunately, there are a number of avenues one can take to escape this problem, short of the dramatic assumptions involved in choosing *a priori* a well-behaved functional form and distribution for Y. One avenue relies upon the idea of a neighborhood. A neighborhood is a parameter δ that defines a local space around a point. When one has sparse (or nonexistent) data, for example, at a given point x_i, instead of relying upon the limited observations (or making no prediction at all) to predict y, one could instead estimate $E(Y \mid x)$ using the observations contained within $(x_i - \delta, x_i + \delta)$, thereby increasing the number of observations available and reducing the variance in the conditional mean of Y. The parameter δ can be adjusted to produce a more or less granular function, depending upon the modeling needs and the number of observations present in the sample.[16]

Sadly, one cannot escape the curse of dimensionality completely. The use of the neighborhood estimate $E(Y|(x_i - \delta, x_i + \delta)$ in place of $E(Y \mid x)$, for example, still becomes problematic as the parameter space increases. Imagine one has 10 independent variables each of which is selected from the Reals [0..1], and the desired granularity for each dimension requires that 10% of the domain of a single dimension make up the neighborhood. In 1 dimension, this means that $\delta = \pm 0.05$, which does not seem too difficult. But, in 10 dimensions, to achieve a hypercube that is equivalent to 10% of the total volume of the parameter space would require .794 of each individual dimension to make up such a neighborhood (i.e., δ would have to increase to ±.397). As noted in Hastie, Tibshirani, and Friedman (2001, 22), "sampling density is proportional to $N^{1/p}$, where p is the dimension of the input [parameter] space and N is the [desired] sample size. Thus, if $N_1 = 100$ represents a dense sample for a single input problem, then $N_{10} = 100^{10}$ is the sample size required for the same sampling density with 10 inputs." Changing the size of the neighborhood can only help so much in grappling with combinatorics of this magnitude.

---

[16] Note that, for an OLS model, the neighborhood for each point x_i is the entire domain of x.

PARTIAL SOLUTIONS FROM THE NONPARAMETRICS LITERATURE

The preceding section has left us with significant problems. Ideally, we would like to be able to construct empirical models that avoid overfitting or underfitting the data. We also would like to sidestep the curse of dimensionality, without resort to extraordinarily limiting assumptions arrived at *a priori*. As argued in the first chapter, assumptions that allow us to "solve" a complex problem are always suspect, especially when they are not organic to the problem under consideration. One must admit that, in many contexts, choosing a particular distribution and functional form is inappropriate (or at the least, atheoretic). Fortunately, there are some things that one can do to arrive at a theoretically appropriate model that nonetheless avoids the problems noted here.

Feature Spaces

As one will quickly learn teaching a graduate research methods class, the modal graduate student sees enormous shortcomings in everything that has been published to date. This, obviously, is healthy, unless one subscribes to the notion that social science has discovered all that can be discovered – we will know we have achieved parity with the physical sciences when we produce our first Roger Penrose. Unfortunately, the most common fault students detect in existing research is that it is incomplete; that is, it is missing essential features or details of the "real-world" process under consideration.

This sort of idea is especially popular in "qualitative research" and the more historical schools within social science. Terms like "process tracing" along with citations to Clifford Geertz and thick description portray situations, which, from the perspective outlined above on the importance of the size of parameter spaces, seem completely impossible as objects of rigorous study. One example of this line of reasoning is exemplified in a thoughtful piece by Buthe (2002):

The institutions within which actors interact are social constructs, as are the aggregate actors that populate so many of our models in political science. Due to factors such as uneven growth, increasing or diminishing marginal utility, and accumulation or ratcheting effects as well as the tendency of actors to attempt to manipulate or escape constraints, the passage of time makes it, *ceteris paribus*, more likely that institutions, actors themselves, and their preferences may change. Recognizing this dynamic aspect of temporality does not mean that everything is constantly in flux. In fact, institutions and aggregate actors can be extremely stable for a long period of time. But the possibility of change implies that explanations of temporally large processes must allow for change in the constitution of actors as well as for change in their preferences. In the sense of the inherent dynamism of temporality, then, history is "the study of changes of things that change." Models of "history" must explain stability rather than assume it. . . . The dynamic quality of temporality suggests that models based on assumptions of stable institutional contexts, stable preferences, and constant units for which we record variable, independent attributes at any given point in time would be unsuited if we are concerned with explaining history, understood as a macroprocess. Endogenizing explanatory variables, however, comes at the expense of parsimony or worse: Scholars who seek causal explanations usually frown upon endogenization because when the dependent variable is not only explained by, but also (partly) explains the independent variables, we run the risk of circular reasoning. Can we avoid this problem? Sequence provides the answer. . . . Sequence allows us to endogenize the explanatory variables without having to abandon modeling and scientific aspirations because it enables us to avoid circular reasoning. Endogenization involves incorporating into the model some variation of causal feedback loops from the explanandum to the explanatory variables. (Buthe, 485; internal citations omitted)

The goal of this article is laudable – how to study historical processes scientifically – but the proposed solution is lamentable, given what we know about the effects of increasing the size of parameter spaces. If one actually believes that a process has actors, preferences, and institutions, none of which can be held constant, introducing time (here defined as sequence, with the possibility of feedback between different time periods) has the unsalutary effect of changing each observation into a statement that is conditional based upon time (i.e., $Pr(X)$ becomes $Pr(X \mid t)$). Simple bean counting of the magnitude of the parameter space, as we have engaged in throughout this chapter, would convince the prospective modeler that this is a bad idea.

Let us imagine, however, that we genuinely believe that time and the possibility of feedback are essential components of a given problem. Simply adding time will not do; the problem must first be simplified to a degree that an additional parameter will not result in a huge increase in the size of the parameter space. A better approach is to reduce the size of the parameter space, such that the addition of a new variable (in this case, time), will not result in a sparsely populated space given the available data. In the artificial intelligence, nonparametric statistics, and related literatures this process is known as preprocessing or feature extraction. Feature extraction can be seen as a transformation of the raw data into a new set of inputs that dramatically reduces the size of the parameter or state space.

It is important to note that feature spaces are not unique; that is, any given input (parameter) space can be transformed in a large number of sensible ways. What is required to transform a given input space is either domain-specific knowledge[17] that allows the researcher to choose a theoretically justified feature space or a data-driven technique (e.g., principal component analysis) that produces an input space of reduced dimensionality and maximum variance on each of the remaining dimensions.[18] A ready example of the utility of feature spaces is provided by face recognition (a topic of much concern, given the world security situation).[19] One might think that better cameras would be useful in an automated system to recognize faces, but this is not obviously the case. Even a lousy camera with a pixel field that measures 100×100 with 8 bits for recording color would have a parameter space of $(2^8)^{10000}$ – allowing for an unimaginably large number of possible faces. Any number of observations would sparsely populate such a parameter space and increasing the resolution or color depth of the camera is the last thing one needs. Even if one argues, as Buthe does for the inclusion of time into historical models, that better cameras

---

[17] Readers may note that domain-specific knowledge is what qualitative researchers and historians are after. If qualitative researchers use their intimate knowledge of the details of a problem to derive better measures, features, and assumptions, so much the better. The argument here is against the idea that there is any free lunch in adding complexity to a causal argument – qualitative models are bound by the same laws as other models.

[18] For good treatments of the prevailing data-driven techniques, see Ballard (1997, Chapter 4) or Bishop (1995, Chapter 8). In additional to principal component analysis, one can rely upon a number of iterative techniques that sequentially discard inputs that fail to contribute to overall model performance.

[19] This example is taken from Ballard (1997, 85–6), who relies upon Turk and Pentland (1991). Turk and Pentland use eigenspaces to identify eigenvectors (features) that stratify different pixel-fields recording faces. The earlier discussion of theoretical feature selection owes much to Bishop (1995, section 1.3) and Russell and Norvig (1995, Chapter 4). In the social sciences, see Master (1988).

would provide details that inferior models miss (e.g., instead of a still shot, one could use a videoclip), without a feature space to reduce the complexity of the inputs, any proposed gain would be eclipsed by the curse of dimensionality.

To extract a useful feature space that would allow the available observations to span the reduced parameter space one might first adopt a data-driven method. The idea is simple: The population of faces follow rules that constrain the possible faces one could observe. The data never span the entire parameter space; rather, a lot of variance exists on a few dimensions but, otherwise, there are huge amounts of empty space. If one could find the reduced space that captures the systematic variance of human faces, one could safely do away with the larger parameter space that includes faces one would never observe in a human population (as opposed to a Martian or Plutonian one – on Earth, for example, we all have at most two eyes). A variety of techniques exist to do just this; a prominent example is principal component analysis. Fortunately, these techniques are familiar to social scientists, but it is important to keep in mind that these are linear transformations. It is possible that one can miss a great deal, even if "most" of the variance is retained in the reduced space.

Of more interest here is a second approach, which for lack of a better term I will call theory-driven feature extraction. Unlike game theoretic and statistical methods texts in the social sciences, artificial intelligence texts, which treat many of the same topics, always include a chapter on feature extraction. Russell and Norvig (1995) is one good example, and they make clear early on that most problems of interest are unsolvable without feature extraction/dimension reduction. In contrast to "uninformed search methods" (which is more or less what game theory equates with human rationality – but, see the next chapter), "informed search methods" are those "in which we see how information about the state [parameter] space can prevent algorithms from blundering about in the dark" (Russell and Norvig, 92). Solving complex problems without feature extraction, whether they are found in the context of a deductive or a statistical model is literally unthinkable within this tradition. Typically, researchers attempt to create feature spaces using domain-specific knowledge.

Using the example of face recognition, what would a theory-driven feature space look like? It would require that researchers deduce a set of transforms to reduce the size of the input space into something much smaller using what we know about human features. Relevant measures might include the distance between the eyes, the size or shape of the nose, mouth, ears, and eyes, the shape of the hairline, and so on. The raw data would be used to form these summary measures and then discarded, resulting in an enormous reduction in the size of the parameter space. It is important to note that theory-driven feature extraction might not work perfectly. Given the size of the parameter space for problems such as face recognition, it is impossible to deductively show whether or not a given feature space will work. But, given the complexity of such problems, no other approach is possible.[20] Adding new variables or thickly describing complex phenomena is not a realistic alternative.

Out-of-sample Forecasting and Deriving Testable Implications

As the preceding section shows, one must strive to reduce the dimensionality of parameter spaces when one confronts complex problems; otherwise, one never has enough data to determine whether a model captures something essential about a problem or only some nonsystematic component of the sample. Determining whether a model "works" is difficult, however, and this difficulty is compounded by the fact that social scientists are loathe to compare models on out-of-sample performance. Rather, it is most often the case that the only results presented for a model are those for a fixed sample. A very persuasive monograph on this topic is provided by Granger (1999), where he notes that

> Cross-sectional and panel models are usually evaluated in-sample whereas time series models are also evaluated post-sample. To illustrate this difference, suppose one is interested in estimating the elasticity of demand for watermelons and has available some appropriate cross-sectional data set I. Two applied econometricians each build models, M_1 and M_2, using the same data and produce elasticity estimates $e_1, e_2 \ldots$ If I ask a group of decision makers for advice, they are likely to expend a great deal of effort in comparing

---

[20] Explicit feature extraction also results in greater transparency. Rather than hiding such details through limiting assumptions – typically given short shrift in papers – one would have to present a case up front for the choice of a particular feature space. This of course assumes that researchers openly present their affirmative arguments for choosing a particular feature set.

the quality of the alternative models. Values of summary statistics such as R^2, likelihood values and model selection criteria, for instance BIC, can be compared and even tested for superiority of one model over the other. Doubtless the properties of the estimation techniques used in deriving the models will be discovered and compared, including (asymptotic) consistency and relative efficiency. Potential problems with the alternative estimating methods will be emphasized. It is possible to ask if M_1 encompasses M_2, or vice-versa, using alternative forms of encompassing. A single model can be viewed in terms of how well it performs under various "specification tests," against specific missing variables or linear trends or ARCH, general malaise such as non-linearity, the t-values of the included variables, can be discussed, and the coefficients of variables queried as to their economic meaning as well as asking if their signs are "correct" according to some particular naïve theory. However, all of this activity is aimed at discussing the (relative) quality of the models and ignores the quality of the outputs which I, as a decision maker, am most concerned about.

In contrast, consider a similar forecasting situation starting with a time series data set. . . . Although it is standard practice to pay some attention to the relative quality of the models, the majority of the evaluation effort is directed to comparing the quality of the forecasts, that is to the outputs. As a decision maker having to choose between two methods of forecasting, it is the quality of the output that is more important rather than the quality of the model.

Why this difference of approach? There seems to be two obvious distinctions. The first is the idea that a decision maker will be using the output of the model for some previously stated purpose and how well the models do in achieving this purpose provides a natural way of evaluating them. . . . A second idea, which I think is now widely accepted by time series econometricians, is that if M_1 produces better forecasts than M_2, it is unlikely that model M_2 will prove to be superior in other tasks such as testing theories or making control and policy statements. (Granger 1999, 63–5)

Note the close similarity between Granger's statement on the purpose of modeling and that of Friedman's discussed in Chapter 1. Models should be compared based upon their stated objective, and not on other grounds. Moreover, this stated objective should be as closely aligned as possible to the dependent variable used in the model, as loose analogies between a model and the empirical referent remain just that (loose).

Equally important is Granger's distinction between the quality of the *model* and the quality of a model's *output*. Discussions centering on model quality obviously consume the greatest share of methodological debate within political science, much to our detriment. Instead of comparing ourselves based upon methodological allegiance (e.g., Bayesian vs. Frequentist), we might do better by comparing the results of our models using real or artificial out-of-sample performance. If novel data exist to decide between competing models, we should focus upon how models perform on these data. If we lack such data, we can divide our sample into a *training set* (i.e., data used to generate a model) and an artificial *test set* (i.e., a surrogate for novel out-of-sample data). One might even adopt a more complicated structure for model testing; that is, set aside 50% of a sample for training models, 25% for a validation set used to distinguish between different candidate models, and then a final 25% held independently to be used as a test set as well as to provide final results.

One might object that for some samples it is impossible to create an artificial test set to be used in generating out-of-sample results, because of a small sample size. In this case, one is pressing up against the curse of dimensionality, and there can be no great confidence in the results. Results, when predicated solely upon a fixed sample/training set, are woefully nonrobust, and usually present a rosy picture of model performance based upon overfitting the sample.[21] Thus, while out-of-sample forecasting, real or artificial, curbs many sins of modeling, it does present additional difficulties. As one increases the number of steps involved in modeling a given problem, it becomes more difficult for other researchers to replicate this process. Put another way, when one is left alone to train many candidate models on a training set, and then chooses among them by resorting to a validation set, and then presents results for a final, (hopefully) independent test set, other researchers require a great deal more information to replicate this process fully.

Out-of-sample forecasting, along with feature selection, offers a great deal of hope for addressing complex problems in the social sciences. But both avenues might inadvertently complicate the hoped for transparency of mathematical models, thereby requiring extra effort on the part of researchers for others to replicate their steps. The next section demonstrates how difficult this process can be, using a

---

[21] Though see Chapter 1, Section 4, and Chapter 5 on Logical Implications for an alternative route in testing models.

recent forum in the *American Political Science Review* as grist for the mill.

AN EXTENDED EXAMPLE: PREDICTING CONFLICT BETWEEN NATIONS[22]

During the 1990s, quantitative security studies became an increasingly prominent and sophisticated area of inquiry within our discipline. In particular, estimators based on the general linear model have been central to the development of extensive literatures on deterrence, the impact of democracy and trade on international conflict, and other issues. In 2000, BKZ offered a sweeping critique of these research programs and argued that nonparametric estimation was more appropriate for predicting the outbreak of war using the Correlates of War data on militarized interstate disputes. This viewpoint was challenged by de Marchi, Gelpi, and Grynaviski (2004), which elicited a response by BKZ (2004). In both their original article and the subsequent exchange, BKZ contend that standard parametric procedures underfit the data, missing systematic components best described as "highly non-linear, massively interactive, and heavily context dependent or contingent (22)." As noted earlier, underfitting the data is typically not a problem with most empirical models in the social sciences; in fact, given the overreliance on the sample (i.e., training set) and the qualitative features of the model rather than the output, it would take a leap of faith to imagine that underfitting had plagued a field for any appreciable amount of time. Too many researchers with too many free parameters (variables, model choices, etc.) have attacked the problem of predicting conflict.

BKZ, however, offer a partially convincing explanation for why underfitting might plague models of conflict. If, indeed, the outbreak of a militarized dispute is caused by highly nonlinear interactions between variables, termwise linear models or close analogs such as a logit specification might systematically miss these interactions, even if researchers designate a few modest nonlinear terms (e.g., by squaring the years a particular dyad had been at peace). Nonparametric techniques such

---

[22] This section borrows heavily from de Marchi, Gelpi, and Grynaviski (2004) and owes a huge debt to our continued conversations on these topics.

as the neural networks used by BKZ would thus pick up on these interactions in a way that more limited functional forms such as OLS could not.

As argued in the preceding section, nonparametric statistics offers a great deal of insight into how empirical research goes wrong and points to several interesting approaches to take in solving these problems. Moreover, the militarized interstate disputes data set offers what seems to be a great opportunity to utilize the approach detailed in section III of this chapter: a focus on out-of-sample forecasting. Given the number of observations in the disputes data set, one can easily divide the sample into several subsamples for training, validation, and testing. On the face of it, BKZ's approach seems reasonable, and their focus on out-of-sample results is noteworthy.

Unfortunately, a closer evaluation of the data and models relied upon by BKZ reveals several flaws in their approach, highlighting how difficult it can be to apply the principles outlined in this chapter without a great deal of care. As we will see, BKZ present results that are likely overfitted, and suffer from a lack of theorizing about what would be an appropriate feature space for predicting the outbreak of conflict. Additionally, BKZ forget one of the simple rules of research developed in Chapter 1: build models to test hypothesis, rather than engaging in atheoretic data mining.

Torturing Innocent Data Always Produces a Confession

The first place to begin is always the data. The data set used by BKZ records the initiation of militarized disputes within "politically relevant dyads" between 1947 and 1989 from the Correlates of War (COW) project.[23] The data include 23,529 dyad years; 976 of these years include a militarized dispute.

Dependent variable: **Dispute**, coded 1 for the presence of a conflict and 0 for peace. The threshold for the presence of a conflict is arbitrary – 1,000 battle deaths, and is somewhat compounded by elaborate coding rules. One example is taken from the codebook for the COW 2 data: "One dispute, 3575 in MID 2.1, was removed from the MID 3.0 data

---

[23] Documentation on the project and the included variables may be found at http://cow2.la.psu.edu and http://www.umich.edu/~cowproj.

set. Papua New Guinea launched a raid against the Solomon Islands on March 12, 1992. Subsequently, Papua New Guinea apologized for the raid, said that it was not authorized and promised to pay compensation. That apology is sufficient for us to delete the dispute" (from the codebook at http://cow2.la.psu.edu). While there are enormous benefits for the scholarly community to agree on one particular set of coding rules, it does complicate matters for evaluating out-of-sample forecasts. The possibility that results are not robust under different codings of this variable is a distinct possibility, especially given the relatively rare nature of conflicts (they account for $\sim$4% of the data). Applying the lessons of Chapter 1 on assumptions, one would not place much confidence in a model that provided varying levels of predictive capability based upon small changes in the threshold of battle deaths.[24]

What is more subtle, however, is to decide what it is that one is predicting when one uses this dependent variable. A naïve answer is that investigations using these data discover high-risk dyads; that is, those pairs of nation-states that are likely to go to war in a given year. This, however, is not quite sufficient for understanding the challenge presented by these data. Given the fact that the data are cross-sectionalized (i.e., time has been stripped away), what one is actually doing is discriminating between the observations in which a particular dyad chose to fight and the larger aggregation of observations in which the exact same dyad did not choose to fight – and all of this with sequence removed from the data!

A brief example will make the point. As part of a larger Arab-Israeli conflict, Egypt and Israel fought a war in 1967. Egypt and Israel, however, are in the data set for each year between 1947 and 1989, including some years when there was a conflict (e.g., 1973) and many more years when there was not. Sequence, obviously, is lost, given that the data are cross-sectionalized, so the real task is to distinguish between observations in which the dyad fought a conflict from observations in which the dyad did not. Under most investigations, Egypt and Israel are a

---

[24] Literally, current models including those of BKZ predict 1,000 or more battle deaths, and not conflict per se. It would be informative to see if one's results were consistent when noise is added to the above variable – for an example of checking for robustness by adding noise to a model, see Axelrod (1984).

high-risk dyad, but a model that "discovered" this fact would not be very informative, nor would it predict the outbreak of conflict with much accuracy in a particular year.

The task of predicting conflict out-of-sample turns out to be quite difficult and its importance is underappreciated in the literature. Simply determining that Egypt and Israel are a high-risk dyad results in a large number of false positives for the majority of observations that do not involve a conflict between the two nations. And, as we will see below, with one exception, none of the independent variables changes from observation to observation within a dyad, complicating this process significantly.[25]

Independent Variables

- **Contiguous landmass**, coded 1 if the nations are contiguous and 0 otherwise.
- **Distance**, coded as the actual distance between states. This has been shown to have a substantial impact on military conflict (Bremer 1992, Maoz and Russett 1993; Oneal and Russett 1999) and was derived from the EUGene program (Bennett and Stam 2000).
- **Similarity of alliance portfolios**, coded as a real from −1 to 1, where 1 indicates maximum similarity and −1 indicates dissimilarity. This variable measures whether or not each state in a dyad has similar relationships with other nation-states.

---

[25] Matters are worse in BKZ's chosen coding of the dependent variable. Their dependent variable includes multiple years of a conflict as observations – e.g., a dyad that participated in the Thirty Years' War would produce 30 observations coded as a war. The problem with this coding is that it violates the assumption of IID observations – and this is never trivial. The result is that BKZ's model (or any other using their dependent variable) only produces true positives (i.e., correct predictions of war at any reasonable threshold) when the Peace Years variable equals 0 (note that this is true even if one drops the classification threshold to very small thresholds – for example, .25, where one finds a huge number of false positives). Put another way, the presence of multiple years of a conflict as "independent" observations means that a flexible technique like a neural network can leverage the fact that if you fought in year t, you are likely to continue fighting in year t + 1. One should thus take BKZ's results in this chapter with an additional grain of salt. Their model does not predict war; rather, it says one should predict war whenever the dyad fought in the preceding year.

- **Alliance status**, coded 1 if the two nations share a treaty and 0 otherwise.
- **Asymmetry of Military Capabilities**, coded as a real from 0 to 1 where 1 represents imbalance and 0 represents parity in the dyad. Most work (e.g., Oneal and Russett 1999) has hypothesized that the relationship between military capabilities is curvilinear. The square of the asymmetry value is used in order to account for this relationship.
- **Major Power Status**, coded 1 if one of the dyad members is a major power and 0 otherwise. It is well established that major power states are much more likely to engage in military conflict. (Bremer 1992; Maoz and Russett 1993; Oneal and Russett 1999).
- **Democracy**, coded from the Polity III data set, and ranging from -10 (autocracy) to $+10$ (democracy); typically, one adds $+11$ to each variable (to eliminate negative numbers) and multiplies them to create a summary interaction of the joint level of democracy in the dyad (Bueno de Mesquita and Lalman 1992; Maoz and Russett 1993; Rousseau, Gelpi, Reiter, and Huth 1996). Additionally, a number of scholars suggest that the impact of democracy on conflict may be curvilinear (Snyder 1991; Mansfield and Snyder 1995; Goemans 2000), so the square of the joint variable is also included.
- **Peace Years**, coded as an integer from 0 to N, where 0 indicates the dyad fought in the previous year and N is the number of years in the data set. This variable is coded oddly, insofar as all states start out at either a 0 (indicating a conflict in 1946) or a 1 (indicating no conflict in 1946 and any number of years before that).

What should be noted about the above independent variables is that they *preclude* the data generating process stipulated by BKZ. Although one might imagine that war is a complex function of nonlinear interactions between variables (i.e., BKZ may be right), the data must allow one to test such a notion. Keep in mind that the real difficulty in this data set is to distinguish observations in which disputes occurred from the much more numerous observations in which peace occurred within each dyad. Merely identifying high-risk dyads is a recipe for large numbers of false positives and little predictive power. Thus, if one's hypothesis is that war is the complex accumulation of factors, the data must support a direct test of this (admittedly nebulous) hypothesis.

Unfortunately, it seems obvious that the above independent variables are poorly suited to the task. This is largely because all but one of these variables do not change significantly from observation to observation within a dyad. For Egypt and Israel, as one example, Contiguity, Distance, Similarity of Alliance Portfolios, Major Power Status, and so on do not change very much between observations. If these variables jointly indicate that conflict is likely, then they must do so for all observations in the data set featuring these two countries. If they fail to indicate that conflict is likely, then peace will be predicted instead for all observations for Egypt and Israel. This represents an enormous problem, and it is mitigated only partially by the inclusion of Peace Years as a variable. As stands to reason, Peace Years *does* change from observation to observation, and not surprisingly, it accounts for most of the performance of all models relying upon these data (alone, through functional transformations, and through modest interactions). Given the coding of this variable, it is necessarily a blunt instrument, but it is all one has in this data set.[26]

Thus, while BKZ might hope to model war with more complicated nonparametric models designed to capture massive nonlinearities and interactions between different independent variables, the data simply do not support such a venture. One should not be surprised to find that a simple logit model using only Peace Years along with splines of this variable yields a baseline for out-of-sample performance that is equivalent to BKZ's original model from 2000, and less than 2% worse than BKZ's subsequent effort in 2004 using a committee of neural networks and the entire complement of independent variables. Moreover, BKZ's 2004 effort represented their third effort at modeling the exact same out-of-sample test set (the data post-1985), which by any notion of forecasting is a violation of the spirit of the enterprise.

BKZ, despite repeated attempts to model conflict, have very little hope of improving upon previous efforts given the limitations of the data on militarized interstate disputes. Complicating their efforts

---

[26] A more sensible coding for Peace Years would be to count backward in time to arrive at real starting values for 1947. That is, instead of coding the United States and Britain as a 1 (indicating that they had fought a war two years earlier), one could code it as 125. If this is too arduous, use the average of Peace Years across the range of 1947–1989 as the starting value, and count from there. Otherwise, one confuses early years with years that genuinely saw violence.

are problems with the idiosyncratic coding of both the dependent variable (which depends upon an arbitrary number of battle deaths) and the most salient independent variable (peace years, which also is coded idiosyncratically given the arbitrary starting values – see the description of this variable earlier). Although there are many useful lessons in their approach to this long-standing problem in security studies (e.g., a focus on out-of-sample forecasting to compare models), this does not mean that one allows the data to speak without any intervention by theory. And to the extend their model does improve upon far simpler models, one has to question whether the improvement of ~2% represents genuine progress or overfitting.[27] Overfitting, even in what is supposed to be an out-of-sample experiment, is much exacerbated by repeated efforts against a fixed and known out-of-sample set. Arbitrary coding rules compounds the problem by calling into question whether one is explaining systematic components of the DGP or simply a small set of observations right at the threshold of 1,000 battle deaths (or the initial values of Peace Years, or any number of other idiosyncratic factors).

Is There a Theory in the House? Not Without a Feature Space...

In large part, BKZ's repeated attempts to model conflict with such paltry rewards is a byproduct of the fact that their theory is not only vague but unsupported by even rudimentary consideration of the data at hand. As noted in Chapter 1, empirical models serve to test theories. Even if BKZ had reaped greater rewards from their neural networks, it is not at all obvious what these solely empirical exercises would tell us.

---

[27] The difference between the best model of BKZ, arrived at after numerous attempts at predicting the same out-of-sample set, is within any reasonable confidence interval of our logit model for summary statistics such as the area under an ROC curve – see Figure 2.4. One should note that the results for BKZ in this table are taken from their published papers – we have subsequently discovered that they normalized their data incorrectly and these results are wrong. To help their optimization algorithm, they took the sensible step of normalizing each input variable to a mean of 0 and a variance of 1. Unfortunately, they normalized the training and predictive sets together – that is, they used a global mean and global standard deviation. The correct procedure is to normalize the training and test sets independently, else one is peeking into the future. BKZ's published results benefited substantially from this mistake.

One might defend the practice of using an atheoretically derived empirical model, especially given their reliance (however imperfect) upon out-of-sample forecasting. There is, however, a problem that is revealed by bean counting. Given the independent variables in the previous section, one can come up with a rough idea of the size of the parameter space by dividing the real-valued independent variables into bins. To accomplish a back-of-the-envelope calculation, I use Stata's formula for histograms:

k = min(sqrt(N), 10* ln(N)/ln(10))
$\qquad$ where N is the (weighted) number of observations.

This results in

$$2 \cdot 43 \cdot 43 \cdot 2 \cdot 43 \cdot 43 \cdot 2 \cdot 43 \cdot 44 = 50{,}570{,}904{,}392$$

possible parameterizations for the models of conflict used by BKZ. If one adds the five splines for peace years and squared terms for joint democracy and asymmetry, one gets

$$= 50{,}570{,}904{,}392 \cdot 43^7$$

total parameterizations. Lest one forget, this already enormous space is further expanded by the choices made in the modeling process. In an OLS or MLE model, the researcher has comparatively few choices to make. But, in a neural network such as the one utilized by BKZ, researchers make an incredible number of choices related to the following features of the model:

i. random number generation and the distribution of seeds for the optimization procedure;
ii. the composition of training/validation/test datasets;
iii. smoothing or penalizing results to account for model complexity;
iv. the number of hidden neurons and the number of layers in the network;
v. the target evaluation function (e.g., maximizing area under the receiver-operating characteristic [ROC] curve);
vi. the type of committee system for producing predictive values.

Including these choices as parameters expands the parameter space even more, and allows researchers to do great damage to the data, usually through overfitting.[28] Thus, 23,529 observations seems like a large number only if one ignores the vast parameter space BKZ ask these observations to span.

In more restricted models such as OLS or logit, one can do an end-run around such data problems if one is testing a theory arrived at before statistical work. In this case, a well-developed theory is buttressed by empirical findings that demonstrate the main tenets of the theory hold, even in an impossibly large parameter space. Think of this as a betting person would – even though the parameter space is large and the data populate a fraction of the total space, finding that the main tenets of the theory hold would increase one's priors about the usefulness/correctness of the overall theory. Simply stating a theory *prior* to looking at the data and then testing it increases the likelihood that one is "right" – inventing a theory *after* finding a statistical model cannot be counted as evidence supporting the theory.

BKZ thus have a problem because that they are not testing a theory, nor even presenting a specific statement about the DGP. Feed forward, multilayer neural networks such as the one relied upon by BKZ have the virtue that they are universal function estimators, but this is offset by the "black box" nature of interpreting these models.[29] Recovering the exact functional form for a particular neural network is impossible. With the huge size of the parameter space, tricks that work for simple models like logit – taking the first derivative for each independent variable and setting the other variables to their medians – fail miserably in a neural network model. The possibility of dramatically nonlinear and interactive functional forms means that one cannot look at a first derivative and recover anything meaningful, as the slope for a given independent variable at a particular point does not provide anything but an estimate for the variable in a narrow neighborhood. Literally anything can happen as one allows the values of the other variables to stray from their fixed, arbitrary values.

---

[28] Defining choices of this sort as parameters is a slight abuse of terminology, but is defensible given that all results are predicated upon these choices.

[29] For a general overview of the black box problem and an interesting mapping between feed forward, multilayer neural networks, and fuzzy rule-based systems (i.e., systems based upon fuzzy logic) see Benitez, Castro, and Requena (1997). Such approaches are obviously a bit far afield from mainline econometrics/statistical methods, and impose significant costs on researchers hoping to interpret the role of the independent variables in a model.

To simplify the coincident problems of an intractable parameter space and hard to interpret independent variables, one should follow the advice of section III of this chapter and derive a theoretically justified feature space.[30] Given the computational costs of estimating a neural network, it is difficult to simply try all combinations and transformations of the full set of possible explanatory variables and modeling choices. Without the "correct" set of explanatory variables, modeling choices, and a theoretically justified feature space, one cannot place much confidence in the output of a neural network or any other nonparametric technique. Studies of the performance of neural networks in the related literature of macroeconomics reveals a quite mixed set of outcomes (Gonzalez 2000), reinforcing the need for theoretical work prior to estimating a neural network. Even though neural networks should in theory encompass and outperform a simple logit model, the results of actual applications in the macroeconomics literature suggest that these models often overfit the data, due in large part to the enormous size of the parameter spaces being tested relative to the number of observations in the data.

Feature sets, as noted in section III, make everything easier, increasing one's confidence that the results of a nonparametric model are in response to systematic components of the DGP as well as allowing for easier interpretation of results. Without feature sets, one is searching in a very large space with a tiny flashlight, and the odds that you are fitting your model to nonsystematic aspects of the sample are heightened (see footnotes 25 and 27). Given the task at hand is predicting conflict, any reasonable feature set would focus upon factors that would discriminate the small proportion of years when a high-risk dyad would engage in a conflict. One would think that the dimensionality of many of the independent variables (e.g., distance,

---

[30] BKZ (2004) seem to confuse normalization with preprocessing/feature extraction. They cite Bishop (1995, Chapter 8) on feature extraction, but, in reality, they merely rescale their existing variables to a mean of 0 and unit standard deviation. If the independent variables have dramatically different scales, normalization can be useful insofar as it simplifies the task of choosing starting values for the optimization procedure used by the nonparametric estimation technique (usually some variant on hill-climbing). But in this data set, few variables are not on a similar scale, typically binary or [0..1]. Only distance has an extraordinary range (integers from 0 to ~12,000), but the log of this is used. The argument here is that BKZ should have engaged in the sort of feature extraction covered in Bishop necessary to reduce the pathologically large parameter space of their model; rescaling does not accomplish this task.

similarity of alliance portfolios, democracy) could be dramatically reduced.[31]

How Do You Know When You Are Right? Evaluating Models

Imagine that BKZ had avoided most of the mistakes listed earlier. How would we know whether their model was better than previous efforts? Almost every mathematical methods book (at least those in the empirical tradition) have a section on model selection. Typically, these sections offer vague advice, because in the most general case, this is a difficult question. Granger (2000), however, offers extraordinarily lucid advice. As noted previously, his focus is on comparing the quality of outputs, rather than features of the model itself. He notes that many models are "the result of considerable specification searching... data mining, or data snooping in which data are used several times" and suffer from the curse of dimensionality. "Unfortunate experience," Granger argues, has led time series econometricians to focus on out-of-sample testing.

Comparing models in this way is easier said than done. First, all parties must agree on a reasonable loss function; typically, mean squared error is used for regression problems, but there are other error functions that are more appropriate for dependent variables that are non-Gaussian.[32] Second, one has to agree on a standard for comparing different models. For mean squared error as the error function, it may seem natural to compare models based upon the ratio of the error

---

[31] Although a pessimist would conclude that most of the independent variables already contained within the COW data are not suitable for discriminating between conflicts and peaceful observations. Changes in economic conditions, demographics, and so on seem far more fruitful than the existing variables, and Peace Years is likely a blunt proxy for these processes. An inability to define a reasonable feature space that corresponds to a well-defined model of conflict is probably a sign that the data are not adequate to the task of testing a model. Yet, even with data of this quality, it is still better to define a feature space, rather than let your statistics package do it for you (atheoretically). Inevitably, you will find that you rarely produce stable models without a feature space.

[32] For example, one can use a Minkowski-R error function to minimize the influence of outliers in fat-tailed distributions (by setting the parameter $R < 2$). See Bishop (1995), Chapter 6, for a selection of error functions. Also note the arguments presented earlier in the chapter for smoothing, which complicates error functions by adding a term to account for model complexity.

functions using an *F*-test, but Granger notes that "there are good reasons for expecting that e_{1t}, e_{2t} [the errors] will be highly correlated" thereby decreasing the value of the *F*-test (Granger 2000, 69). Alternately, one could generate a linear regression comprised of two competing models M_1 and M_2:

$$x_{test} = \alpha + \beta_1 M_1 + \beta_2 M_2 + e_{test}, \quad \text{where } e \, \hbar \, N(0, \sigma^2)$$

If β_1 is significant and β_2 is not, one can conclude that M_1 dominates M_2; the converse also holds (Granger 2000, 69–70). Or, it may be the case that neither model dominates, but a committee of models (in this case, the number of members = 2) performs better than any individual model.

Fortunately, the special case in which one has a *binary* dependent variable is considerably simpler than the general case, though a bit of explanation is required to make this point. Once again, I will use the work by BKZ and de Marchi, Gelpi, and Grynaviski on predicting militarized interstate disputes to examine model comparison with a binary dependent variable.[33]

As BKZ (2000, 21) correctly note, out-of-sample results indicate whether a model reflects the "true" causal process driving the phenomena of interest and guards us against "taking advantage of some idiosyncratic feature of the data." Predictive success against a binary dependent variable, however, should never be judged on the basis against an arbitrary 0.5 probability threshold or a single classification table. BKZ, by relying upon such a poor standard for adjudicating out-of-sample performance, diminish their contribution to the literature.

In general, the use of any arbitrary cutoff point to discriminate between "peace" and "war" or "success" and "failure" in classification tasks is risky, and may simply be inappropriate (Greene 1997, 892–3; King and Zeng 2001, 11–13; Swets 1988, 1285–93). Theoretical work on international conflicts provides us with an additional worry in choosing such a threshold. Statistical models provide the predicted probability of a conflict, *but this probability may be low in all cases.* As noted in Greene, "0.5, although the usual choice may not be a very good value to use for the threshold. If the sample is unbalanced – that

---

[33] This subsection follows the "Evaluation of Dichotomous Forecasts" section of de Marchi, Gelpi, and Grynaviski (2004).

is, has many more 1's than 0's, or vice versa – then by this prediction rule, it might never predict a 1 (or 0) . . . The obvious adjustment is to reduce [the threshold]" (892).[34]

Even wars that ultimately *do* occur may have been generated by circumstances where the *ex ante* probability of war was less than 0.5 (Fearon 1995). For example, if we view war as "off-equilibrium" behavior (Gartzke 1999), then the precise timing of the outbreak of military conflict may result from some combination of idiosyncratic events. In this case, any attempt to build systematic statistical models that generate high *ex ante* probabilities of military disputes will inevitably become an exercise in overfitting a particular data set, especially given the nature of coding rules such as those used for the dependent variable (i.e., 1,000 battle deaths constitute a dispute) and the key independent variable Peace Years (i.e., the arbitrary starting values for all dyads).

A better alternative would be to use the criterion developed in de Marchi, Gelpi, and Grynavisky: examine the trade-offs between false-positives and false-negatives for a variety of predictive thresholds, and do not penalize a model predisposed to predictions biased too high or too low. One way to look at different thresholds would be to generate a huge number of classification tables. A better solution, however, is to use ROC curves. ROC curves are diagnostics that are able to cope with the trade-offs between false positives and false negatives in model assessment (Swets 1988). These curves plot the proportion of conflicts correctly predicted on the x-axis and the proportion of nonconflicts correctly predicted on the y-axis. The intuition behind the graph is that any threshold used as the cutoff between a conflict or peace prediction will correspond to a single point on this curve. The area below a single point on the curve corresponds to the proportion of true negatives for that cutoff, while the area above the point indicates the proportion of false positives. Similarly, the area to the left of a point corresponds to the proportion of true positives, while the area to the right of the point represents the proportion of false negatives. For example, if the cutoff is zero, then all disputes (but no cases of peace) are predicted correctly. Finally, as the cutoff varies over the range between zero and one, the

---

[34] See Morrow (1989) for an early attempt to address this problem with international conflict data.

curve will be negatively sloped, as fewer conflicts and greater numbers of peaceful dyads are forecast correctly.

The key point to glean from a pair of ROC curves used for model comparison is that the curve with more area underneath it corresponds to a greater proportion of successful predictions, regardless of what arbitrary threshold is settled upon for predicting the dependent variable. In the absence of a specified optimal threshold based upon decision-theoretic criteria (see Granger 2000, Chapter 3, or de Finetti 1974), the area under an ROC curve provides a useful summary statistic that can arbitrate between competing models.

As an example of how necessary ROC curves are, consider the model presented in BKZ (2000). They discover that neural networks predict wars with a probability greater than 0.5, whereas prior logit models do not. One might conclude that this demonstrates the superiority of the particular brand of nonparametric techniques used by BKZ at the expense of simpler logit models.[35] The question then is how does one compare models of conflict to make this determination? For this example, I present several models, ordered from the least complex to the most complex:

- a very simple linear discriminant in which each class is assumed to have an equivalent covariance matrix;
- a logit model derived from the existing security studies literature;
- (tie) a feed forward neural network presented in BKZ (2000) using an incorrect error function based upon the number of correct classifications at the 0.5 threshold;
- (tie) a neural network from de Marchi, Gelpi, and Grynaviski (2004) using the correct error function of area under the ROC curve;
- BKZ's 2004 committee of three neural networks estimated using the correct error function of area under the ROC curve.

Results are presented for two different test sets. One of these is the test set originally reported in BKZ (2000), consisting of all dyads in the years after 1985. A second test set was created by drawing a

---

[35] BKZ correct this mistake in their 2004 publication. As noted in this section, the choice of error function is crucial. BKZ in 2000 did not use MSE; rather, they used a weighted function that rewarded true positives and true negatives. Maximizing the area under the ROC curve is the correct error function for this problem, however.

Model	Forecast Set	Uniform Draws (Pre-1985) & selected 95% confidence intervals	Post-1985 & selected 95% confidence intervals
Peace Years (+ splines)		0.805	0.904
Linear discriminant		0.815	0.872
Logit		0.837 [0.77 ... 0.9]	0.915 [0.89 ... 0.94]
Single neural net - classification		0.801	0.87
Single neural net - ROC area		0.856 [0.77 ... 0.91]	0.869 [0.79 ... 0.94]
Committee of neural nets		0.871 [0.82 ... 0.92]	0.927 [0.91 ... 0.95]

Figure 2.4. Area Under ROC Curves

5% uniform random sample of the dyad-years from 1947 to 1985. The latter test set was used to test for robustness, and serves as a useful tool to determine whether the particular cutoff of 1986 might be fortuitous, aiding or hurting different models. Second, I do not present results from the training set; to do so may artificially inflate the models' apparent performances and deflect attention from their out-of-sample performance.

Note that these models range from the simple linear discriminant to a very complex committee comprised of three different neural networks. Given the increase in the parameter space intrinsic to complex models, and the difficulty in understanding the moving parts in a complex model, it is always useful to see whether or not the complexity of a model is warranted by the data at hand. When in doubt, one should follow Friedman and Granger's advice and choose the simplest "best" model.

How do these very different models perform? Figure 2.4 reports the area under the ROC curves for all the models detailed above and Figure 2.5 plots the ROC curve for selected models. As Figure 2.4 indicates, the committee of neural networks that maximized the area under the ROC curve in the training set outperformed all of the other models in this forecast set for both the uniform draws test set and the post-1985 test set.

Given the rarity of militarized disputes, one should not dismiss even a modest increase in forecasting accuracy, but one cannot avoid the impression that the difference between all of these models is quite small. Figure 2.4 reports that the committee of neural networks had the greatest area under its ROC curve at 0.9271, while the logistic regression had the second greatest at 0.9152. Figure 2.5 demonstrates

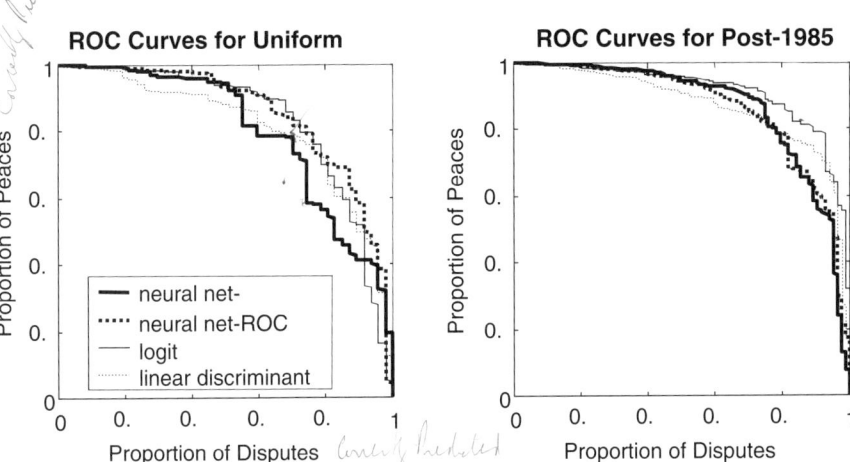

Figure 2.5. ROC Curves for Neural Net (classification), Neural Net (ROC) Logit, and Linear Discriminant Across Uniform Draw and Post-1985 Test Sets

that for practically any given tolerance of false positives, the logit model was nearly indistinguishable from its rivals. The overwhelming impression left by this set of results is that there is little difference between the various neural networks, logit and discriminant analysis in terms of their ability to distinguish between dispute and nondispute cases, once one controls for a model's inherent bias toward predictive probabilities that are either too high or too low.

But, as with many methodological ventures, such impressions may be wrong. How could we explicitly test whether or not one model outperforms another based upon the results of the ROC curves? Fortunately, there is an easy answer to this question. One can compare different ROC curves by using a chi-square test, or a number of related techniques such as the Kolmogorov-Smirnov test (see Scott and Fasli 2001) or the algorithm developed by DeLong, DeLong, and Clarke-Pearson (1988).[36] All of these approaches make no assumptions about the distributions in question, and are appropriate to comparing ROC curves. As one might guess from inspecting Figures 2.4 and 2.5, the differences between the competing models are in fact not significant (not even at the $P = 0.20$ level). Given the limitations in the data and

---

[36] See the Stata Reference Manual, Rel. 8 (2003). The latest version of Stata has implemented very robust code for computing ROC curves as well as comparing different models with either correlated or independent ROC curves.

the overall level of performance of all the models (which is quite high), this should not be seen as surprising.

As noted in Chapter 1, a better approach by far would be to use a genuinely new out-of-sample set, such as the recently released 1990–2001 data, in which the differences between the models would likely be far greater. Repeated efforts to achieve marginally better performance on the 1986–1989 data, by contrast, runs counter to the entire predictive enterprise.

A GENERAL STATEMENT ON MODELS

As noted in the first section, the problems discussed in this chapter are by no means limited to empirical modeling. Since the next chapter will concern itself with game theoretic and computational models, I will limit myself to three brief remarks.

First, just as one would argue that empirical models can overfit the data, so, too, can deductive models "overfit" a desired end result. With a combination of limiting assumptions, information restrictions, and equilibrium concepts, one can achieve any desired result with a formal or game theoretic model. The fact that one can prove something to be true is not of itself useful; there are an infinite number of models that prove any given result is true. As with empirical modeling, the task is to discriminate between competing models. As I argued in the first chapter of this book, one must avoid what Friedman defines as a "retreat into purely formal or tautological analysis."

Second, one must bean count for analytic models in much the same fashion as the preceding sections have bean counted the various parameters involved in formulating empirical models. Parameter spaces are parameter spaces, and to the extent that one is making choices for a deductive model, the stability of the result depends upon both how many choices are made as well as the nature of these choices.[37] A reasonable question to ask is how robust one's deductive results are given perturbations in any of these assumptions. And, if one believes in the epistemological arguments from Chapter 1, we should be particularly worried about technical assumptions or assumptions that seem unrelated to the empirical referent.

---

[37] See the section in Chapter 1 on conditions that should be placed upon assumptions.

There is, perhaps, a more subtle point to be made here. Unlike empirical models, deductive models do not depend upon stochastic components in producing results; that is, assumptions are not noisy in the way that data are. If you have a set of rotten assumptions in an empirical model, confronting that model with the data will immediately reveal this fact. For a deductive model, however, one might arrive unknowingly at a set of knife-edge values for what seem to be trivial or purely technical assumptions but account entirely for the result. Perturbing any of these assumptions may produce drastically different outcomes for the model.

As I will argue in Chapter 3, this is a real problem, especially if one adopts the normal science notion that models should build upon previous research (and previous models). Fragile models make this goal difficult. What one requires is a theory of *equivalence classes* for formal or game theoretic models. Much of the remainder of the book attempts to build such equivalence classes, so I will say no more about it here.

Third, one has to test deductive models. I believe most researchers would accept that the work of BKZ is incomplete given the fact that there is no real model being tested. So, too, must one be wary about deductive models that are "proven" with case studies or qualitative anecdotes. The exact same standards should apply to deductive work: When the parameter space of a deductive model is large, one needs a plentiful supply of out-of-sample data or a set of novel logical implications to test the deductive model. To the extent that the data do not span the deductive model's parameter space, we have less confidence in the utility of the deductive model. Granger's admonition that the consideration of empirical models should focus on the outputs and not characteristics of the modeling process also applies to deductive models. The attractiveness of one equilibrium concept over another, or whether the result was generated with one set of assumptions over another, is only so useful.[38] One should instead focus on how well models do when confronted with their empirical referents.

---

[38] In large part, it seems the conflation of "rationality" with game theory has diverted attention from the theories generated by game theoretic models. The rational choice debate, in Granger's terms, concerns features of the modeling process, not the quality of the results.

A final point concerns these outputs. It is often the case that the mapping from a deductive model's results to an empirical referent is attenuated. To the extent that a deductive model has only loose application to an empirical referent, we should ignore it, as no real testing can proceed. As noted in the first chapter, one obvious example is the iterated prisoner's dilemma. What, exactly, are the predictions of this class of models given the plethora of equilibria one can generate? That people in some settings cooperate?

APPENDIX: PERL CODE FOR THE CURRENCY GAME

```
1.  use Math::BigFloat;
2
3   # parameters
4
5   $loops=100;        # number of times program is repeated
6   $N=10;             # population size
7   $ep=0.50;      # mutation rate
8   $time=100;         # length of horizon
9   $early=$N/2;       # number of early adopters/those changing
    each time period; must be <= $N
10
11  # do file I/O; in this case, output only
12
13  open DATA_DUMP, ">>dump.txt";
14  select DATA_DUMP;
15
16  # print header for data 1x
17  # print "NUMBER of regime shifts | OVERALL MEAN of
    populations | Delta |
      N | Mutatation Rate | Time \n";
18
```

```
19  # repeat program $loops times; output at the end of the
    program body
20
21  for ($z=0; $z<$loops; $z++)
22  {
23
24  # initialize population - uniform draws
25  $pop_mean=0;            # population mean
26  $current_standard=0;    # either 0 or 1 based upon pop`mean
27  $regime_shifts=0;       # number of regime shifts
28  $pop_total=0;           # keeps total population values for
    use later in determining mean
29
30
31  for ($i=0; $i<$N; $i++)
32       {
33       if (rand()<0.5){
34                  $agents[$i]=0;
35                  }
36                  else {$agents[$i]=1; $pop_mean++;}
37       }
38
39  if ($pop_mean>$N/2) {$current_standard=1;} else
    {$current_standard=0;}
40
41  # start main loop; pick one agent at random and allow
    change
42
43  for ($i=0; $i<$time; $i++)
44       {
```

```
45          # set temp_regime to existing standard for later
            comparison at loop end
46          $temp_regime=$current_standard;
47
48          for ($e=0; $e<$early; $e++) # start loop of switchers
49             {
50             # draw the agent who considers change
51             $temp=int(rand($N));
52             $val=$agents[$temp];
53
54             # draw the epsilon
55             if (rand()<$ep) {$agents[$temp] = sprintf
                ("%.0f", rand ()); }
56             # otherwise, act like a sheep
57             else    {if ($agents[$temp]!=$current_standard)
58                      {$agents[$temp]=$current_standard;}
59                     }
60
61             #check for change, update $pop_mean and $current_
                standard
62             if ($agents[$temp]>$val) {$pop_mean++;}else
63                      {if ($agents[$temp]<$val) {$pop_mean--;}}
64             if ($pop_mean>$N/2) {$current_standard=1;}else
       {$current_standard=0;}
65  }          }# end $early loop for all switchers
66
67             # save pop_total and print out values of interest
68             $pop_total=$pop_total+$pop_mean;
69
```

```
70              # print "Pop_mean: ", $pop_mean, "Standard: ",
   $current_standard, "\n";
71
72              # check to see if a regime shift occurs
73              if ($temp_regime!=$current_standard) {$regime_
                shifts++; }
74
75          }
76
77 # determine overall pop mean
78 $pop_total=$pop_total / $time;
79
80 # print data
81 print $regime_shifts, " ", Math::BigFloat->bceil
   ($pop_total), " ", abs(Math::BigFloat->bceil($pop_total)
   -$N/2), " ", $N, " ", $ep,," ", $time, " \n";
82
83      }       # end $loops
84
85 close DATA_DUMP;      # close output file
```

3

From Curses to Complexity

The Justification for Computational Modeling

INTRODUCTION

The study of international conflict, like many fields, has hosted a longstanding debate between rational choice theory and its critics.[1] Rational choice, in this debate, is in some sense a misnomer, as the critics almost solely reference game theoretic models in which the nation-state is the primary actor. The overall question, however, raised by critics of game theory is whether or not three decades of formal modeling has helped us to understand complicated phenomena such as the causes of war and alliance formation.

In this chapter, I will review the main positions taken in this debate, using some of the more prominent game theoretic models as illustrations. It will become obvious that I am critical of the efforts of game theory to date, despite my support for the idea that one must engage in modeling as an enterprise to understand complicated phenomena. My focus, however, is not solely on the limitations of existing models nor is it on any particular substantive area (although problems in security studies will be used as examples); rather, it is to investigate these models with the goal of determining which complications systematically hamper their effectiveness when applied to difficult problems. Obviously, game theory has been tremendously effective in solving other problems, so one must wonder where the stumbling blocks lie in

---

[1] See, in particular, Walt (1999a) which launched the thousand ships, and Walt (1999b), which is a response to various defenses of game theory in a special issue of *International Security* (Vol. 24:2, Fall 1999). The most salient defenses were written by Bueno de Mequita and Morrow (1999), Niou and Ordeshook (1999), and Powell (1999).

complex problem areas like security studies and what the implications are for game theory more generally.²

As we have seen in the previous chapter, there are two problems that complicate empirical research. First, the curse of dimensionality hampers one's ability to test the results of complex models. Second, one needs to avoid brittle models, in which seemingly trivial changes to a model's assumptions cause huge swings in the results. This chapter demonstrates that these problems affect game theoretic models in exactly the same fashion as empirical models. Fortunately, the solutions to these problems are much the same for game theory as they were for empirical models. We will see that one must develop feature spaces that encode problems in a parsimonious fashion. Further, without the development of equivalence classes, it is difficult to engage in cumulative research.

I will thus present an approach that borrows from both game theory and computational political economy, and, as such, will likely cause some discomfort to both methodological "camps." To illustrate the promise of a combined approach, I use two examples that serve as illustrations of how to apply the proposed methodology. The first example (beginning in this chapter and continuing to the next) concerns the problem of alliance formation. The second example (in Chapter 5) examines nonseparable preferences and survey data.

A DETOUR: A BRIEF CRITIQUE OF GAME THEORY (AND SUNDRY COMMENTS ON MACHINE CHESS)

In the debate between formal modelers and their naysayers, modeling complex processes such as war is most often framed as a dichotomous choice between game theoretic models, on the one hand, and qualitative/historical work, on the other.³ It is worth repeating that

---

² One example involving a complicated auction would be Binmore and Klemperer (2002). In April 2000, they organized the license auction of Britain's third-generation mobile phones. The total revenue of the auction was equivalent to 2.5% of Britain's GNP. There are, of course, other examples of the utility of game theory.

³ As argued in the first chapter of this book, there is a third approach, which is to adopt Friedman's (1953) maxim that models and their assumptions are not worth arguing over; rather, one should be ecumenical with regard to models and base comparisons solely upon their out-of-sample performance. Sadly, most social scientists

game theory has been widely accepted in large part due to analytic simplicity and broad applicability. Most would believe that game theory deserves the name – all games are potentially representable within the confines of game theory.

Thus, if game theory is to work as advertised, we have to have some way to encode most of the games we are interested in studying; or, more in the vein of mathematics proper, build upon previous efforts to derive increasingly complicated models that achieve more verisimilitude with the problem at hand. It is worth summarizing what is required by game theory to encode a given problem. To accomplish this task, game theory requires three moving parts. First, one needs an instantiation for the problems that humans confront, and ideally this encoding represents what players know at different points in the game. In game theory, this instantiation is most often an extensive form game, where the innovation of information sets provides a nice vehicle for understanding how knowledge impacts play. Second, one needs explicit utility functions that represent how players evaluate the outcomes of the game. Last, one needs a solution concept and an algorithm that "solves" a given problem; game theory typically utilizes a Nash equilibrium (or a refinement) as the solution concept and backwards induction as the algorithm. Given an extensive form and a utility function, one can readily apply backwards induction and test for the existence of a Nash equilibrium.

Although I am working toward a critique, I would like to distinguish the current work from the approach taken by most critics of game theory (and rational choice more generally). There are two main streams of criticism. The first has focused upon whether humans can actually frame problems correctly (i.e., can we satisfy information requirements?) or apply the appropriate solution concept (i.e., can we satisfy computational requirements?). The consensus of this line of research is that humans are quite stupid compared to the ideal rational choice player, even if the humans in question are heads of state.

The problem with the standard criticism is that it (bizarrely) concedes that the definition of human rationality coincides with a game theoretic player, and this is what Green and Shapiro (1994), and other critics of rational choice theory, have failed to recognize. Humans are in

---

have fetishized the different methodological approaches at the expense of focusing upon results and predictive performance.

many ways limited or less good than *homo economicus*, but it is also the case that humans typically make choices in difficult environments with limited information. Kahneman and Tversky (1979) style experiments point to our obvious flaws in relatively simple tasks; but up the ante a bit by presenting humans with more complicated games and the tables turn quite dramatically. We "outperform" rational choice players, and there is no reason to suspect that game theoretic models have much to say about certain (complex) classes of human games and decision contexts. So although we may sometimes make mistakes calculating simple expected value problems, it is also true that we thrash rational choice players at games like poker.[4]

The second, equally critical line of research, focuses upon the supposed ahistoric, simplifying assumptions relied upon in most game theoretic models.[5] The argument from proponents of a more historical approach is that the models are assumption driven, and that careful attention to case studies is a more appropriate avenue toward understanding complex problems.

History, regrettably, seems less than fruitful as a model of how to conduct research in the social sciences, unless one wishes to give up on any notion of causality.[6] If one adopts a King, Keohane, and Verba sensibility about the nature of epistemology underlying both mathematical methods and historiography, one has to admit that "case studies" of itself is not a methodology.[7] Much as some would wish, the use of history does not somehow avoid problems inherent in models of any kind (game theoretic or not). As I have argued in Chapter 2, a parameter space is a parameter space, whether the parameters involved are quantitative or qualitative.

Despite my belief that game theory, as currently employed, is inadequate to the challenge posed by many important problems in the

---

[4] The most ambitious poker research project is currently run by the University of Alberta Computer Poker Research Group. See http://www.cs.ualberta.ca/~games/poker/ for more details.

[5] For an overview in the security studies literature, see Walt (1999a); for an attempt at a general synthesis of game theory with case studies, see (Bates et al. 1998).

[6] For a considered treatment of the role of causality in historiography, see Novick (1998).

[7] Typically, proponents of qualitative/historical methods state that one should match assumptions with reality, incorporate dynamic/path dependent elements, and be sensitive to the possibility that preferences or institutions may change through time. Typically, they are not troubled by the complications that ensue due to a loss of IID observations and the explosion of the parameter space.

social sciences, I do believe that mathematical modeling is the best of all approaches, so long as we remember the arguments presented in Chapter 1. Models should be compared by examining how fruitful their predictions are, rather than the supposed accuracy of their assumptions. This implies that models should provide results that correspond to the real-world phenomenon that is being measured with a dependent variable; qualitative assessments and analogies that aim to "bridge the gap" between the model and the data are troubling.

Extensive Game Forms, Utility Functions, and Feature Spaces

In Chapter 2 of what is perhaps the most important book ever written in economics, Von Neumann and Morgenstern state what has now become a tenet of belief for most of us:

> It should be clear from the discussions of Chapter I that a theory of rational behavior – i.e., of the foundations of economics and of the main mechanisms of social organization – requires a thorough study of the "games of strategy"... in the process of this analysis it will be technically advantageous to rely on pictures and examples which are rather remote from the field of economics proper, and belong strictly to the field of games of the conventional variety. Thus the discussions which follow will be dominated by illustrations from Chess, "Matching Pennies," Poker, Bridge, etc., and not from the structure of cartels, markets, oligopolies, etc. (1944, 46–7)

There is, however, one point of difference between the program specified by Von Neumann and Morgenstern and that advocated by more modern game theorists. The games Von Neumann and Morgenstern viewed as "essential" to any theory of rational behavior have been dramatically dumbed down or truncated from modern game theory – bridge and poker, for example, are not active research concerns. And it is not as if Von Neumann and Morgenstern were alone in their earlier belief that game theory's domain should involve complex human games. John Nash, famously, was interested in Go, and invented the game Hex while he was at graduate school at Princeton.[8] Ken Binmore, after finding one of Von Neumann's poker models counterintuitive (yet helpful for actual play), also decided to study game theory.[9] Many of

---

[8] See, for example, Kuhn and Nasar (2002, Chapter 3).
[9] Personal communication with Binmore and Binmore (1992, 573). As Binmore details in Chapter 12 of *Fun and Games*, many other game theorists were interested in poker, including Borel and Shapley.

the brightest game theorists had, at some point, a desire to use the tools of game theory to study real, human games.

Ironically, Go, Hex, chess, and poker are largely immune to game theoretic treatments. The main reason that the tools of game theory (and the early research program of Von Neumann and Morgenstern) have failed so completely is because of the encoding used to study games. What is wrong with using a normal form or extensive form to encode games? To understand the issues involved, a brief detour to machine chess is necessary.

Of all the games noted here, chess, on the face of it, is by far the most amenable to game theoretic treatments. Chess also has the beneficial feature that decades of work have been devoted toward building a machine player that is the equivalent of human masters. Periodically, one can measure the success of this program by taking stock of the frequent matches between machines and human opponents.

Of all these matches, the most famous is the second tournament between IBM's Deep Blue and Garry Kasparov that occurred in the spring of 1997. After watching Kasparov lose to Deep Blue, chess masters went on record with statements such as:

"Nice style!" said Susan Polgar, the women's world champion. "Really impressive. The computer played a champion's style, like Karpov," she continued, referring to Anatoly Karpov, a former world champion who is widely regarded as second in strength only to Kasparov. "Deep Blue made many moves that were based on understanding chess, on feeling the position. We all thought computers couldn't do that." (New York Times, "Computer Defeats Kasparov, Stunning the Chess Experts," May 5, 1997)

The problem, of course, is that Deep Blue does not represent a triumph for artificial intelligence, a fact the IBM team is quite up-front about (though the media has not been). From the official IBM FAQ on Deep Blue:

Does Deep Blue use artificial intelligence?
The short answer is "no." Earlier computer designs that tried to mimic human thinking weren't very good at it. No formula exists for intuition. So Deep Blue's designers have gone "back to the future." Deep Blue relies more on computational power and a simpler search and evaluation function. (Deep Blue FAQ. *http://www.research.ibm.com/deepblue/meet/html/d.3.3.html*)

Even though Deep Blue is not what one might expect from artificial intelligence – a learning, strategic algorithm – Deep Blue *is* (rather surprisingly) the ultimate game theoretic player. By this, I mean that Deep Blue approaches the problem of chess in much the same way a game theorist would recommend. It uses an extensive form for chess positions, and "solves" this tree with a variant of backwards induction (i.e., alpha-beta pruning, which is computationally more efficient than backwards induction).

So, Zermelo had it right all along; at some point, chess will be conquered by computers, given any reasonable increase in the power of hardware. And more important for the argument here is that chess has been conquered by an encoding and a solution algorithm that look very much like game theory. One could argue that success in such a complex game is an indication that game theory is an appropriate tool for studying all human games and decision contexts.

The problem is that looks are deceiving in this case. Two characteristics in particular of Deep Blue (and machine game players more generally) distinguish it from game theory proper; moreover, these distinctions are instrumental in highlighting what goes wrong when game theorists approach complex problems.

The first characteristic worth noting is the use of *idiosyncratic utility functions*. Chess, obviously, has a well-known utility function with three elements {win, lose, draw}. Unfortunately, encoding chess with game theory requires the ability to match strategies with outcomes; given the combinatorics of chess, this is not feasible. It is also obvious, to anyone who plays the game, that human players are able in most cases to evaluate a game before the terminal nodes are reached, based upon features such as material, position, pawn support, and the like. These features are mysterious, insofar as they bear no obvious connection to the ultimate utility function (or strategies) of the game as encoded by game theory.[10]

But perhaps after reading Chapter 2 they are not so mysterious to us! The terms of the utility function used in models of chess can be seen as analogous to the features described by Bishop and other researchers in non-parametric statistics. Just as in empirical models, not all features

---

[10] Concepts such as "material" do not bear any relation to the rules of chess either, thereby compounding the mystery. Whether one assigns a single point to a pawn and three to a bishop or entirely different values is not, in any way, deducible from the rules of the game.

in machine chess are created equal – a random feature of chess, such as how close to the center of a square one places one's pieces, would probably not be useful. Machine algorithms thus incorporate an insight that is common to both empirical and analytic work: By utilizing (linear) combinations of features that characterize utility derived from intermediate actions taken within the game, one can reduce the parameter space of an impossibly complex game. Without such a simplification, no analytic work would be possible.

Thus, one surmounts a logical problem. Even though Deep Blue could calculate hundreds of millions of moves a second, all of this processing power would be for naught unless it could span complete strategies. Game theory, as noted earlier, requires complete extensive forms, so that one can map terminal nodes to payoffs – an impossible feat in chess. Instead, Deep Blue used its formidable computational power to generate *partial* extensive forms (e.g., a tree that represents 10 moves out from the current game state) and assigned the terminal nodes of these partial extensive forms values taken from idiosyncratic utility functions. "Idiosyncratic" is taken here to mean a utility function comprised of features that bear no necessary relation to the utility function or rules of chess but are nonetheless helpful in evaluating intermediate positions in chess.

Where does such a utility function come from? The researchers involved used a combination of domain specific knowledge of chess to choose the terms in the utility function, plus empirical work drawn from past games of human chess masters:

The evaluation hardware has four components. A piece placement evaluation scores pieces according to their central placement, their mobility and other considerations. A pawn structure evaluation scores pawns according to such parameters as their mutual support, their control of the center of the board and their protection of the king. A passed-pawn evaluation considers pawns that are unopposed by enemy pawns and can therefore be advanced to the eighth rank and promoted to queens. A file structure evaluation assigns values to more complicated configurations of pawns and rooks on a particular file.

We also began to consider ways of tuning the evaluation function's 120 or so parameters, specified in software. Traditionally, programmers had hand-tuned the weights that programs assigned to material – pawns and pieces – and to positional considerations. We believe ours is the only major program to tune its own weights automatically.

We acquired 900 sample master games and arbitrarily defined the optimum weights as those that produce the best match between the moves the machine judges to be best and those that the masters actually played. (Hsu et al. 1990, 18)

Essentially, the researchers relied upon a combination of hill-climbing and OLS estimation to provide a fit between feature weights and optimum play, where "optimum" is defined as a correspondence between good human play and the idiosyncratic utility function's evaluation of intermediate strategies.[11] A combination of deductive (particularly for the end game) and computational work thus chose the features, while clever empirical work using a data set comprised of expert human play determined the weights of these features in a linear function.

The second characteristic that distinguishes machine chess from game theory proper concerns the use of *components*, which may be thought of in similar terms as a subgame. The distinction between the two concepts is that subgames, starting with a node in the extensive form, include all possible histories generated from that node (i.e., all actions from the starting node to the corresponding terminal actions). Component games, in contrast, are here defined as any linked collection of actions, whether or not the partial strategy includes terminal actions.

In machine chess, components often are used to simplify play. In fact, independent algorithms are defined for different components that added together form a complete game of chess. One example would be opening move libraries; another would be a specialized algorithm for end games in chess. What should be obvious is that the use of components dramatically reduces the combinatorics of strategies by decomposing them into computationally independent parts. It should be equally clear that doing so represents an enormous leap of faith, insofar as the independence of components does not at all follow from the extensive form of a game.

---

[11] Hill-climbing refers to a computational technique akin to a gradient search. One defines a neighborhood as a number of perturbations originating from a given action, then chooses a perturbation that results in the greatest increase in utility. By following the "best" perturbation from each action's neighborhood, one can computationally determine the location of local optima. Note that the idiosyncratic utility function defined above is a real-valued function defined on incomplete extensive forms, while the actual utility function for chess is {win, lose, draw} defined on the complete extensive form. There will be more discussion of optimization in the next chapter.

Components, like subgames, have associated utility functions, but, as noted earlier, they do not necessarily include terminal nodes as in game theory. This complicates the issue of assigning utility to strategies taken in a component game, as one cannot simply use the overall utility function of the complete game for the partial strategies of a component. The lack of complete strategies demands that "solving" any given component rests upon the assignment of an idiosyncratic utility function tailored to that component. As we have seen, these utility functions have no necessary relationship to the overall utility function of the game itself.

One example of the relationship between components and idiosyncratic utility functions would be the idea (probably correct, but perhaps wrong) that a rook's-pawn opening is inferior to a king or queen's pawn opening. If our component is taken to be the first N moves of the game (spanning most opening move libraries), and our idiosyncratic utility function is taken as outlined earlier (some combination of position, attacks on central squares, etc.), rook's-pawn openings are inferior. In game theoretic terms, this kind of statement is impossible to make given the combinatorics involved – and would be quite suspect if made informally. After all, it is possible that an equilibrium strategy for white for the complete game of chess starts with a rook's-pawn move.

Machine chess thus provides a great deal of insight into how one might go about modeling complex games using feature spaces and domain specific encodings. One starts with deductive models to gain insight into a problem using transparent, tractable methods; one also may use deductive methods to solve "easy" parts of a problem (e.g., the end game in chess readily succumbs to purely deductive approaches). Instead of resting at this point, however, one should try to build cumulative models that add verisimilitude, which I have defined as a model that provides results directly connected to empirical tests (whether they be out-of-sample data or analytic implications of the model). This may well mean that early deductive models are expanded using computational models; in machine chess, this process was aided by empirical work that chose the key parameter values of the idiosyncratic utility functions. At the end of the day, the "closer" the final model is to the real-world referent, the better. After all, one would be far less impressed with machine chess algorithms if they did not actually play the game but instead yielded vague aphorisms about cooperation, bluffing, and the like.[12]

"Brittle" Encodings and Equivalence Classes of Games: Empirical Implications

A quite different problem with the application of game theory to security studies concerns the "brittleness" of game theoretic models. But what does this mean? Simply put, it means that game theory should be able to model a broad range of games, and moreover, scale well with the different sorts of complexity one finds as problems in subfields like security studies. Else, we run into the difficulty that we model what we can and depend upon loose analogies to talk about the problems we are really interested in.[13]

This is potentially quite embarrassing, and much like the situation of teaching the IPD to undergraduates. In every class, at least one student, dissatisfied with the outcome of the single-stage game, attempts to change the payoffs.[14] We patiently explain that changing the payoffs, or the strategy sets, results in a *different* game; moreover, the "novel" game bears no obvious relationship to the original. This runs counter to most students' intuition and for good reason: Game theory demands a high level of precision because of the way it encodes games. The problem, of course, is that all this precision usually goes out the window when we make analogies and derive empirical implications of our models. One cannot assume that a two-player, complete information game of interactions between nations is useful for understanding the

---

[12] Note that there is an enormous "peace dividend" of writing models that play the actual game, rather than relying upon simplifying assumptions that change the game under consideration. By forcing modelers to focus on chess (rather than some simpler game that one believes, through unprovable analogies, is "like" chess), one can use data from real games to improve one's models.

[13] One example of this phenomenon is the short, unhappy literature on Colonel Blotto-type games. Despite enormous interest by military planners and think tanks, the literature petered out when results were not forthcoming. There is, however, relatively recent work (in the style of Axelrod's tournaments with the IPD) by the mathematician Jonathan Partington.

[14] You want to partially reward this type of behavior – at least it shows an understanding of the logic of the game, and there are examples where this type of skullduggery is rewarded. See, for example, Kreps and Wilson 1982 and their modification of the chain store paradox (Selten 1978).

nondyadic conflicts of the real world. Small changes (e.g., increasing the numbers of players) matter a lot; to date, there is no aspect of game theory that readily lends itself to theory that persists across "equivalence classes" of games.

The work of Signorino (1999) details exactly how disastrous this is for the empirical study of international conflict. On the one hand, Signorino notes that the measures typically employed in quantitative studies of conflicts (e.g., the balance of military forces) fail to "capture the structure of that strategic interdependence – that is, the set of states interacting, their sequence of decisions, options at decision points, the factors that influence their incentives, and the equilibrium effects of this interdependence on outcomes" (280). Further, if more than two states are involved in a conflict, using dyadic observations (as most everyone does), means that "each N-nation interaction becomes $N(N-1)/2$ independent observations, greatly expanding the size of the data set without adding any additional information to it" (280).[15] Given these problems, Signorino does the only sensible thing, and builds an empirical model that is more closely connected to the strategic game responsible for conflict.[16]

On the other hand, the obvious merit in including the structure of a game in the empirical specification leads to an unexpected difficulty in evaluating the predictive power of the model:

We know that small changes to a theory (e.g., the number of players, the sequence of their moves, the choices and information available to them, and their incentives) can have large consequences in what the theory predicts. If a theory is vague, then it is unclear what statistical model would be consistent with that theory. Therefore, if we want to ensure consistency between a theory and a statistical model, we must be as precise as possible in the specification of the theory. Given the requirement for theoretical precision, how are we to specify and test strategic theories without doing so formally? ... although the call for increased formalization of theories may be welcomed by many positivists, the importance of structures also seems to cut the other way. Consider the typical derivation and analysis of a positive theory. One major assumption

---

[15] I would quibble with the characterization of these expanded observations as independent – they are not IID, and this obviously sows confusion for empirical models.
[16] Essentially, he assigns probabilities to histories of the extensive game form. To avoid the problem of null probability histories, an error term is attached to these probabilities.

generally held – indeed, held throughout this article – is that the structure of the model remains constant across all observations in the data.... It does not seems unreasonable to suspect, however, that the true game structure changes over time and place. If even small changes in structure can make a large difference in likely outcomes, and if the true structure of the strategic interaction changes from observation to observation in our data, then what are we to make of any statistical results predicated on the assumption of a fixed game? (294–5)

One could easily expand the above point to include the possibility that the game in question is not quite right. Absent any theory of equivalence classes that would describe "similar" games, one has to suspect that empirical "verification" of a game has more to do with building a game to match a preconceived idea of the correct outcome than any genuine understanding of the causal processes involved. There are, after all, a universe of possible games. For any given empirical outcome, 10 different researchers might construct ten different games that all yield the "right" answer. Unless we have a source of novel data, it would be impossible to discriminate between them.

How brittle are game theoretic results? In the next section, I will review one of the more prominent models of international conflict, and see how well it holds up under the sorts of criticism advanced in this section.

AN EXISTING MODEL OF CONFLICT INITIATION

Perhaps the most famous paper that uses game theory to examine conflict is Fearon's (1995) "Rationalist Explanations for War." A game theoretic paper by Brito and Intriligator (1985) and work in military history by Blainey (1988) predate the work by Fearon in political science, and along with several decades of work in labor economics, all of these papers make essentially the same argument: wars, given what we know about bargaining theory, are not "rational" enterprises, insofar as one could always transfer resources rather than incur the costs of a conflict. Wars are thus the byproducts of incomplete or asymmetric information; or, as Gartzke (1999) puts it, "War is in the Error Term."

To make his argument, Fearon relies upon a standard bargaining game (see Osborne and Rubinstein 1990, for an overview) and makes the following assumptions to justify the claim that completely informed, rational players do not initiate conflicts:

1. war is costly for both participants;
2. two nations constitute the set of players;
3. the game is a single-stage, not repeated;
4. there exists a single fungible, continuous resource (i.e., no non-separabilities or discontinuities exist over multiple issues).

Given the bargaining model and requisite assumptions employed by Fearon, is there any reason to place much stock in his conclusions?

A fair answer has to be "no." The problem, as noted by Signorino, is that the conclusions of Fearon's work are very much dependent upon the structure of the formal model; if any of these assumptions are incorrect (or simply different), one can make no prediction about the effect this perturbation would have in generating his conclusions. And as I argued in the first chapter, one has to be especially wary of models that do not have the property of result convergence; that is, if minor perturbations of assumptions produce dramatically different results, one cannot place much confidence in the model.

His first assumption, that war is costly, is far from obvious in the macroeconomics peace literature. In their review of the macroeconomics literature, Isard and Anderton (1999) detail the impact of defense spending and conflict on various measures of the domestic economy, including GDP, inflation, unemployment, and technological investment. This overview makes clear that it is difficult to discern what the overall impact of military spending or a conflict is, especially if one understands that "the good" is not a single feature (e.g., GDP might go up if the resources used for the military were optimally reallocated but unemployment might rise). If one adds more dramatic but longer term effects such as a nation's overall technology for war and the experience gained from fighting, the picture becomes murkier still.[17] Last, Fearon is reluctant to identify who the relevant agents are in his model – who,

---

[17] See Diamond (1997) or Kennedy (1987). While one can take issue with the analysis presented within these volumes, they do serve as warnings to how difficult it is to evaluate the costs and benefits of military resource allocations over long time spans. Of the more memorable examples of how decreased military spending can result in dramatic, unexpected costs is China's self-mandated destruction of its naval resources in the 15th century.

in particular, receives utility from conflict (or its avoidance)? As Goemans (2000) has pointed out, it may in fact be beneficial for state leaders to engage in conflict in some circumstances, and they are but one candidate for the agent under consideration in Fearon's work.[18]

Fearon's second assumption limits the set of players to two nation-states. This adds obvious analytic tractability but at the cost of compromising any general conclusion generated by such a model. It is worth repeating that war is often nondyadic, and models that assume dyadic conflicts cannot be expected to have anything general to say about nondyadic conflicts (i.e., structure matters). As noted earlier, N-player games are difficult, in most circumstances, for game theory to encode; thus, formal modelers often make the choice of making analogies to the multiplayer case from a two-player game.

Fearon's third assumption is equally injurious if one wishes to derive general conclusions from his work. Conflicts in the international system are not single-shot games; and again, we should have no expectation that a model with repeated plays would generate the same conclusion. In fact, working from similar assumptions but generalizing to the repeated case, Garfinkel and Skaperdas (2000) show that it is often "rational" to initiate conflicts. The reason for this is easy to understand – following Fearon's setup, if nation A has epsilon more power than nation B, it could extract some amount from B so long as this total is less than the cost to B of fighting. Unfortunately (for B), if the game is iterated, the extraction of resources by A would certainly continue, and the gap would grow while B's chances of winning a conflict would decrease monotonically. B's best chance, then, of winning a conflict would be on the first round. By considering the repeated game, one arrives at an equilibrium result that is exactly the opposite of that presented by Fearon in his section on "Preventive War."

The final assumption, which seems trivial, is that nations may exchange resources in a transferable, continuous commodity. Imposing the assumption of unidimensionality in this way avoids a problem that Fearon himself notes: If the issues at stake are discontinuous or nonseparable, war may be the inevitable result of an inability to reach a bargaining outcome all sides prefer to war. Fearon dismisses this as unlikely, but surely, this is an empirical question, and issues such as the

---

[18] One also could look to Machiavelli's *Discourses* for a distinct viewpoint on the costs and benefits of war for a republic.

status of Jerusalem in the Israeli-Palestinian conflict might lead one to reconsider this assumption.

At this point, one might object that attacking assumptions in this manner is counterproductive, and cite the treatment of Friedman (1953) in Chapter 1 of this book as proof of this position. Friedman's version of instrumentalism is consistent, however, only if one heeds his call to compare models based upon their predictive power, rather than the verisimilitude of their assumptions. Fearon's model has no hypotheses that one could test, so under Friedman's terms it would be impossible to support or reject his model by tying the results to existing (or even hypothetical) sources of data on conflicts.[19] Assumptions, in this case, are all we have, both for evaluating the model and for generating substantive conclusions. Slight changes in the assumptions result in huge changes in the conclusions, and that should be a cause for alarm, especially when the assumptions fail to comport with the phenomenon in question.

Put another way, *all* conflicts are characterized by asymmetric/ incomplete information. But not all nations fight wars. For Fearon's model to be useful, one would have to provide a measurable dependent variable that could falsify the model.[20]

On a theoretical front, it seems that the state of affairs has not advanced much past the description offered in Niou and Ordeshook (1991):

For those who are not a party to it, the debate between realists and neoliberals seems a curious circus. While realists struggle with the specification of state goals and with alternative conceptualizations of balance of power, neoliberals offer vague admonitions that goals depend on context. Realists see cooperation as secondary to the conflictual processes of politics even though stability

---

[19] As noted in Chapter 1, one might also test a model by deriving nonobvious implications of the model, especially for problems that are data-poor.

[20] This is not to say that all purely deductive models are without merit – contrast Fearon's model with Arrow's (1963) seminal work. For Fearon, one needs to be confident that one is observing a two-player noniterated game where war is costly. For Arrow, *any* preference aggregation mechanism fails to satisfy a set of conditions one would like to be true of democracy. Absent any way to directly test a deductive model, one must consider the breadth of the theory. In Fearon's case, it seems fair to say that the model does not obviously describe anything about the world. To the degree it is a simplification of reality, one needs to map the results of the model back to empirical work to see if the simplification is a useful one. In the case of Arrow's impossibility result, it applies to all conceivable voting rules, which clearly covers any real-world case. Empirical work is thus beside the point.

requires some minimal level of cooperation to maintain alliances, whereas neoliberals, aside from references to examples in game theory that do not necessarily model any specific international process, fail to define precisely the necessary and sufficient conditions for cooperation.... Neoliberalism argues that institutions matter because they somehow modify the actions of decision makers both directly by altering the costs and benefits of actions and indirectly by modifying goals, whereas realism has difficulty explaining the institutions and patters of cooperation that characterize human affairs. (481–2)

In large part, many of the debates about the nature of the international system stem from the underlying difficulty of modeling processes such as alliance formation and the initiation of conflicts. Fearon's model was used here because it is widely recognized as one of the better efforts to model conflict initiation; one should not be deceived, however, into believing that better models exist elsewhere.[21] What is needed is a different approach that avoids the shortfalls noted earlier.

A final note to the wary is in order. Critics of game theory often depend upon unstated assumptions about the nature of reason or other matters of taste. That is not the case with the criticism presented here. What is at issue is whether or not game theory, as one encoding of many that exists for investigating human games, is particularly effective in generating predictions or explaining current strategic problems. My answer is that it is not, and to make this case, I depend upon an examination of existing models.

Additional weight may be added to the argument presented here by borrowing from analytic results into the nature of the encoding offered by game theory. Conitzer and Sandholm (2002) have shown

---

[21] Powell's (1993) work on the trade-off between domestic spending and military allotments is less a well-stated game than it is a set of parameters, where Powell picks parameter values (by assumption) that allow him to make his argument. The Markov Perfect Equilibrium is also superfluous in this paper, as it does not serve to refine the equilibria past what a subgame perfect equilibrium would do. Niou and Ordeshook's (1991) paper is the best of the existing models, as it tries to incorporate N players with the possibility of coalitions. Unfortunately, the results are driven by the twin assumptions of a single, continuous resource and the fact that the game terminates when one coalition achieves exactly one half of the available resources. The main strategy, given this condition, is for the losing nations to achieve a coalition with exactly one half the resources, thereby artificially terminating the game before one nation dominates. Both of these papers violate the spirit of my arguments on the nature of assumptions in Chapter 1, insofar as technical assumptions (or parameter choices) unrelated to the phenomenon in question drive the results.

that for many classes of "simple" games, finding a Nash equilibrium (or a related refinement) is a nonpolynomial (or, NP) hard problem:[22]

Noncooperative game theory provides a normative framework for analyzing strategic interactions. However, for the toolbox to be operational, the solutions it defines will have to be *computed*. In this paper, we provided a single reduction that 1) demonstrates *NP*-hardness of determining whether Nash equilibria with certain natural properties exist, and 2) demonstrates the #*P*-hardness of counting Nash equilibria (or connected sets of Nash equilibria). We also showed that 3) determining whether a pure-strategy Bayes-Nash equilibrium exists is *NP*-hard, and that 4) determining whether a pure-strategy Nash equilibrium exists in a stochastic (Markov) game is *PSPACE*-hard even in invisible games (and remains *NP*-hard if the game is finite). All of our hardness results hold even if there are only two players and the game is symmetric. (10)

What does this result imply? It means that as the size of even the simplest games increase, the number of computations that must be performed to check for the existence of a Nash equilibrium increases in nonpolynomial time (i.e., greater than polynomial). And yes, this is a very, very bad thing. Again, simple bean counting of the sort performed in Chapter 2 comes in handy. Fearon's model, despite the apparent simplicity, has a quite large parameter space, where almost any deviation from his assigned parameter values causes substantially (and unpredictably) different results.[23]

---

[22] For an overview of computational theory, see Papadimitriou (1994).
[23] For his basic bargaining model, you have the following parameter space:

  a. N players (set to 2 in Fearon's model)
  b. A single issue with a real value from the set [0..1]
  c. An ideal point for player A and B (or N in the most general case)
  d. A choice of utility function for A and B
  e. A number of iterations (set to 1)
  f. A rule for conflict (in Fearon's model, a simple statement of probability p)
  g. Costs C_a and C_b for the two players (assumed to be >0)
  h. An equilibrium concept (perfect Bayesian, a refinement of the Nash)

One could quite easily generalize Fearon's model by resorting to a computational model, thereby increasing one's ability to track how changes in parameter values modify the results Fearon presents. Using a deductive model with a particular set of parameter values as Fearon does is a valid first step to gain intuition about a problem. The argument in this and subsequent chapters of this book is that building a more general model is an essential second step in this process, even if this means abandoning a purely game theoretic approach and moving toward computational models. The final step, of course, is empirical work to test one's results.

AN ALTERNATIVE METHODOLOGICAL APPROACH

Game theory is a powerful tool, but, as I have argued here, it has limitations that prevent it from aiding us in understanding some of the more complex human games and decision-making contexts. In this section, I will start to build a methodological approach that aims to:

a. allow researchers to explicitly model more complex games and build upon prior efforts using feature spaces and domain-specific encodings;
b. avoid brittle encodings that limit the generalizability of results (i.e., develop an equivalence class for your model);
c. introduce a methodology to model component games and their associated (idiosyncratic) utility functions.

So what should one do differently if one wishes to study more complex games that model conflict initiation, alliance formation, and the like? As noted earlier in this chapter, machine chess offers a great deal of guidance in solving this problem using the tools of computational political economy. Accordingly, I will argue that a combination of methodological approaches yields better answers for complex problems in the social sciences.

Is Computational Political Economy Different?

I have presented a number of examples of computational modeling in this book, focusing on problems ranging from standing ovations to machine chess. As I have argued, the best examples of computational models often model things as they are, without relying upon simplifications that distort the problem of interest. The merit in computational methods is that the space between the model and the empirical referent, as in machine chess, is entirely absent. This allows for a much easier transition to empirical tests, which curbs many of the problems of mathematical modeling highlighted by this book. Further, computational models can also serve as bridges between different methods. In the alliance game presented later in this chapter, game theory will provide most of the intuition about this problem, which will then be expanded on using computational methods.

It is, however, true that many computational models fall short of the research design standards presented here. Just as in game theory, researchers are often content to present a model that is more of an existence proof than anything dispositive. To take one example, consider the investigation of state formation by Cederman (1994). In his computational model, there are roughly two dozen parameters chosen for convenience; changing them produces qualitatively different results than those found in the paper.[24] As with Fearon's model of conflict, one needs out-of-sample work to increase confidence that the model has something genuine to say about the world.[25]

Combinatorial Game Theory

In addition to the computational political economy literature, a source of inspiration is the almost unknown (in the social sciences) combinatorial game theory literature.[26] Combinatorial game theory studies human games with the following properties:[27]

1. there are two players;
2. moves are sequential (rather than simultaneous);
3. there is complete information;
4. strategies are finite;
5. there is an ending condition, which specifies a constraint that determines the winner. Typically, a player loses if she cannot move; for example, checkmate in chess;

---

[24] Some of these parameters are reported in the paper and some are only found in the code. A more thorough treatment of the fragility of Cederman's model and the implications for computational political economy is the subject of ongoing research by a team of graduate students at Duke University (look for a paper by Jolly, Reifler, Tofias, and Warren in the near future). In Cederman's defense, his practice of using computational models essentially as existence proofs is no different from the standard practice in game theoretic articles. For a more modern computational model, see Lustick, Miodownik, and Eidelson (2004). Like Cederman, Lustick has constructed a brittle model without any empirical tests, but there is the advantage that Lustick has made the code available with an interface that allows one to modify the parameters easily.

[25] Predictive tests aside, one can still improve on current practice in choosing parameter values. Instead of relying upon a magician's hat or convenience, why not choose values based upon real-world data? One may still go wrong (e.g., any particular sample may be misrepresentative), but a bet placed on data trumps bets placed on fancy. Rabinowitz, MacDonald, and Listhaug (2004), for example, develop a computational model of issue voting using parameters derived from the 1989 Norwegian Election Study. Another compelling alternative is to use qualitative or historiographical methods to choose parameter values.

[26] For an introductory text, see Conway (1976).

[27] This partial list is taken from Berlekamp, Conway, and Guy (2001). The list included in their volume is somewhat more restrictive, but relatively recent work in the field has relaxed some of their assumptions (which I have dropped).

6. there is an effort to build equivalence classes for all results; that is, to see whether one's results apply to other games.

This strain of game theory has been the province of mathematics departments, and at first glance, seems to have much in common with game theory or even represents a quite drastic domain restriction of game theory.[28]

What is less obvious, however, is the way the above tenets are translated into practice, which *is* quite different from game theory in the social sciences:

   I. encodings are specific to particular games;
  II. rules are often expressed as constraints rather than a set of strategies and associated utility functions;
 III. failing equilibrium play, the goal is for "better" play, typically measured against human performance;
  IV. the focus is upon more complex games that humans actually play; for example, hex, Go, or poker.

A trade-off is taking place here. By giving up a ubiquitous encoding and an emphasis on backwards induction as the solution algorithm (with the goal of finding equilibrium play), the above approach has more latitude to attack harder problems. The cost for more verisimilitude, as we will see, is a change in the nature of the conclusions we may draw from our models and complications in encoding the model (see Chapter 4). Combinatorial game theory and computational political economy thus share common goals; the following examples will demonstrate how to apply these abstractions to research questions in the social sciences.

A Return to the Currency Game

Machine chess, as outlined earlier, is an example of a computational approach to modeling. What this entails may not be entirely clear, however, without an example from the social sciences. Let us return to the currency game of the preceding chapter to see what distinguishes computational modeling from game theory.

In the last chapter, I developed a model of the currency game using the programming language Perl. Building a computational model of

---

[28] It does, however, have a great deal to do with constraint satisfaction problems/logic programming, a field of artificial intelligence.

this kind was a straightforward process of translating the dynamics of the game into Perl – in many respects, this is much easier than constructing a game theoretic model of comparable complexity. What do the results of a computational model look like?[29]

In my initial presentation, epsilon (the parameter for mutation) was held constant while N (the parameter for population size) was allowed to vary in a limited range. Despite the fact that the game has only two parameters, it is complex enough such that one's intuition can be wrong. Young (1998), from whom I borrowed the setup of the currency game, is in part led astray because he considers a very small subset of the parameter space in his initial forays into modeling the game. His claim is that the currency game is useful in studying path dependent processes, such as competing technologies (see Arthur 1989):

> Qualitatively, this process evolves in the following manner. After an initial shakeout, the process converges quite rapidly to a situation in which most people are carrying the same currency – say, gold. This norm will very likely stay in place for a considerable period of time. Eventually, however, an accumulation of random shocks will "tip" the process into the silver norm. These tipping incidents are infrequent compared to the periods in which one or the other norm is in place (assuming ε is small). Moreover, once a tipping incident occurs, the process will tend to adjust quite rapidly to the new norm. This pattern – long periods of stasis punctuated by sudden changes of regime – is known in biology as the *punctuated equilibrium effect*. (Young, 11–12; emphases in original)

Along with the text, Young provides graphs of his experiments with the currency game, illustrating how one sees multiple regime shifts when the game is allowed to run through 30,000 iterations. Unfortunately, for the experiments he details in the text, he relied upon small population sizes ($N = 10$) and a very high mutation rate ($\varepsilon = .5$) to generate his intuition about the properties of the game.

Young's intuition that the currency game generates relatively long periods of convergence characterized by sudden shifts to the

---

[29] I should caveat this to say what the results of a "good" computational model do look like. As noted in Chapter 1, some computational modelers present qualitative results based upon a limited sample of synthetic data. This practice should be avoided. To have any hope of understanding a computational model of any complexity, one needs to develop a theoretically justified feature space and present statistical work for the parameters that make up that reduced space. Results are thus specific to a feature space.

alternative currency is supplemented by a deductive result he derives later in his book. The theorem is short enough to be stated here:

Let G be a 2 × 2 symmetric coordination game with a strictly risk dominant equilibrium, and let Q_m, ε be adaptive learning in the playing the field model with population size m, complete sampling, and error [mutation] rate ε, $0 < \varepsilon < 1$. For every $\varepsilon' > \varepsilon$, the probability is arbitrarily high that at least $1 - \varepsilon'/2$ of the population is playing the risk dominant equilibrium when m is sufficiently large. (Young, 76)

What this theorem states is that if you have a suitably large population, a majority of the agents will be playing one currency. This majority is largest when ε is small. This adds quite a bit to his earlier chapter, but many readers might not be certain about what the properties of the currency game are for different values of n (m in Young's notation) and ε. Interpreting this theorem is elusive, even though it is deductively true.

Contrast Young's deductive approach with a computational model. In the appendix to Chapter 2, I list the Perl code that implements the currency game. The choice of language (Perl) is a matter of personal preference; what matters is that the goal of a computational model is twofold:

I. encode the rules of the game as accurately as possible;
II. iterate the computational model through a wide range of parameter values.

Once this process is accomplished, one has a tidy data set comprised of the following observations:

$$\text{mean regime shifts} \sim N, \varepsilon.$$

The final step is then to investigate the relationship of N and ε on the dependent variable (mean regime shifts) by estimating a statistical model. As noted in Chapter 2, a good model for the data generated by the currency game is a Poisson regression, which for a large number of observations spanning much of the parameter space described by N and ε is:[30]

---

[30] For the empirical work presented here, I generated 1,600 observations allowing N to range between [10...10,000] and ε to range between [.05....5]. This is not in actuality anywhere near enough observations for an accurate representation of the underlying DGP, but it is close enough for the purposes of this exposition.

Table 3.1. *Results for the Currency Game*

Poisson regression				Number of obs	=	1600
				LR chi2(2)	=	19492.69
				Prob > chi2	=	0.0000
Log likelihood = −2244.3969				Pseudo R2	=	0.8128
Num_reg	Coef.	Std.Err.	z	P > |z|	[95% Conf.	Interval]
N_pop	−.0351948	.0007884	−44.64	0.000	−.03674	−.0336496
Mutat_rate	15.4024	.9942932	15.49	0.000	13.45362	17.35118
_cons	−4.148296	.4970227	−8.35	0.000	−5.122443	−3.17415

The above model has a reasonable fit to the data and the residuals are normally distributed with very little variance. These results are different in character than Young's deductive work and easier to interpret. For a Poisson regression, the predicted values are given by e^{xb}. By examining representative values, it is easy to gain a more complete understanding of the currency game. For example, Young's preliminary analysis of the game is misleading, insofar as it only applies to very small populations. For $N = 10$ and $\varepsilon = .5$, $E(\cdot) = 0.015$ – in 1000 iterations of the game, this indicates that one would expect to see 15 regime shifts. If one considers a larger population and a smaller mutation rate – which more closely mirrors the nature of the real-world problem Young is using the currency game to investigate[31] – one quickly discovers that regime shifts never, ever happen. For $N = 100,000$ (still a tiny population) and $\varepsilon = .05$ (a reasonably high mutation rate), E(regime shifts) = 6.89E-1534 – and that is a lot of 0's.

As argued in the concluding remarks of Chapter 1, purely deductive investigations are most useful in starting an investigation and gaining some insight into how a problem works. Young's work is certainly helpful in understanding the dynamic process by which one regime, subject to small mutations, can move to another regime because of the nonzero probability that an arbitrarily large number of mutations will accumulate, pushing the system into a different regime. The possibility

---

[31] For example, the adoption of competing technologies such as a Wintel computer versus an Apple.

102 *Computational and Mathematical Modeling in the Social Sciences*

of regime changes, however, and the usefulness of this particular model is better understood when one develops a full-fledged computational model with the appropriate statistical analysis of the results. By doing so, one avoids intuition based upon a very small subset of the parameter space and brittle assumptions.

An Example Alliance Game

From the preceding example, we have seen how computational modeling can complement game theory; what we have not seen is what one does when presented with a more difficult problem. Often, computational and complex systems research in the social sciences has addressed different sorts of problems, such as path dependency, massively interactive social games, and the like. There are, however, domains of problems, such as those represented in security studies, where the focus is on complex interactions between highly motivated actors engaged in strategic games such as alliance formation and conflict. It is my contention that the lessons of computational modeling and combinatorial game theory offer insight into classes of difficult problems that elude purely game theoretic approaches.

To illustrate how one might develop models of complex phenomena in security studies, I now present an alliance game:

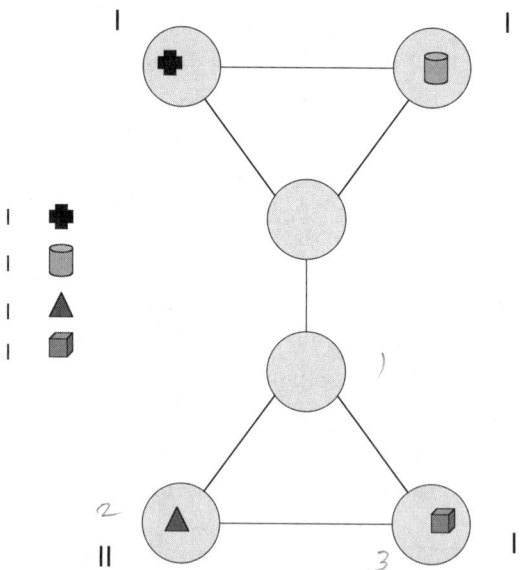

Figure 3.1. The Simple Diplomacy Game

Instead of representing this game as a set of strategies and their associated payoffs, one should note that Figure 3.1 uses a graph to represent the game. Additionally, the rules associated with this game are, in the spirit of combinatorial game theory, defined without explicit reference to the set of strategies:

The Alliance Game

1. The alliance game is represented by a graph G with a set of vertices X and edges U. There are six vertices in Figure 3.1; each vertex represents a location for a military unit. Each vertex also represents a supply (or resource) for building/maintaining a unit. Edges in G represent allowable moves for the units in the game.
2. Four players exist; each has a "home" territory where he or she starts with one unit on a vertex of the graph G (depicted with different shapes and colors on the graph). The home vertex is the only territory on the graph where a player may add units during Build/Remove (see below).
3. Each turn has three phases of play: Spring, Fall, and Build/Remove.
    a. Spring: units may move (change location between vertices), support (aid another unit in staying at a location or in moving to a new location), or do nothing (hold). *One action per unit is allowed per turn.* Territories captured (green circles on graph above) do *not* count for unit totals during the Spring turn.
    b. Fall: the allowable moves are identical to the Spring turn, except that territories captured DO count toward unit totals. If you capture a territory it remains yours unless another player occupies it for a Fall phase (n.b., moving into a territory in the Spring and leaving before Fall does *not* change ownership of a territory).
    c. Build/Remove: Count up the number of territories you own. Ownership, as noted above, is established by holding a territory for a Fall move (one also includes the starting territory). Ownership does not require a unit to stay in a territory; it is only disrupted by a different player occupying the territory for a Fall turn. If one owns more territory than one has units on the board, one adds units to the home territory (if it is owned by the player). If one owns less territory than one

has units on the board, one removes units from any territory on the board (player choice).
d. More than one unit of the same side may occupy a territory; but different players may not "share" a territory.
e. Units may support units of another player, as well as their own. Support may be given to defending units as well as to attacks.
f. When units come into conflict (i.e., different players move to the same territory, or a player attempts to dislodge a unit in a territory), numerical superiority – *adding all support orders* – wins. Losing units must retreat to an empty territory or be eliminated. For example, if two units attack a territory with one unit, the single unit must retreat. If another unit supported the defender, a tie would result and none of the four involved units would move.
g. *Ending condition*: the player who captures all six territories wins the game.[32]

It should be apparent that this game would be extraordinarily difficult to analyze within the confines of game theory. The strategies are (potentially) infinite, and despite the simple structure of the game, four players plus the ability to cooperate through support moves makes the combinatorics of this game quite ugly. One could, perhaps, argue that a few simplifying assumptions would somehow help one to gain leverage, but it is difficult to imagine what the complexion of these assumptions would be (unless they completely violated the spirit of the game).

So let us imagine we want to study this game, with the hope of improving our play against sophisticated human opponents or for developing insight into the dynamics of n-player alliances. Two definitions will help in examining the alliance game presented here:

Component game: A component of the game in Figure 3.1 is any proper, connected subgraph of G.

Component (idiosyncratic) utility function: Given that strategies are not necessarily finite (even in a component game), one needs to assign reasonable payoffs to actions taken in component games.

---

[32] This game is a simplification of the Avalon Hill game of Diplomacy, which is the study of some research in the artificial intelligence community.

One thus has to solve two problems before assigning payoffs to actions taken in a component game. First, one needs to choose an interval for analyzing payoffs; this can be difficult given the potential for nonterminating strategies. Second, one needs to choose a function that represents "progress" in the context of the component. For the purposes of the alliance game represented in Figure 3.1, one example of a component utility function has a horizon of one complete year, and the payoff is an integer that represents the delta of units in the last year (e.g., $0 =$ no change in the number of territories/units; $+1 =$ one territory gained; $-2 =$ two territories lost).

Some Example Components

So how does the forgoing discussion aid us in examining games like the alliance game? The (brief) inspection of several components will illustrate the main lessons of this section, and lay the groundwork for the more technical material in Chapter 4.

Example 1: Friends and Enemies, Together Forever. Figure 3.2 presents a typical component; in fact, this component eliminates the other two players of the game and focuses on one's own neighborhood. What, given this truncation of the game, would constitute good play? Given that we have already decided upon our component game, we also need to specify a component utility function. For the sake of the example, imagine we adopt the straightforward function that counts the delta in territories after each turn for each player (i.e., an integer from -1 to $+1$ for Figure 3.2). What type of play might transpire?

On the face of it, "safe" play might involve each player using their single unit to attack the other, as noted by the gray arrows in Figure 3.2.

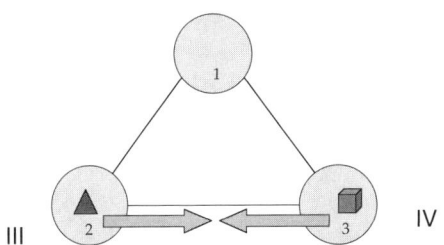

Figure 3.2. Friends and Enemies, Together Forever

What would the outcome of these actions be? Under the proposed utility function, the outcome would be 0 for both players. This infinite strategy {attack, attack,...} would be supported in part by the fact that moving away in the Fall turn would give the other player your home territory, thereby awarding an additional unit to your opponent along with your home base. Mopping up the remaining territory would be easy at this point.

There is one caveat to the play proposed here. Suppose that the players on the other side of the board have not read a book on game theory, and for whatever reason, they fight and one of them wins their half of the graph. While you continue with a self-reinforcing strategy, the lucky (or foolish?) winner on the other half of the graph will then have superior forces with which to attack your half. This should cause some concern with the forgoing analysis and illustrates how difficult the selection of a component and corresponding utility function can be.

Example 2: For Better or For Worse? Does the strategy set forth for both players in Example 1 constitute an equilibrium of sorts? Imagine that one of the players "defected" from the strategy on a Spring turn, resulting in Figure 3.3. At this point in the game, the all-important Fall turn is about to occur, and one would like to know which player has the advantage. At first glance, many people evaluate Figure 3.3 by awarding the advantage to player 4; he does, after all, occupy player 3's home territory, and stands to gain a unit as outlined above.

It is important to remember that any such evaluation depends upon an (often unstated) component utility function. As always, the component we are studying bears no obvious relationship to the final outcome of the game, and so any associated component utility function is in some sense unsupportable within the context of the complete game. Given

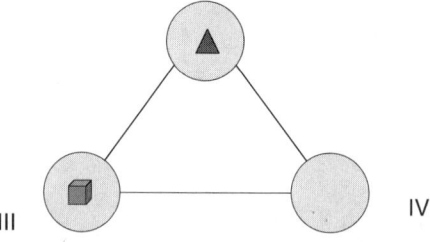

Figure 3.3. For Better or For Worse

the arbitrary nature of components and their utility functions, let us consider two candidates for a utility function:

Candidate 1: $u_1(\cdot) = \{-1, 0, +1\}$. This represents the delta in territories after the Fall move. It is plausible, insofar as gaining territory has to be seen as "good" and losing territory as "bad."

Candidate 2: $u_2(\cdot) = \{-1, 0, +1\}$, where $-1 =$ your opponent has more territory than you do at turn end; $0 =$ equal territory; and $+1 =$ you have more territory. Again, this is plausible, as it incorporates some notion of relative gains.

It cannot be overemphasized that there are a universe of utility functions that might be paired with any given component; these are simply two choices from that set. But, it is not the case that any component utility function will do – some are clearly better than others, though at this point it would be difficult to say why.

Nonetheless, what sort of action is implied by the two-candidate payoff structures? As in the preceding example, game theory will be used to build our intuition about the component game and these payoff functions.

Table 3.2. *Component Game u_1*

	Hold	Attack Open Territory	Attack IV's Home
Hold	(0,1)	(0,1)	(1,0)
Attack III's home	(0,1)	(0,1)	(0,0)
Attack IV's home	(0,0)	(1,0)	(0,1)

Nash Equilibria: [hold, hold]; [attack III's home, hold]; [attack IV's home, hold]; [attack IV's home, attack open territory]; [attack IV's home; ½ attack open territory and ½ attack IV's home]

Table 3.3. *Component Game with u_2*

	Hold	Attack Open Territory	Attack IV's Home
Hold	(−1,1)	(−1,1)	(1,−1)
Attack III's home	(−1,1)	(−1,1)	(0,0)
Attack IV's home	(0,0)	(1,−1)	(−1,1)

Nash Equilibrium: [1/3 hold and 2/3 attack IV's home, 2/3 hold and 1/3 attack IV's home]

108 *Computational and Mathematical Modeling in the Social Sciences*

With component utility function u_1 one finds multiple equilibria, and it would be difficult to guess what the outcome would be (or what strategy would result – see Binmore's (1992) discussion of chicken, 2825–6). One would imagine that player III would very much prefer the equilibrium [attack IV's home, attack open territory], but that player IV might well dissent given the comparative wealth of equilibria that advantage her.

With component utility function u_2 one finds a different outcome – a unique mixed equilibrium exists. Under this utility function, player III is at a disadvantage – his expected value is $-1/3$, while player IV can expect to receive $+1/3$.

Again one must raise the question of which utility function is "better." On the face of it, it would seem the second candidate does a better job capturing the reality of the game, but the only way to demonstrate the superiority of this selection would be to somehow show it results in better play (where "better" is defined as improving one's chances in the overall game).

Example 3: Tough Choices... The last example, displayed in Figure 3.4, represents a tough choice for both players III and IV. Ostensibly, they are potential enemies (i.e., there are no exogenously determined alliances), and player III has the opportunity to eliminate

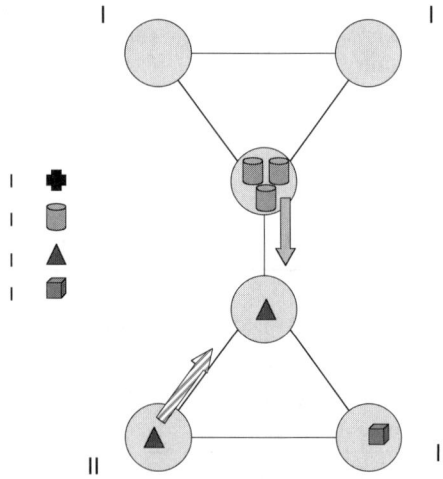

Figure 3.4. Tough Choices...

player IV from the game. Player II is dominant, however, on the northern half of the graph, and will win the game (by taking the open territory on the southern half of the graph) before player III completes his conquest.

There is, however, one possible play that would salvage player III and IV – it would involve player IV supporting player III at the open territory and player III holding. One could pick a component utility function that would result in precisely this play, but it is hard to imagine this particular utility function performing well when player II is not threatening the southern half of the graph – in most cases, player III should eliminate player IV. If player IV supports player III and player IV refrains from attacking player IV, one would have to admit that this unmistakably represents an alliance, given that these actions are costly (in the short term) to both players.

What is needed (for players III and IV) is an indicator of what is happening on the other half of the graph. When no clear victor exists on the northern half of the graph, player III should crush player IV and player IV should seek allies elsewhere (perhaps in attacking the open territory held by player III). When there is a victor, as in Figure 3.4, players III and IV should instead be the best of friends.

CONCLUDING REMARKS ON A METHODOLOGY FOR CHOOSING COMPONENTS AND IDIOSYNCRATIC PAYOFFS

If one has been counting, I have so far defined three sets in the previous section. First, there is the set of all possible component games; even in the relatively simple alliance game, there are a great number of components; for example, the number of combinations with one to five vertices is 62. Second, there is the set of component utility functions, which in most cases is infinite, although usually this set is limited by and naturally formed by the rules of the game. For example, the rules of chess would naturally constrain the terms of the component utility functions to the squares of the board, the pieces, and relations between the pieces. Last, there is the infinite set of indicators that might aid a player's selection of components or utility functions in different states of the game. What is one to do?

Before proceeding, consider the alternative. One could define a simpler game that is "solvable" using the encoding and algorithms of standard game theory and avoid the difficulties detailed earlier. Accordingly, one would then be forced to resort to analogies to discuss the behavior one is actually interested in. In the case of the alliance game, it would be difficult to imagine that the simplifying assumptions necessary for a game theoretic treatment would result in a game that had anything at all to do with the original version. And, as it stands, the unmodified alliance game presented here seems to illustrate alliance formation and conflict over resources in a much more realistic context than existing game theoretic treatments of these phenomena.

Seen this way, the preceding section has only made explicit what has been there all along – a huge search space (in terms of the combinatorics) that we can either account for in our models or assume away. We thus find ourselves in exactly the same situation as the last chapter when we considered empirical research. The curse of dimensionality and the possibility of brittle encodings are difficulties that models should grapple with. As we will see in the next chapter, developing a feature space that accounts for the complex strategic considerations highlighted in the preceding examples without running afoul of these difficulties is not easy. But, working through different encodings does develop a real understanding about the problem; this is to be contrasted with a game theoretic approach that would focus on deriving a set of limiting assumptions to produce an analogous game.

What methodology, then, is appropriate for constructing complex models with more verisimilitude? Given the difficulties in making analogies from existing game theoretic models to empirical tests, it is my belief that the only avenue available for studying more complex classes of games involves the use of computational models. As with the example of machine chess, a combination of deductive modeling to get one's feet wet and solve "easy" parts of the problem, computational modeling that builds upon this and adds verisimilitude, and statistical work to fix parameters and examine model performance, seems appropriate for most games.

This, in brief, would mean taking the following steps for the alliance game:

1. Use game theory to examine several candidate component games and associated utility functions, thereby developing

intuition about the problem. For each possible encoding, examine the implied parameter space to see if it is reasonable.
2. Define a population of agents, their selection of components, associated utility functions, and features of the game's state space. In preliminary trials, components that result from most specifications are quite simple – the reason for this is that larger components (i.e., with a greater number of vertices) make learning more difficult and are selected against in an evolutionary framework. The same general rule also seems to be true of features. Within components and their associated utility functions, the preceding examples make clear that a good deal of "deductive" or game theoretic reasoning is employed by agents in the model. The main thrust of the computational work is to reduce an incredibly complex game into bite-size fragments (fit for chewing by limited game theoretic agents).
3. Optimization theory would be employed to traverse the space of possible components and idiosyncratic utility functions. For example, if one used a genetic algorithm, less "fit" members of the population would reproduce proportionately less than more fit members. Operators such as mutation and crossover would be applied at the level of component selection and the idiosyncratic utility functions. One might, of course, use an alternative stochastic optimization technique such as hill-climbing, simulated annealing, or genetic programming.
4. The results of the computational model would be probabilistic assessments of favorable components (i.e., those most often employed by agents in the population), idiosyncratic utility functions, and features.
5. To test for stability, one would test populations against "similar" games or against human play (which provides an infinite supply of novel data) – if a population was robust under perturbations in the model's form and diverse human strategies, one would have more confidence that the model was not overly brittle. E.g., one could expand the alliance game in Figure 3.1 to include N players (where N is even) by adding symmetric components that match the existing component games defined in Figures 3.2 and 3.3. In all the games of this class, one would expect that the components

discussed in the previous section and their utility functions would have similar properties.

As noted earlier, the knowledge that results from this approach is probabilistic in nature (i.e., regressions would be used to demonstrate the utility of different components, their associated utility functions, or indicators), much as it was for the computational model of the currency game above. Further, results from computational models, while not as brittle as a game theoretic treatment, would be specific to classes of similar games – there would not be a universal encoding suitable for all possible games.[33] This represents a trade-off, insofar as the qualitative character of our knowledge of games would change dramatically under this methodology. In compensation, however, one arrives naturally at a way to provide equivalence classes of games, which I have argued is necessary if one is to link deductive or computational models to their empirical referents.

In the next chapter, we will explore these issues further, and I will detail both the optimization theory and computational tools necessary to derive computational models of the sort hinted at above. As an extended illustration of this methodological approach, I will develop the specific algorithms that instantiate component games and the associated utility functions that provide an encoding for the alliance game. Examining the choices involved in developing such an encoding will demonstrate the advantages and trade-offs between computational modeling and purely deductive work.

---

[33] As we will see in the next chapter, components and their associated idiosyncratic utility functions will be useful (i.e., robust) under many modifications to the structure of the alliance game. For example, if one defines an equivalence class by adding additional players in a symmetric fashion (i.e., groups of three nodes akin to those found in the current game) thereby expanding the number of players from 4 to higher multiples of 2, most of the results of the simpler game carry over without modification.

4

Why Everything *Should* Look Like a Nail

Deriving Parsimonious Encodings for Complex Games

INTRODUCTION

In this text, there have been a number of models presented, ranging in complexity from the currency game to the alliance game. On the simpler end of things, the currency game (in Chapters 2 and 3) can be implemented with 85 lines of documented Perl code.[1] The alliance game, by contrast, represents a much more significant undertaking. If, in fact, one set out as I did for the currency game, fired up a text editor, and typed in the code without any prior planning, disaster would certainly result. While it may well be the case that Perl would serve for this project, one would need a different paradigm for building a computational model to accommodate the complexities of the alliance game.

The goal of this chapter is to cover some of the material that would allow a researcher who is not an expert in computer science to derive

---

[1] Perl is a programming language derived from C and originally used for system programming in the Unix environment. It is often referred to as the "Swiss Army Chainsaw" of programming languages (this last is attributed to the hacker Harry Spencer). For more on the origin of Perl, see the FAQ at http://www.perldoc.com/perl5.6/pod/perlfaq1.html. For our purposes, it is important to note that Perl does not impose a specific paradigm of programming (e.g., object oriented); rather, it is an easy-to-use language for many jobs. It is worth noting that after assigning this project to some smart undergraduates, I discovered that one can produce a smaller (though more opaque) program in about half the size of my version (see the appendix to Chapter 2). Instead of recording the preference of each member of the population in a vector, one can instead store only the proportion of gold adopters and modify this scalar value as the result of single agents changing their preferences. If one wishes to extend the model to allow social networks, for example, then one has to return to a vector representation.

their own computational models for both simple and complex problems. I see this as fundamental to the methodology. If researchers take the alternative route – letting someone who is skilled in computer science derive models for them – there is a high likelihood that the final results will be difficult for the original researcher to interpret or verify, much less an outsider. There are simply too many choices made in the process of coding a model for the primary researcher to be disengaged from the process. Often, a qualitative final result will be desired, and the contract programmer will produce a model that achieves this result. But as is obvious from the previous chapters, with the size of the parameter spaces in question for most problems of interest, this is a trivial task. One can always produce a desired result; the subject of social science should be to pick the particular model that has the best chance of representing something genuine about the DGP. Moreover, when you do not build your models, you are unaware of how sensitive the results are to different encodings of the problem or parameter choices. If we believe the arguments in Chapter 1 on the nature of technical assumptions, it is imperative that the researcher be aware of the influence of these modeling choices.

For this reason, I am presenting a "work in progress" in this chapter. My research on the alliance game from the last chapter and alliance formation more generally is not finished, but because of this it provides an ideal opportunity to examine the choices made in deriving an encoding that specifically addresses the complexities of the alliance game. I hope it will become apparent that the choices involved in building a computational model are worthy of debate and constitute the core of any serious research endeavor. One should not "contract out" these choices or resort to limiting assumptions.

An additional goal of this chapter is to illustrate the process of constructing a computational model, along with some of the technical apparatus needed for such an enterprise. Given that much of this will be unfamiliar to social scientists, Appendix 1 to this chapter lists additional resources that are available to new computational modelers.

In addition to covering some of the computer science skills necessary for engaging in a computational modeling project, I also will provide a very brief overview of stochastic optimization theory. Most computational models are at core an exercise in optimization, and although there are very good mathematical treatments of optimization, it is easiest to understand the main issues from an algorithmic perspective – for example, how does one write a model that meets the requirements for implementing a genetic algorithm?

RULES OF CODING

The good news is that nearly everyone trained in a social science department has done some coding. Writing scripts in Excel, using a statistical package such as Stata or using an applied mathematics package such as Matlab all involve coding. Some of these packages make things quite difficult and have poorly implemented programming languages (e.g., SAS), while others are relatively easy to use and are based upon modern programming languages (e.g., S-Plus is similar to C/C++). Just as with scripts or statistical packages, computational models demand an attention to detail that is uncommon in human languages. Typically, when we speak or write something for human use, there is a large amount of redundancy built into our efforts. Making small errors does not make it all that difficult for someone to understand you. For example, *f y rmv th vwls frm ths sntnc, y cn stll rd t wtht mch trbl*. If, however, you type a line into Stata with just one mistake, you get an error that terminates your program.

The bad news is that the number and variety of programming languages and programming environments (i.e., the actual tool you use to create programs in a given language) are bewildering. There also are quasi-religious conflicts fought over which language/environment is the "best" for a particular type of application, further complicating the issue. The position taken here is that of the Luddite: Use the simplest tool that will get the job done with maximum transparency. Ideally, we would like to build models that other people can read and experiment with; the advice provided here thus serves that goal, and is not as concerned with more technical matters such as which programming paradigm is "best."

Choice #1: Programming Language

The first choice is not as important as you might think. Although there are a huge number of programming languages, most languages share a large subset of features. If you learn one language, you have in effect learned them all. Each programming language provides the ability to create:

i. data structures ranging from scalars (e.g., `int fred=99;` is a single integer) to arrays (e.g., `int fred[100];` generates a vector of 100 integers; `fred[50]` is one of them);
ii. user-defined functions (e.g., finding the maximum value in a vector);
iii. conditional statements (e.g., `if ($pop_mean>$N/2){$current_standard=1;} else {$current_standard=0;}`);
iv. loops (e.g., `for ($i=0; $i<$time; $i++) {// do something a number of times}`);
v. input and output, typically to flat data files for use in a statistical package.

As you may guess from this list, constructing a computational model is not entirely dissimilar to constructing a proof. Functions, conditional statements, and loops are purely deductive in nature, and one can read a program in much the same way one reads a proof. The most salient difference is that the size of most computational models is an order of magnitude or two larger than a proof, thereby making it very difficult to "comprehend" an entire body of code. While there are examples of published proofs that are wrong, it is far more likely that insidious mistakes of logic lurk within a large computational model, undetected by anyone.[2] There is also the subsidiary problem that journals do not have the space to print an entire computational model, thus compounding the difficulty in evaluating these models.

Given these problems, my advice in choosing a programming language is thus motivated by transparency rather than current ideas about what constitutes "the good" in computer science curricula. For other people to evaluate your work (and hopefully catch some of your

---

[2] It may not be obvious to new programmers that even if your program executes, you may still have logical mistakes in the code. This means that although your model is producing results, they are not the results you were looking for.

errors), it seems important to focus on languages that are widely used, readable, and parsimonious.[3]

I would thus recommend Perl, Python, or C as a starting language. Although there are excellent reasons for adopting an object-oriented language such as Java or C#, the barriers to entry for these languages are relatively high and it is more difficult for nonprogrammers to read your code. Many programmers, once they learn a simple language such as Perl, Python, or C, will have an easy time learning another language and will have the background to evaluate the other available choices. But if the goal is to start building models with a minimum of training in computer science, Perl, Python, or C are good choices.[4] By learning one of these language, you also will join a larger community. This, of course, means that you can share code with other researchers.[5]

Choice #2: Development Environment

As noted, social scientists have two goals in building computational models: The models must be transparent (i.e., other researchers can

---

[3] For example, to write the standard introductory program that prints out the message "Hello World!," Java requires some code that looks like this:

```
public class helloworld {
      public static void main(String[] args) {
            System.out.println("Hello World");
      }
}
```

To do the same task in Perl, you need:

```
print "Hello World";
```

While there are excellent reasons for the overhead in the Java program that become more apparent in a larger project, it is clear that for a novice, the Perl code is much easier to interpret (or show to a colleague).

[4] An additional benefit of C is that C is the parent of many other languages (including Perl).

[5] One key example of the importance of sharing code is the "Numerical Recipes" series of books by William Press. This series contains algorithms for mathematical and scientific programming and as such is an enormous time-saver (e.g., pretend you want to write a random number generator, or a Normal distribution, or . . .). The series has algorithms for C, C++, Fortran, and Pascal, but there are differences in how much attention is paid to each language. The latest C++ edition is from 2002; C and Fortran are 1992; Pascal is 1989. Though there are numerous libraries for scientific programming in Java or Pascal, the user community is not at this point in time as large as the C/C++ community (and closely related languages).

look at the code) and easy to manipulate (i.e., others can change parameters/explore the model). Ideally, computational models should be made freely available for every publication and have an interface that allows complete novices to adjust parameter settings and produce novel data.[6]

The Quick and Dirty Approach: The easiest way to begin programming would be to use a scripting language such as Perl or Python along with a quality editor/debugging tool. The editor for a development environment is typically a customized Microsoft Word style of program. Features include auto-indenting the bodies of loops and other stylistic modifications applied to what you type, thereby making it easier to read the source code. The debugger allows you to do things like watch the values of different variables as your program executes and set stop-points in the code so you can halt execution and see what is transpiring. ActiveState Komodo for Perl and Python is my current favorite, but there are many other editor/debugging tools on the market.[7]

The only disadvantage to this approach is that the support for mathematical and scientific programming is not as robust as in C/C++ or Java, and one will be forced to reinvent the wheel in some cases. An additional consideration is that the equivalent program in Java, Perl, or Python is typically much slower than a program written in C/C++ or C# for many mathematical or scientific applications.[8] When you are trying to traverse a large parameter space, this actually matters despite advances in hardware.

The Pay to Play Approach: Perhaps the best way to build applications is to provide a Windows OS-based Graphical User Interface (GUI), so that programming novices can easily modify your parameter

---

[6] All of the latest versions of the source code and computational models used in this text are available on the author's Web site http://moria.poli.duke.edu/overallpage.htm.
[7] Komodo runs on Windows, Solaris, and Linux operating systems.
[8] It is worth noting that for computationally intensive models, all languages are not created equal. For my simple currency model, there were large differences in the speed of executables. For a parameterization with a population of 10,000 agents, 1,000 iterations, and one agent changing per iteration, a Windows application written in C++ (with the Borland Builder compiler) took 3 seconds. A console application written in Perl took 13 seconds, and a Python program profiled with the Psyco tool took 6 seconds. Java would likely finish somewhere between the Python and Perl programs. These measures are, of course, hardware specific.

values. Both the Borland Builder series of development environments and the Microsoft Visual Studio are excellent tools for building Windows OS applications. Both tools provide a palette of Windows features (e.g., menus, toolbars, etc.) that allow a relative novice to produce a graphical interface for their application. Although there is an opportunity cost to learning these tools, the payoff is that one can produce a computational model in which it is easy to modify parameters without requiring that someone fiddle with a compiler.

The largest negative for pursuing this course is the startup cost. To program for the Windows OS, you have to learn a smattering of object-oriented programming, as all the elements of the GUI are objects. Windows OS applications are also driven by events – for example, a mouse click or a menu choice – and program execution is not a straight-forward progression from point A in the code to point B.[9] Finally, if you use the Microsoft Visual Studio, you are constrained to producing applications for one hardware platform and one operating system.[10]

Once you choose a programming language and a development environment, the next step is to start programming. One good option would be to replicate (without peeking) the currency game detailed in this text. Given that the outcome is known (see the results in Chapter 3) and the code is straightforward (see the appendix to Chapter 2), this would be a feasible first project. It also would be worthwhile to buy an introductory text on programming – my favorites are offered by O'Reilly Press.[11] Be warned, however, as even introductory texts cover a huge amount of material. Learn the absolute basics (see the list above under *Choice #1: Programming Language*) and start coding! For an additional set of books you should add to your programming library, see Appendix 1 to this chapter.

---

[9] In many C-based languages, there is a main() function where the program starts execution, though in Python this is implied rather than explicit. In event-driven programs in a graphical user interface type of operating system, your main() function will often be the result of the user selecting a menu item or clicking on a button to start execution of the main block of code. In standard console applications (e.g., for Unix command shells), one explicitly declares a main() function where execution begins.

[10] The Builder package adds the ability to produce Linux applications.

[11] http://www.oreilly.com/

A final note is warranted whatever approach one adopts. Whenever possible, *use functions*. In this respect, my Perl code in Chapter 2 for the currency game is quite poor, as it has no functions. A good practice in coding models is to make certain that each function is correct, rather than continuing to add code. If you have an error in your code (and you will), and your code is divided into a logical set of functions, you only have so far to look to discover the error. If, however, your code is not divided into functions, it is impossible to know where the errors lie. You will have to search the entire body of code for every error, which substantially complicates the process of debugging. My Perl code would be much better if I had one function to initialize the population, one function to draw an agent and update the agent, and another function to check for regime shifts and output the data. With this framework, I could have tested and debugged each function independently – a huge savings in debugging effort.[12]

An example of how to use functions is in Appendix 2 of this chapter.[13] For this example, I used Python instead of Perl, but, as you will note, the code is very similar, reinforcing the point that getting started using any programming language is better than delaying. Once you know one language, it is almost always possible to read another language. The size of the program is increased somewhat over the Perl code,[14] but it has improved readability and one could more easily use these functions for other projects. In addition to using functions to aid in debugging, breaking up the code in my Python program allowed me to profile the code and see where it was slow. My initial program used integer random number functions in the init_all() function, which were poorly implemented in the Python libraries. The result was an executable program that was three times slower than the version presented here that uses real valued random number functions. By commenting out my functions one by one, a

---

[12] But, for small projects, one sometimes cuts corners ...
[13] In Perl, functions start with the keyword sub, for subroutine. In Python, def accomplishes the same task. Python is also unusual insofar as it uses the tab key to declare blocks of code, while Perl follows the more traditional approach of using brackets (i.e., {and}).
[14] Note that the Python code does less than the Perl program. It does not allow for printing to a file, nor does it allow for multiple agents to choose each time period.

helpful individual on the *comp.lang.python* newsgroup discovered the problem.

BUILDING COMPUTATIONAL MODELS[15]

In this section, I will use the alliance game to demonstrate how one goes about building computational models. There are two main issues involved in most computational models that warrant treatment here:

I. What is the best encoding for the problem? That is, how does one represent stategies and utility functions for the popluation of agents that will play the game?
II. How does one search this population for good strategies? That is, what stochastic optimization technique is appropriate for the problem?

Answers to these questions are rarely cut and dried, and for that reason, a computational modeler will continually revise these answers until useful results are achieved. Empirical work is thus a necessary part of modeling; without it, little progress is possible and it is difficult to discern how much of the heavy lifting is being done by assumptions rather than the core logic of the model.

As noted in the previous chapter, the alliance game is not an "easy" problem. Strategies are infinite and backwards induction is impossible. An additional complication is that a naïve parameter space is pathologically huge – without a good encoding and concomitant feature space, any results would likely be fragile. It is necessary to emphasize a point raised above. Problem encodings and feature spaces are not unique; different (and reasonable) researchers may arrive at very different computational models. This is why, to a large degree, I adopt a modified view of Friedman's epistemology in Chapter 1 and insist on the importance of out-of-sample tests and equivalence classes of games. Models need to be immune to minor perturbations in how different researchers encode the problem. Further, models should have as little distance as possible between the model result and the real-world

---

[15] This section assumes some familiarity with a modern programming language. Most of the example code aims at simplicity (over parsimony or elegance), however.

referent. Without the same empirical referent (that is, the same dependent variable), comparisons between models become impossible.

Fortunately, humans can play the alliance game, and one additional benefit of dealing with the actual game rather than an analogy that is amenable to game theory is that one can test results against human play. This is a huge benefit, as it allows the researcher to use novel data to continually revise the computational model without running afoul of the prohibition on overfitting models.

A Failed Encoding for the Alliance Game

The main idea behind the the alliance game encoding discussed in Chapter 3 is straightforward. Agents playing the game have a set of component games and utility functions, so that in any given state of the game they produce a strategy for that state. A number of key details necessary for implementing these ideas in code were not, however, developed in Chapter 3. The trick to studying the alliance game is to arrive at a representation of possible strategies and payoffs that results in a tractable parameter space. To see why this is important, it is useful to examine an attempt (on my part) that failed to produce an encoding that was parsimonious enough.

The goal of a successful encoding is to initialize a population of agents that will search for effective strategies to play the alliance game. As I argued in Chapter 3, agents playing the game will rarely "look" at the complete graph and will instead focus on component games as a way to defeat the curse of dimensionality. Because components represent a partition of the game graph, the encoding needs to be flexible enough to represent arbitrary component games for different agents.[16] Each component has a corresponding idiosyncratic utility function so that component strategies can be evaluated. For player $i \in N$ ($N = 4$ for the version of the alliance game considered here), we have a set of components C_{ix} where $\bigcup_x C_i = G$, x is an index of components and G is the graph of the entire alliance game. Each C_{ix} has an associated U_{ix}, which

---

[16] The reason is that we do not know *a priori* what the good components or idiosyncratic utility functions are. We thus choose an encoding, generate a large population of agents with a variety of different component games and utility functions, then use a stochastic optimization algorithm to find good components / utility functions.

is an idiosyncratic utility function for that component. Each agent is thus represented as a pair ⟨C_i, U_i⟩ and will be randomly initialized at the start of the model. Note that, at this point, it is not obvious what terms will make up the component utility functions (though see below).

My first attempt at modeling component games was to partition the game graph and develop a normal form game representation for the components. The main parameter in such an encoding is the horizon for the normal form game – that is, how many turns into the future should be used to generate the strategies for the normal form game? The structure of the game might lead one to the conclusion that agents should consider an entire turn in their components. Strategies for both the spring and the fall move would thus be included in the normal form game. After each spring and fall phase the game updates how many units each player possesses, thereby creating a powerful argument for a horizon that includes both phases.

To see how this possible encoding would work, consult Figure 3.1 and assume it is the fall phase after which new units are added. Recall that player III's unit is represented on the figure by a triangle and player IV's by a square, and the component game includes three vertices (the lower half of the overall game) labeled {1,2,3}. As a final step, assume the component utility function is a calculation of how many units are gained or lost by the players.[17] The normal form of the game for the fall move would be:

Table 4.1. *Component Normal Form for the Alliance Game*

	□ holds at {3}	□ → {1}	□ → {2}	□ s {1}	□ s {2}
▲ holds at {2}	(0,0)	(0,+1)	(0,0)	(0,0)	(0,0)
▲ → {1}	(+1,0)	(0,0)	(0,+1)*	(+1,0)	(+1,0)
▲ → {3}	(0,0)	(+1,0)*	(0,0)	(0,0)	(0,0)
▲ s {1}	(0,0)	(0,+1)	(0,0)	(0,0)	(0,0)
▲ s {3}	(0,0)	(0,+1)	(0,0)	(0,0)	(0,0)

Note: → indicates an attack and s indicates a support order. * represents a lost starting vertex.

---

[17] This component utility function is of course not unique. Another candidate would be the actual number of units available to each player after the fall update, or the delta between the two players' unit counts, or some consideration of whether or not the player has lost their starting vertex (in the normal form used as an example in the chapter, these payoffs are marked with an *).

Throughout this chapter, the example code will be in the programming language C. One should note that the syntax is almost identical to Perl or Python code and instantiating normal forms in C is quite easy.[18] One only needs to declare a two-dimensional array and store each player's payoffs:[19]

```
enum strategy {hold, attack, support}; // list possible
strategies
struct payoff {
// record player 1 and player 2's payoffs -- one could use
doubles instead of ints
int p1;             // record player 1's payoff
strategy p1_strat;  // record player 1's move
int p2;             // record player 2's payoff
strategy p2_strat;  // record player 2's move
};
payoff normal_form[5][5]; // declare normal form for component
game
```

For bookkeeping, I have added the strategy of each player to the payoff matrix. Otherwise, the only (perhaps) unfamiliar piece of code in the above declaration is the use of the enum statement; this allows one to declare an ordered list of names that can be used in assigning variables. Implicit in this declaration is a one-to-one correspondence with the integers [0...n], for the n elements in the enum statement. As an example, if player 1 holds for a unit, one can write very readable code:

```
Normal_form[0][0].p1_strat = hold;
// this is much better than Normal_form[0][0].p1_strat=0;
// where you have to remember that 0 = hold
```

The idea behind this code may not be apparent unless you have previous experience with computational models.[20] At this point, we have empty arrays representing normal form component games. What

---

[18] Lines preceded by // are comments; that is, the compiler ignores them as whitespace. Brackets ({,}) denote blocks of code. Semicolons (;) denote the end of a block or a line.

[19] This snipped of code features a custom data type defined by the modeler starting with the keyword struct, which stands for structure. Structs are common in many languages, though sometimes they go by different names. And sometimes, to confuse new programmers, languages rename keywords. In C#, for example, structs are a type of object.

[20] One can find a very clear presentation of how to initialize agents in the case of the IPD in Axelrod (1984).

is missing is a set of payoffs for each element in the array. One could certainly choose (by hand) a utility function for each agent, though as we will see, this turns out to be too costly given the parameter space for the problem. An easier way to define payoffs would be to randomly initialize each cell, and trust that if we have a big enough population of agents and a reliable optimization technique, we would select out agents with "good" utility functions. Yet another approach would be to define a feature space that takes the state of the game as an input and produces a preference ordering for possible moves. Each agent would have slightly different weights on the elements of this feature space, as was the case with the chess example in Chapter 3 (see the section on Fitness Functions later in this chatper for more on this technique).

To expand this approach to an encoding that includes both the spring and the fall moves together in the component would require a larger normal form game consisting of a 25 × 25 matrix. This is still tractable, but keep in mind that what we are modeling is the smallest of special cases – the component game in Figure 3.2 has only two units. To be truly general, we would need to plan for the possibility that a player had up to five units in the component game.[21]

As advocated in Chapter 2, one should at this point determine the approximate size of the parameter space implied by this encoding of the alliance game to see whether one is running afoul of the curse of dimensionality. In the component game of Figure 3.2, each unit has five options: {hold, attack the other two vertices, support the other two vertices}.[22] Thus, the number of entries in the normal form matrix would be 5^5 for the player with five units and 5 for the player with one unit for each spring/fall phase; an encoding which had a horizon that spanned one year (i.e., both phases) would have 5^{12} elements in the normal form matrix.

While we could certainly try to be clever and strip away a large number of these elements, 5^{12} is far too large a parameter space, and we have only modeled part of the game. Given the logic of the preceding chapter on component utility functions, it would be desirable to

---

[21] One does not need to plan for six units, as at that point the game is over.
[22] If one changes the component, this calculation will not be invariant. For example, in Figure 3.4 of Chapter 3 one might decide an appropriate component adds the nearest middle vertex. This would expand the number of options for units on the middle vertex to seven possible strategies.

126 *Computational and Mathematical Modeling in the Social Sciences*

avoid "picking" a particular utility function for each component, and instead allow different agents to arrive at different component utilities. A natural way to do this with the normal form games presented here would be to assign random utilities to the payoffs of the normal form matrix that would result in a total ordering. But, with 5^{12} elements in the array, this approach to encoding the alliance game is impossible.

The main advantage of using game theory to model player actions within each component is that strategy is based upon a consideration of the other player's possible actions and incentives. One way to reduce the size of the game's encoding would be to go the route of the machine chess models detailed in Chapter 3, which sacrifices a consideration of the opponent's future moves for utility functions that are essentially "blind" to strategic considerations.[23]

A Better Encoding

The preceding encoding is a failure, but it is useful to think about why it failed. Take a moment and think about what is responsible for the explosion in size of the parameter space. The first complication involves the joint consideration of a player's strategies. With, for example, four units and five possible actions for each unit, considering the units in concert as one would do if one relied upon a normal form game involves 5^4 possible actions and up to 25 actions for opponents. A slightly bigger graph for the alliance game with the possibility of more units would complicate matters enormously, even though the new game might be fundamentally similar. It would be difficult to argue that this encoding would allow one to investigate a very large class of games or produce results that were insensitive to small changes in the game (i.e., the results would not apply to an equivalence class of similar games).

The second complication involves the horizon for a component game. As noted, the most natural encoding would model decisions

---

[23] The idiosyncratic utility functions for chess included terms such as material, position, and the like, which reduces the parameter space substantially. As soon as one includes terms for the opponent's actions, the parameter space explodes. In terms of the component game that is the subject of this chapter, one could adopt this approach by encoding strategies for each player without regard to opponent strategies. The resultant parameter space would be then be 5^{10} in the worst case scenario (i.e., a player has 5 units), a considerable reduction but still not enough.

for spring and fall simultaneously. The fact that units are updated after a complete year is likely important, but again, there is a cost for the parameter space. Whatever choice one makes for strategies must be squared if one choose a horizon spanning a complete year. Four units with five actions each thus balloons into 5^{12} possible outcomes when the horizon is extended.[24]

The main advantage of thinking about problems in this fashion is that it forces the researcher to confront the unique complexities of the problem itself. Limiting assumptions, in contrast, deflect attention from what makes a problem difficult and turns the focus to the mathematical technique. Assumptions may allow you to "solve" a game using the tools of game theory, but the cost is obvious: You are no longer studying the problem you set out to understand, and you will not generate results that directly map to the empirical referent. Whatever encoding one finally settles upon for the alliance game, it is necessary to produce a set of results that let you play the game directly. Without this standard, it would be difficult to test one's results.

With this said, the encoding I have currently settled upon has a few subtleties designed to incorporate as much of the complexity of the game as possible within a parsimonious framework. The first "trick" involves disentangling the moves of multiple units. A player would like to use units in concert – for example, an attack with one unit might benefit enormously from the support of other units. To capture this behavior without the enormous costs of the forgoing approach, I use an encoding where strategies for units are decided upon sequentially, but with a small innovation. Each unit of a player after the first has the additional information of what the preceding unit in the sequence chose to do. For example, if the first unit moves to a vertex, the second unit has that action as a parameter.[25] The question then is how large is this strategy space?

If, in the worst case scenario there are five units and the first unit has five possible actions. The second and all subsequent units have five actions that are conditioned by the possible actions of the

---

[24] More generally, the parameter space increases exponentially as the horizon is lengthened.

[25] One could instead have all units access the action of the first unit. Preliminary tests indicate that accessing the $(n-1)th$ unit is a better encoding.

first unit. This results in 105 elements in the parameter space, and instead of expanding exponentially as in the encoding that relied upon the normal game form this encoding is linear in the number of units.[26]

The second simplification in this encoding is that the explicit strategies of opponents are not accounted for. Rather, I use a feature space that stores the opponents' likely actions in a far more economical manner without completely ignoring their strategies. The preceding strategies are parameterized for the following features of each vertex on the board:

i. the owner = {the player, an opponent, empty};
ii. the number of units = {0..5}.

The number of elements in this feature space is equal to the number of vertices in the component multiplied by the forgoing two parameters. For the example component considered here, this would be $3 \cdot 3 \cdot 6 = 54$, which also scales as a linear function of the number of vertices.[27] This encoding thus considers the location and the number of the opponents' units as a proxy for their strategies. If one knows how one's opponents have allocated their forces, one can assume the worst and make plans accordingly.

The complete parameter space for the example component used in this encoding would thus be $108 \cdot 54 = 5832$ elements. This is not by any means small, but, compared to 10^{12}, one has to be happier. More to the point, this is close to a size that is small enough to model computationally with confidence that optimization algorithms will be effective.[28]

---

[26] This is equal to *(n units)* · *(5 actions)* · *(5 actions for unit n − 1)* + *(5 actions for unit 1)*.
[27] This is equal to *(m vertices)* · 9.
[28] In subsequent (and ongoing) revisions of the computational model, I have simplified the encoding further. For the ownership parameter, I removed "open" and expanded the category of "opponent" to include open vertices – they are now recorded as an opponent's vertex with 0 units. For the number of units, I replaced {0..6} with {0, 1, 2+}. Since at most 6 units can exist at any time in the game and this total is subdivided between components, this alteration has had no negative effect on performance. Finally, the graph G is symmetric, so I do not have multiple components for each agent. Rather, if the agent uses a 3-vertex component (like the one used for the example in this section) the "optimal" play that results from the first component is applied to units on the other half of the graph. I also use this approach to modeling 2- and 4-vertex components, even though there is some overlap of vertices. Finally, I run tournaments of each component game separately, and "piece together"

The final complication involves the horizon. We would not, by including both spring and fall together, want to square the forgoing parameter space. In general, choices that involve exponential expansions of the parameter space are to be avoided – imagine if we wanted to include a longer horizon. The feature settled upon here to model time without significantly expanding the parameter space uses a binary variable to record whether it is spring or fall. This doubles the parameter space, but the hope is that conditioning the strategy selection on which part of the year it is hopefully captures most of what we are after.

Optimization in the Alliance Game

Now that we have a rough idea of what the encoding for component games will look like, we have to address the related problem of conforming our encoding to a stochastic optimization procedure. Instead of deducing what good play looks like for one player with enormous ability, computational models typically model a population of limited agents evolving strategies through time. The optimization algorithm employed here will be a genetic algorithm, and our encoding will need to provide agents in a format that allows the genetic algorithm to function.

Before we examine how well the preceding encoding conforms to the requirements of a genetic algorithm, it is necessary to sketch a bit of optimization theory. Many readers are probably familiar with analytic optimization methods such as a gradient search or Newton's method. Both of these require a continuous, differentiable function and have difficulties with local optima. In contrast, stochastic optimization algorithms, such as simulated annealing and genetic algorithms, do not require well-behaved functions and to some degree overcome the presence of local optima.[29]

---

meta-agents with multiple components at the end of these tournaments. An open question for this ongoing line of research is how much the parameter for {spring, fall} helps performance. Because it doubles the parameter space, I am investigating ways to remove it. See the author's Web site http://moria.poli.duke.edu/overallpage.htm for more details and the latest source code.

[29] For good introductory texts on optimization, see Ballard (1997), Chong and Zak (1996), Mitchell (1996), and Sundaram (1996). Ballard is the best introductory treatment, though Chong and Zak is nearly as readable and covers more territory in optimization proper. Mitchell's text is an excellent union of theory and practice, but focuses solely upon genetic algorithms. Sundaram is the most theoretical of the lot and is geared toward the economics literature.

For the encoding detailed for the alliance game, a genetic algorithm is appropriate. The parameter space utilized by the agents playing this game is a complex function that is not suitable for analytic methods; the hope is that a stochastic method such as a genetic algorithm will produce tolerable solutions comparable to nonexpert human play.

Genetic algorithms, like all stochastic optimization approaches, have two essential elements.[30] The first element attempts to optimize locally by searching within a neighborhood of the current location in the parameter space. The second element perturbs locations to jostle solutions from local optima.

To see how this works, it is easiest to first consider the simpler hill-climbing algorithm.[31] Hill-climbing involves searching within a well-defined neighborhood of the current location. The direction of greatest improvement in that neighborhood is selected as the new location; this process is then iterated until every point in the neighborhood is inferior to the current location. The way hill-climbing avoids local optima is by repeating the search algorithm for different starting values. The hope is that one of the starting values achieves a global optimum (or something close to it), but there is always the chance that in a rugged landscape, one will never succeed.[32] It is, however, easy to see that hill-climbing locally optimizes through an iterated exploitation of neighborhoods and perturbs away from local solutions by repeatedly trying new starting values. Figure 4.1 shows a very simple fitness landscape (not least because it is one dimensional) where there are two local optima and one global optimum. Note that where you end up is sensitive to your initial condition – for example, if the pink ball had started a bit further to the left, it would have ended at the leftmost local optimum. Only by dropping multiple balls do you have any confidence you will find the global optimum. This is why, in the context of a complex problem

---

[30] What follows is a gross simplification, although I hope a useful one. This is not a text on optimization, but I believe the main issues involved in stochastic algorithms are simple enough to be understood in the terms presented here. You have been warned.

[31] Hill-climbing is very similar to a gradient search but does not require that the function be differentiable.

[32] Another problems concerns the selection of a step-size for the algorithm. Imagine that a large step was chosen for Figure 4.1 – it is possible the ball might miss an optimum by stepping over it. For a real-valued function, it is obvious that one cannot pick a step size small enough to completely avoid this problem, so one is in essence betting that the function is well behaved.

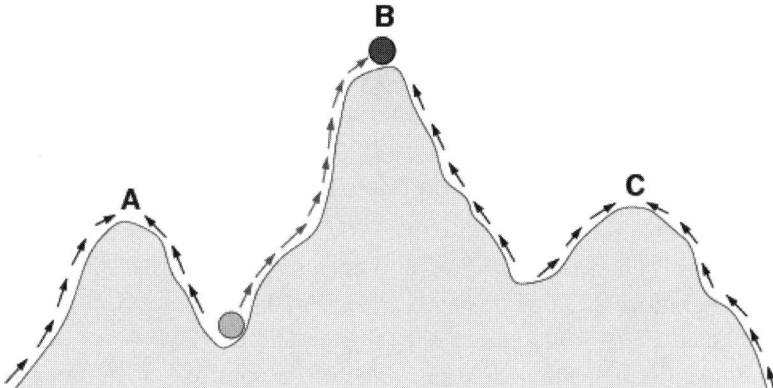

Figure 4.1. An Example Fitness Landscape
Note: Illustration by Claus Wilke (http://nemus.dllab.caltech.edu/~wilke/). Reproduced with permission.

such as the alliance game, one uses a population of agents to search for good strategies, each with a different starting set of components and idiosyncratic utility functions.

Genetic algorithms approach the problem of optimization a bit differently, though the two main elements of the simpler hill-climbing algorithm are still present. They optimize locally through the operation of crossover, which involves combining pieces of different agents into a new agent. Figure 4.2, for example, demonstrates how crossover in theory is effective. In this figure, there are two agents that are represented by a set of six binary parameter choices.[33] The gray-shaded parameter values are "good" choices, insofar as they add to the overall utility of the agent, while the white choices are poor. Crossover picks one or more points and swaps material from the two agents, thereby creating two new agents. Note that in this example, the swap was particularly fortuitous for the topmost agent – it received both of the good halves of the parent agents and will likely do quite well compared to either parent. The bottom agent, in comparison, received both of the poorly performing halves and will likely have very low fitness. If reproduction

---

[33] One can think of each parameter as a gene. In this figure, the genes are independent/separable. If genes impact the expression of other genes, matters are more complicated – see the next chapter for details. In terms of Figure 4.2, imagine what would happen if the genes in each parent were *not* independent! It would be impossible to predict the fitness of the offspring.

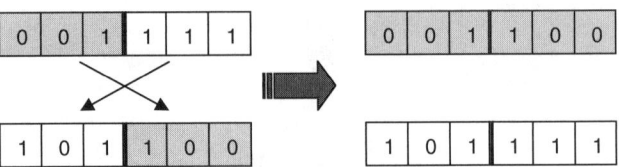

Figure 4.2. The Crossover Operator

of agents is unequal (or one kills off agents below a certain threshold each iteration), the top agent will expand in the population.

Effective crossover involves picking a number of crossover points and identifying where crossover should be performed. Crossover points can themselves be treated as parameters and allowed to evolve in a population; in the biology literature, these are called "hot spots." Mitchell (1996) offers more details on this and other issues pertaining to crossover. For our purposes, the natural location for crossover to act on the agents in the alliance game encoding is between different component games and idiosyncratic utility functions (but see later).[34]

The other element of genetic algorithms perturbs solutions so that local optima are not traps. This operator is mutation, and is easy to understand. At some constant rate (yet another parameter value), a parameter in an agent is perturbed to a new value chosen uniformly from the domain for that parameter. Since most genetic algorithms rely upon binary encodings, this usually involves flipping a single bit. Mutations help populations avoid getting trapped on some subset of the optima in a fitness landscape, much in the same way that random initial values aid hill-climbing.

Given that I rely upon a genetic algorithm to search for good strategies for the alliance game, it must be verified that the encoding settled on above works within this framework. Figure 4.3 is a visual representation of how the encoding is instantiated in a genetic algorithm: The good news, from a programming perspective, is that that the agents in the population are all simple vectors. Note that the figure differentiates

---

[34] It is worth noting that the theoretical work behind genetic algorithms is incomplete. The schema theorem advanced by Holland is almost certainly false. Analogies to n-Armed Bandit problems demonstrate that when the arms are not independent, nothing really works as advertised.

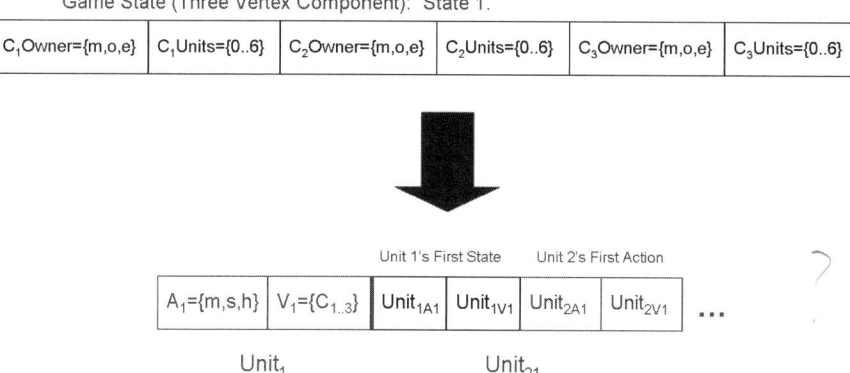

Figure 4.3. An Encoding of the Alliance Game

between states (represented in gray) and actual parameter values that would be stored in the program's data structures (in black boldface). The vector only records parameter values and the code "remembers" the ordering of the array, such that a correspondence is created to the underlying states in the encoding. The figure thus displays one particular state of a component game that is described by the owner and number of units in each of the three vertices. For this component game there is an associated strategy that consists of the first unit's action along with the second and subsequent unit actions. Note that within this strategy there are also states for the second and subsequent units that correspond to the $(n-1)$ unit's action. As noted earlier, crossover points can occur between each unit or between larger groupings like complete components, while mutation is applied with a fixed (small) probability to each individual parameter.

This encoding does much of the heavy lifting, and initializing a population of agents is a simple task of randomly assigning starting values from a uniform distribution to the above arrays. One final complication remains, however, involving the fitness functions for the alliance game.

FITNESS FUNCTIONS AND EQUIVALENCE CLASSES

The final choice involved in using a genetic algorithm (or any other optimization procedure) concerns the selection of a fitness (or objective) function. For many tasks, both the problem encoding and the associated fitness function are straight-forward; one example is the iterated prisoner's dilemma, where the fitness function is based upon the payoffs of the game. But for other tasks, such as the alliance game, it is not obvious what the right form is for either the encoding or the fitness function. While I have described the process by which one arrives at an encoding for a complex game, I have not yet matched this encoding to a fitness function. Given that strategies in the alliance game are potentially infinite in length, one cannot simply use the actual payoffs of the game and hope for the best.[35]

In the examination of idiosyncratic utility functions used in machine chess research from Chapter 3, the fitness functions were arrived at empirically by matching a set of features with expert human play using OLS regression. For the alliance game I follow a similar strategy, though this is a matter of ongoing research.[36] Fitness, like the above encoding for component games, is represented on a horizon of one phase (i.e., spring and fall phases are separate) and relies upon two measures:[37]

i. $\delta(units_i)$: how many units are gained or lost by player i during the year
ii. $[units_i / max(units_{n/i})]$: the number of units player i owns divided by the next highest unit total for the other players.

These two features are weighted by coefficients idiosyncratic to each agent in the population. The coefficients are real-valued numbers

---

[35] As one might expect, in early versions of the computational model using the game's payoffs as the utility function the population had a difficult time learning strategies for the early/middle parts of the game. In essence, the histories of play were simply too long to develop a correlation between early/middle actions and final payoffs.

[36] What one would like is a function that takes the game rules as an input and produces a set of features for the fitness function. Given that different features produce different metrics in the resultant fitness landscape, this turns out to be a difficult problem.

[37] The fitness function has to be matched to the encoding for the component game actions, otherwise it would be impossible for the genetic algorithm to select "good" actions. The oddity is that spring actions are evaluated in exactly the same fashion as fall actions, even though the agents do not actually update units at the end of the spring phase. To do otherwise would (as usual) result in a much larger parameter space. Finding a way to look further into the future (e.g., as in sacrificing play in chess) would be desirable.

from [0..1], with the constraint that they sum to one.[38] One should note that a parameter representing these weights must be added to the forgoing agent encoding, somewhat expanding the parameter space.

The derivation of these features is by all lights inexplicable, but, as argued in Chapter 3, the proof of their usefulness (or that of features like them) in constructing fitness functions is ultimately decided by success against human players. Intuition suggests that evaluating agent strategies every phase (as opposed to waiting until the game's termination), allows for learning that would not otherwise be possible in the early and middle parts of the game. Moreover, it is not unreasonable to believe that the change in units during a phase is correlated with success in the overall game and that the ratio of the player's unit total compared to the nearest competitor serves as a measure of strategic threat. As in machine chess models, I could use expert human play as a guide to picking the coefficients for the above features, or I could allow the genetic algorithm to improve random starting values in a population of agents. But the best intuition can be wrong, and one needs a final check on all of the choices that go into a model. Plentiful data from play against humans provides this check in the case of the alliance game.

One might feel some discomfort with the seemingly arbitrary nature of these features and their coefficients – other features might better capture an essential aspect of the game or the list may not be expansive enough. What I hope to demonstrate, however, is that the choice of an encoding and component utilities revolves around a consideration of the game itself. This is to be contrasted with assumptions typically relied upon in purely formal work, where the assumptions serve the quite different purpose of detailing a new and simpler game amenable to the fixed encoding and solution algorithm of game theory. This chapter thus shows how one can arrive at an encoding and feature space for

---

[38] That is, they function like weights $\langle p, (1 - p) \rangle$. With this form, one needs include only one parameter in the agent arrays. Agents thus "improve" their fitness based on these local weights. When I construct meta-agents that play the complete game, however, fitness is derived directly from success in the overall (i.e., not component) game G. A two-stage fitness function, in which one is idiosyncratic to the agent, is an alteration of normal practice using genetic algorithms.

fitness functions that reflect a deep consideration of the problem itself, rather than some desired equilibrium property or belief about human rationality. Since the computational model produces results that map directly to the actual game, it is possible to test the results against human play, which is a great source of out-of-sample data. Only by developing such a close correspondence between the model and the empirical referent is this possible.

Although there are trade-offs involved in following the approach advocated here (e.g., one might reasonably disagree with all of the choices I have made in this chapter for encoding the game), there is one additional and subtle benefit that should not be overlooked. As discussed in Chapters 1 and 3, equivalence classes of games should be the focus of research, especially if one agrees with the statistical arguments presented in this text on the nature of out-of-sample testing and its role in inference. One natural outcome of deriving an encoding that depends upon components for a complex game and a set of features that describe component utility functions is that in effect one gets equivalence classes for free. Abstracting away from the game itself is thus a useful step in building equivalence classes. As a concrete example, imagine that I add additional players and subgraphs to the alliance game like those in Figure 3.1, keeping the overall nature of the game similar to the base game. Because this expansion of the game maps to and is invariant within the encoding/feature space outlined earlier, I would not have to derive a new computational model to deal with the additional complexity. Therefore, if one solves the base game, any other game that has a correspondence to the components used in the encoding and the feature space used to produce component utility functions fits within the equivalence class described by the computational results.[39]

---

[39] If you are interested in the ongoing research on the alliance game, the latest source code and results are posted on my Web site, along with data from human players. Currently, I am investigating how to divide a player's units into subsets to reduce the combinatorics of the encodings detailed here. The possibility of 5 units (or more if you consider related games that add players and territory) greatly expands the combinatorics of many encodings; it may well be the case that component games limited to two or three units are superior. One would then apply these smaller encodings to subsets of units until a complete strategy is arrived at.

SELF-DESTRUCTION IS THE ANSWER

Throughout this book, I have been very critical of existing approaches to modeling; my hope is that many readers will turn the tables and examine the work I have presented in this chapter just as closely. After all, it seems more than fair to subject my work on the alliance game to the standards developed in the first three chapters of this book. There is more than fairness at stake, however. I believe that the best way to improve modeling in the social sciences is to apply these standards to all modeling efforts, including my own.

One reading of this book is that game theoretic and statistical models are often very poor and that computational models are a panacea for all the ailments of mathematical methodology. This, however, is *not* the argument I am making. What I am trying to show is that very different modeling approaches can all be examined using the same critical framework. The most pressing reason to do this is to force models to focus on the substantive problem, rather than the technique. If, for example, a game theorist and a computational modeler both want to investigate the alliance game, they should model the game as it is, with a focus on providing comparable empirical tests. Otherwise, the different practitioners will simply talk past one another, making it very difficult to engage in cumulative knowledge building.

In all likelihood, the flaws in the game theoretic and computational models will be different. Thus, while we do not necessarily get a complete understanding with either model alone, we get two understandings with different weaknesses and strengths. Most important, if both models address the same empirical referent, we can learn from both despite their different vantage points.

So, without further ado, what are the biggest problems with my preliminary efforts to solve the alliance game? My first encoding attempted to implement the logic of game theory and arbitrarily established that the component games would have a horizon of one year. This approach was adopted because it was a direct way to produce components that incorporated the strategic considerations necessary for good play. Unfortunately, the number of possible units, locations, and strategies made this encoding unworkable; that is, the parameter space for the encoding was much, much too large. Worse still, the encoding depended upon an arbitrary parameter choice for the length of the component game horizon, and given the size of the resultant parameter space, it would be difficult to generate enough data to be comfortable with this choice.

My current encoding reduces the dimensionality of the parameter space, but at the expense of doing away with a straightforward game theoretic implementation of strategy. Instead of explicitly modeling how a player's choices are conditioned upon the actions of the other players, the current model resorts to a series of parameter choices that limit the amount of strategic flexibility in the component games. The mitigating factor, as noted in the preceding text, is that the parameter space is now small enough to use stochastic optimization to generate desirable components.

The domain restrictions imposed upon the component games are severe, but the weakest part of the computational model is the approach taken to generating idiosyncratic utility functions. I would much rather create a flexible model that accepts the game rules (in some form) and produces a set of features that measure good play. Unfortunately, the model now depends upon constructing features by hand (though the weights are endogenous). These also must be considered as parameter choices, and by their nature, they are exceptionally brittle – that is, a lot depends on correctly evaluating the component games, so one should be very suspicious of these component utility features. Only by repeatedly testing the model against a wide variety of human players would one gain confidence in these choices.[40]

Finally, while it is the case that the alliance game is orders of magnitude more complex than the sorts of games one usually studies using the tools of game theory, it is still arguable that the intuition generated is not qualitatively different from the previous generation of toy games (e.g., the IPD). If one were to make any broad claims about results for the alliance game, it is worth noting that important work remains

---

[40] To bolster the results from human play, I have used game theory to test the utility measures in a way that may seem novel. Since many components are small enough to be solvable with game theory, one can test the choice of idiosyncratic utility functions (along with the quality of the component encoding) by seeing if the resultant strategies identified as highly fit match up with game theoretic outcomes. In this way, a combination of techniques – computational modeling with game theory – allows for a rate of progress that is not possible with a single approach.

undone. One would have to provide a set of empirical tests using real data from the international system before these results would gain any credibility, and I have provided no guidance on how to accomplish this task. Thus, at this stage, the alliance game is more of a laboratory for building modeling techniques for complex games rather than a dispositive statement on alliance formation in the real world.

One might ask at this point why are we any better off with the computational model. First, and most important, this chapter has always focused upon the alliance game itself, which represents a problem that would not yield to traditional methodological approaches. There are a large number of assumptions and parameters underlying the model, but at every point they have been chosen by focusing upon the difficulties presented by the alliance game, and not some atheoretical notion of what constitutes human rationality or mathematical tractability.

Second, this approach demonstrates how computational political economy, game theory, and empirical work can be coordinated. Choosing a reasonable encoding for the alliance game depended upon game theoretic investigations of strategy in the sample component games; proof of the reasonableness of different parameter values was provided by game theory (i.e., does one achieve results from the computational model that match our intuition from game theory) along with statistical work. Fortunately, by modeling the alliance game as it is, I have been able to conduct experiments to see how the strategies discovered by the most fit agents fare against human play. Without this plentiful source of data, I would have a very difficult time distinguishing my multiple attempts to generate successful encodings and idiosyncratic utility functions from the worst examples of curve-fitting.

Third, even though generalizing from the alliance game to actual alliances between states is a stretch, the question remains as to whether or not studying a complex game is worth the loss of analytic certainty. To the extent that one disagrees with the sentiment of Von Neumann and Morgenstern that one way to understand complex reality is to model the games people actually play, my efforts here along with almost all of game theory would have to be rejected. The question is where to draw the line between a reasonable abstraction (blemishes and all) and a toy model that provides little insight; upon this distinction there may be continuing disagreement. This said, efforts to model more complex phenomenon directly and to build cumulative models seems worthwhile, as the only possible answer to the forgoing charge that a model lacks sufficient verisimilitude is to build a more complex model. Because we lack the methodological tools to do that, the ongoing enterprise of computational political economists to build better models is desirable whether or not the payoff is in sight.

The next chapter continues the arguments presented here, but instead of focusing upon how one derives an encoding and fitness function for an ongoing research problem, it is geared toward developing results from a completed computational model. In particular, I will show how one can derive a logical implication to test the main implications of a complex model with less than ideal data.

APPENDIX 1: A BEGINNING PROGRAMMING LIBRARY

1. Reference for the programming language. O'Reilly Press (http://www.oreilly.com), as noted previously, has excellent reference and instructional volumes on almost all programming languages.
2. Numerical algorithms: The standard has long been William Press's Numerical Recipes series of books (http://www.nr.com). Additional help for numerical algorithms can be found in James Gentle's *Elements of Computational Statistics* and the companion volume *Number Generation and Monte Carlo Methods* or Kenneth Judd's *Numerical Methods in Economics*.
3. Computational Methods/Optimization Algorithms: The standard reference (which includes pseudo-code for many applications) is Stuart Russell and Peter Norvig's *Artificial Intelligence: A Modern Approach*. For genetic algorithms, Melanie Mitchell's *An Introduction To Genetic Algorithms* is comprehensive and covers a good deal of the analytic work (and resulting ambiguities) behind genetic algorithms. Dana Ballard's *An Introduction to Natural Computation* is an excellent reference for computational modeling.

APPENDIX 2: PYTHON CODE FOR THE CURRENCY GAME, WITH FUNCTIONS

```
1  #!/usr/bin/env python
2  import random    # import random number library
```

```
3 import psyco     # import code profiler for generating faster executables
4 psyco.full()     # call profiler
5
6 pop=[]           # popluation of agents; initially empty list
7 N = 10000        # population size
8 ep = .05         # mutation rate
9 its = 100        # number of times through the main loop
10 gold=0          # initial number of gold adopters; (1-gold) = silver adopters
11 standard=0      # either 1 for gold or 2 for silver
12 shifts=0        # number of regime shifts
13
14 def init_all():          # init globals
15 global pop, gold, standard  # tell interpreter to change globals, not locals
16 pop = []
17 gold = 0
18 for i in range(N):
19       if random.random()<0.5:  # assign to gold or silver uniform draw
20              pop.append(1)
21              gold=gold+1
22       else: pop.append(2)
23 if gold>N/2: standard=1
24 else: standard=2         # if tie, silver wins
25 # end function init_all
26
27 def one_choose():
28 global pop, standard, gold, shifts # change globals, don't create locals
```

```
29 for i in range(its):              # horizon / how many agents per its
30     temp = random.randint(0,N-1)  # choose one member of population to change
31     tempval = pop[temp]
32     old_stand = standard
33     if random.random()<ep:        # if epsilon, then change uniformly
34         if random.random()<0.5:
35             pop[temp]=1
36             if tempval!=pop[temp]:
37                 gold=gold+1
38                 if gold>N/2: standard=1
39         else:
40             pop[temp]=2
41             if tempval!=pop[temp]:
42                 gold=gold-1
43                 if gold<N/2: standard=2
44         if standard!=old_stand: shifts=shifts+1 # check for regime shift
45     else:      # if (1-ep) then change to majority if not already there
46         if gold>N/2:
47             if pop[temp]!=1:
48                 pop[temp]=1
49                 gold=gold+1
50                 if gold>N/2: standard=1
51         else:
52             if pop[temp]!=2:
53                 pop[temp]=2
```

```
54                  gold=gold-1
55                  if gold<N/2: standard=2
56      if standard!=old_stand: shifts=shifts+1 # check for
regime shift
57 # end function one_choose
58
59 # start main loop
60
61 for i in range (1000):
62          init_all()       # call init function
63          one_choose()     # call draw function
64 print "Number of regime shifts:," shifts # print to console
```

5

KKV Redux

Deriving and Testing Logical Implications[1]

INTRODUCTION

For most of this book, the focus has been on the necessity of conducting out-of-sample statistical work to sort between competing models. Models are unfortunately not unique, even when they produce identical results. We thus face the task of choosing the most likely model from the class of logically consistent models using out-of-sample comparisons. But, as detailed in Chapter 3, it is often the case that the gap between the model and the empirical referent does not allow for dispositive tests. Or worse still, the amount or quality of available data precludes out-of-sample testing with statistical methods. In these situations, deriving logical implications of a model is a parsimonious way to test the model when the data are not accommodating.[2]

King, Keohane, and Verba (1994) – henceforth KKV – emphasize the importance of deriving the logical implications of models, and I borrow heavily from their treatment in Chapter 1 of this book. Like KKV, I depend upon examples from physics to demonstrate that logical implications can be an alternative to statistical modeling. The problem, however, is that there are few examples in the social sciences of this

---

[1] This chapter owes an enormous debt to Dean Lacy, Emerson Niou, and George Rabinowitz.

[2] As we have seen in Chapter 2 with the study of militarized international disputes, repeated attempts against the same sample often go awry. To test a model under circumstances when no new out-of-sample data is available, one should resort to testing the logical implications of the candidate models. Of course, if one cannot reconstruct the theory underlying the statistical model, this is impossible.

approach to testing a model. KKV do not provide an extended example, and to this point, neither have I.

To address this shortcoming, I will return to the problem of nonseparable preferences featured in the Prelude. The focus will, however, shift to a topic that is more interesting to social scientists than recipes for hot fudge sundaes: voter preferences. As has been my tack throughout this book, it seems better to choose a difficult problem than an easy one to make a point about methodology, and nonseparable preferences in the context of voting certainly qualifies. The study of voter preferences is a long-standing research concern in American politics. Unfortunately, most survey work assumes that preferences are separable, thereby confining a matter of great theoretical interest to an unjustified assumption about the DGP.[3] This is not because survey researchers are malicious; rather, it is yet another example of the curse of dimensionality in practice. Imagine what a survey that attempted to measure nonseparable preferences would look like. If, for example, a survey wanted to measure your opinion on the use of military force in Iraq, it would have to simultaneously measure your preferences on every potentially related issue. No sensible respondent would want to say "go in with guns blazing" without also stipulating that the war would have to be funded at a certain level, and this funding would have obvious implications for policies such as tax cuts and spending.[4] There is the additional question

---

[3] There is considerable empirical support for the presence of nonseparable preferences. Lacy (2001a and 2001b) derives a general model that accounts for the presence of nonseparable preferences in individual-level responses to public opinion surveys. Lacy, along with Gerber and Lewis (n.d.), also furnish evidence that preferences in a variety of contexts, including public opinion surveys and votes on referenda, do not always obey the simplifying assumptions of separability. Lacy distinguishes between the effects of preference complexity and bounded rationality explanations; in particular, he shows that ordering effects can be attributed to nonseparability and not priming. Gerber and Lewis note that most models of legislative representation characterize districts with a simple summary statistic, such as the mean or median preference. Using proposition voting data from Los Angeles County, they argue that better measures of district complexity are more useful indicators of electorate preferences, and allow for more variegated research into the relationship between legislative outcomes and electorate preferences (see also Fiorina 1974, and Brady and Bailey 1998).

[4] One way to conceptualize nonseparability using these issues is to create a two dimensional space, where the X axis represents war in Iraq and the Y axis represents defense spending. If both the X and Y axis are scaled so that positive values represent conservative responses (that is, pro-war and pro-defense spending are positive values), one would expect that voters might be found in quadrants 1, 2, and 3, but not 4. In words,

of who does the fighting, and this touches on policies dealing with race and class. Leaving open the possibility of nonseparable preferences would hideously complicate survey work, but it may well be that the nature of voter preferences demands this kind of survey. How would we investigate this problem given the limitations of existing surveys?

In addition to the problem with survey data, most of the models of electoral decision making depend upon the simplicity separable preferences afford.[5] Spatial voting (Downs 1957), for example, assumes that voters pick the candidate that is closest to them in policy space. If preferences are separable, this is a relatively easy thing to model. Simply place the candidates and voters in an N-dimensional policy space. Each voter would then use Euclidean distance to determine which candidate is closest and vote accordingly. Improvements to the basic spatial model such as ideology (Hinich and Munger 1994) and directional theory (Rabinowitz and MacDonald 1989) do not alter this key assumption.

Why would anyone care about this technical assumption given the analytic tractability it provides? I would argue that despite reasonable performance, all of these models have left something on the table. Typically, regressions explaining candidate approval yield in-sample results with R^2's of well under 0.50; out-of-sample tests are not commonplace.[6] Either one can conclude that voters are dim and that everything systematic has been explained, or that the models are incomplete.

There are thus two reasons to be skeptical of existing models of electoral behavior. First, they violate the constraint developed in Chapter 1

---

quadrant 1 stands for pro-war and pro-defense spending; 2 stands for anti-war and pro-defense spending; and 3 stands for anti-war and anti-defense spending. Quadrant 4, which stands for pro-war and anti-defense spending, is not a platform that would attract much support. It is worth noting that in the 2004 campaign, Bush repeatedly tried to paint Kerry as a candidate located in quadrant 4 (that is, he voted for the war and against defense spending).

[5] Milyo (2000) and Lacy and Niou (1999) detail the importance of discerning the true structure of preferences instead of simply assuming the presence of Euclidean preferences. Milyo (2000) reviews the formal literature in political science and economics and correctly notes that the assumption of Euclidean preferences is both ubiquitous and in almost all cases unjustified. Niou and Lacy (1999) explore different voting rules and the quality of resultant outcomes when voter preferences are nonseparable. In particular, they note that confidence in the outcomes of referenda is misplaced when voter preferences are nonseparable.

[6] Additionally, proximity (i.e., spatial models using policy scales) and directional models add party identification, race, region, and other control variables.

that there should be an equivalence class for all crucial assumptions. Nonseparability drives results, and without it, voting models provide little intuition even in cases where there are small deviations from this assumption (e.g., some pairs of issues might be related). Second, current models are compared solely based upon in-sample performance. Once again we find ourselves in a situation where the models are brittle, no out-of-sample work exists to test these models, and even the in-sample performance is not terribly compelling.

Before we go any further, it seems reasonable to ask if there is any easy way to explore this question using existing survey data. After all, a large number of models depend upon the assumption of separability and for good reason. Allowing for complex preferences would complicate modeling throughout the social sciences, and if there is no real payoff, it is not worth the effort. We are, however, faced with the problem that existing survey data assumes separability. What is one to do?

In this chapter, we will take the alternative route of using the logical implications of various models of electoral behavior to examine their plausibility. Our first question then is to determine if voters act according to the logic of spatial models. A straightforward implication of spatial voting is that voters have separable preferences and choose the "closest" candidate. Some issues are likely so complicated that voters may get confused easily, so why not choose a salient, simple issue where the parties have taken extremely clear positions?[7] Abortion thus seems to be a good candidate, and the implication we are testing is whether or not Democrats line up on one side of the issue and Republicans on the other. The American National Election Survey (A-NES) has used the following question in 1988, 1992, 1996, and 2000:

WHEN SHOULD ABORTION BE ALLOWED BY LAW
There has been some discussion about abortion during recent years. Which one of the opinions on this page best agrees with your view?

VALID CODES:

1. By law, abortion should never be permitted.
2. The law should permit abortion only in case of rape, incest, or when the woman's life is in danger.

---

[7] For an extended treatment of the important of an issue's salience and complexity, see Canes-Wrone and de Marchi (2002).

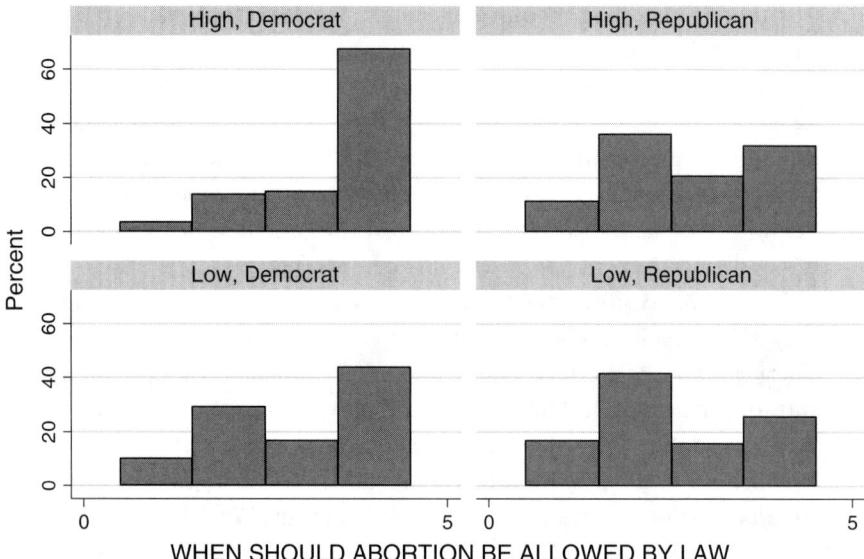

Figure 5.1. A-NES Abortion Positions 1988–2000. Graphs by Education and Party.

3. The law should permit abortion for reasons other than rape, incest, or danger to the woman's life, but only after the need for the abortion has been clearly established.
4. By law, a woman should always be able to obtain an abortion as a matter of personal choice.

It is not a huge leap to assume that Democratic candidates for office usually line up somewhere between response 3 and 4, while Republicans locate between 2 and 1. Using the respondent's choice of president as a way of dividing up the sample between Democrats and Republicans, one should find that Democrats overwhelmingly choose positions 3 and 4 while Republicans choose 1 and 2.[8] Figure 5.1 presents these results: What is interesting is that only a bit more than half of the electorate is consistent. Figure 5.1 also demonstrates that even when one confines the sample to highly educated voters (here defined as a

---

[8] One can also partition using self-reported ideology or party identification – the results do not vary.

college degree or more), just under 20% of Democrats and over 50% of Republicans are inconsistent.

One could at this point say that the forgoing is not surprising. Voters may be ignorant of abortion policy, or they may attach little salience to it. But without more effort, neither of these claims seems terribly convincing, both due to the historical context of the issue in the United States as well as the fact that even highly educated voters are inconsistent.[9]

To buttress the case for reexamining our assumptions about preferences, let us develop another implication of the basic spatial model. If, as we find here, abortion is an issue where a number of respondents are inconsistent, does this have any necessary implication for their location on other issues? Put another way, if I look at the group of Republicans who favor abortion, would I find that their positions on other issues vary from the Republican platform in any systematic way? If one confines oneself to separable preferences, one would have to say "no" to this question.[10]

Again, using data from the A-NES between 1988 and 2000, I looked at questions measuring the major political issues facing the American electorate and compared consistent with inconsistent respondents to see if any systematic differences on other issues than abortion were present.[11] Figures 5.2 and 5.3 present pro- and antiabortion respondents in both parties, segregated by education level.

Contrary to expectations, voters that are inconsistent on abortion are also inconsistent on a set of other issues, regardless of their level of education, party affiliation, or choice of president. For both Democrats

---

[9] Although it may seem counterintuitive, highly educated voters are more ideological and more partisan than less educated voters (Zaller 1992).

[10] Jennifer Harrod and Michael Munger (personal communication) argue that, if anything, one would expect that the inconsistent group is closer to the party platform on other issues, given that spatial models assume separability and the use of Euclidean distance. One way out of this conundrum is to believe that salience is the determinant factor, but salience does not seem to help voting models and is not commonly included on surveys.

[11] Because the sample sizes were large, I used a cutoff of one half to distinguish the responses of the groups rather than a chi-square test. Not surprisingly, a chi-square test finds that the groups are different on most issues, but this is not an appropriate use of the test. A cutoff of one half, although arbitrary, does represent a real difference in terms of policy given that the questions use either 5- or 7-point scales.

Democrats, High Education		Anti	Pro			
A-NES Code	Question	Mean	Mean	Delta	Min	Max
VCF0104	RESPONDENT GENDER	1.52	1.53		1	2
VCF0106a	RESPONDENT RACE	1.60	1.38		1	5
VCF0111	URBANISM	1.89	1.82		1	3
VCF0301	PARTY IDENTIFICATION	2.46	2.39		1	7
VCF0838	WHEN SHOULD ABORTION BE ALLOWED BY LAW	1.80	3.82	2.02	1	4
VCF0803	LIBERAL-CONSERVATIVE 7PT SCALE	4.00	3.22	0.78	1	7
VCF0834	R POSITION 7PT WOMENS EQUAL ROLE	2.15	1.49	0.66	1	7
VCF0843	R POSITION 7PT DEFENSE SPENDING	3.72	3.07	0.66	1	7
VCF0876a	STRENGTH OPIN LAW TO PROTECT GAYS	2.30	1.72	0.59	1	5
VCF0854	MORE TOLERANT OF DIFFERENT MORAL STDS	2.63	2.06	0.57	1	5
VCF0830	R POSITION 7PT AID TO BLACKS	4.38	3.92	0.46	1	7
VCF9046	FOOD STAMPS SPENDING -FEDERAL SPENDING	2.21	1.99	0.22	1	7
VCF0809	R POSITION 7PT GOVT GUARANTEED JOBS	4.26	4.05	0.21	1	7
VCF9049	SOCIAL SECURITY - FEDERAL SPENDING	1.38	1.57	0.19	1	7
VCF0604	HOW MUCH DOES R TRUST FEDERAL GOVT	2.49	2.37	0.12	1	4
VCF0887	CHILD CARE - FEDERAL SPENDING	1.43	1.32	0.11	1	3
VCF9047	ENVIRONMENT - FEDERAL SPENDING	1.33	1.32	0.01	1	3
VCF0890	PUBLIC SCHOOLS - FEDERAL SPENDING	1.21	1.22	0.01	1	3
VCF0806	R POSITION 7PT GOVT HEALTH INSURANCE	3.29	3.29	0.00	1	7

Democrats, Low Education		Anti	Pro			
A-NES Code	Question	Mean	Mean	Delta	Min	Max
VCF0104	RESPONDENT GENDER	1.55	1.57		1	2
VCF0106a	RESPONDENT RACE	1.78	1.53		1	5
VCF0111	URBANISM	1.09	1.92		1	3
VCF0301	PARTY IDENTIFICATION	1.95	2.23		1	7
VCF0838	WHEN SHOULD ABORTION BE ALLOWED BY LAW	1.74	3.72	1.98	1	4
VCF0834	R POSITION 7PT WOMENS EQUAL ROLE	2.66	1.99	0.67	1	7
VCF0803	LIBERAL-CONSERVATIVE 7PT SCALE	4.03	3.65	0.38	1	7
VCF0876a	STRENGTH OPIN LAW TO PROTECT GAYS	2.56	2.20	0.36	1	5
VCF0854	MORE TOLERANT OF DIFFERENT MORAL STDS	2.52	2.34	0.18	1	5
VCF0830	R POSITION 7PT AID TO BLACKS	4.49	4.31	0.18	1	7
VCF0887	CHILD CARE - FEDERAL SPENDING	1.50	1.37	0.13	1	3
VCF0809	R POSITION 7PT GOVT GUARANTEED JOBS	3.85	3.97	0.12	1	7
VCF9047	ENVIRONMENT - FEDERAL SPENDING	1.42	1.47	0.05	1	3
VCF0604	HOW MUCH DOES R TRUST FEDERAL GOVT	2.40	2.45	0.04	1	4
VCF9046	FOOD STAMPS SPENDING -FEDERAL SPENDING	2.07	2.03	0.04	1	7
VCF0843	R POSITION 7PT DEFENSE SPENDING	3.87	3.90	0.03	1	7
VCF0890	PUBLIC SCHOOLS - FEDERAL SPENDING	1.28	1.26	0.03	1	3
VCF9049	SOCIAL SECURITY - FEDERAL SPENDING	1.37	1.39	0.02	1	7
VCF0806	R POSITION 7PT GOVT HEALTH INSURANCE	3.20	3.21	0.00	1	7

Figure 5.2. Policy Positions of Democrats

and Republicans, sizeable differences exist on policy preferences concerning women in the workplace, gay rights, and tolerance. Additionally, highly educated Democrats differ on aid to African Americans and defense spending. In all cases, inconsistency on abortion signals

KKV Redux 151

Republicans, High Education		Anti	Pro			
A-NES Code	Question	Mean	Mean	Delta	Min	Max
VCF0104	RESPONDENT GENDER	1.42	1.44		1	2
VCF0106a	RESPONDENT RACE	1.29	1.17		1	5
VCF0111	URBANISM	2.15	2.02		1	3
VCF0301	PARTY IDENTIFICATION	5.93	5.76		1	7
VCF0838	WHEN SHOULD ABORTION BE ALLOWED BY LAW	1.76	3.61	1.85	1	4
VCF0834	R POSITION 7PT WOMENS EQUAL ROLE	3.03	1.95	1.08	1	7
VCF0876a	STRENGTH OPIN LAW TO PROTECT GAYS	3.56	2.88	0.68	1	5
VCF0854	MORE TOLERANT OF DIFFERENT MORAL STDS	3.37	2.72	0.65	1	5
VCF0803	LIBERAL-CONSERVATIVE 7PT SCALE	5.47	4.98	0.49	1	7
VCF0806	R POSITION 7PT GOVT HEALTH INSURANCE	5.02	4.79	0.22	1	7
VCF0890	PUBLIC SCHOOLS - FEDERAL SPENDING	1.70	1.53	0.17	1	3
VCF0887	CHILD CARE - FEDERAL SPENDING	1.97	1.83	0.14	1	3
VCF0830	R POSITION 7PT AID TO BLACKS	5.20	5.09	0.11	1	7
VCF9047	ENVIRONMENT - FEDERAL SPENDING	1.80	1.69	0.10	1	3
VCF0604	HOW MUCH DOES R TRUST FEDERAL GOVT	2.35	2.46	0.10	1	4
VCF0843	R POSITION 7PT DEFENSE SPENDING	4.35	4.26	0.10	1	7
VCF9046	FOOD STAMPS SPENDING -FEDERAL SPENDING	2.51	2.54	0.04	1	7
VCF0809	R POSITION 7PT GOVT GUARANTEED JOBS	5.34	5.37	0.03	1	7
VCF9049	SOCIAL SECURITY - FEDERAL SPENDING	1.80	1.80	0.00	1	7

Republicans, Low Education		Anti	Pro			
A-NES Code	Question	Mean	Mean	Delta	Min	Max
VCF0104	RESPONDENT GENDER	1.55	1.47		1	2
VCF0106a	RESPONDENT RACE	1.27	1.20		1	5
VCF0111	URBANISM	2.28	2.09		1	3
VCF0301	PARTY IDENTIFICATION	5.75	5.42		1	7
VCF0838	WHEN SHOULD ABORTION BE ALLOWED BY LAW	1.71	3.62	1.91	1	4
VCF0834	R POSITION 7PT WOMENS EQUAL ROLE	3.20	2.29	0.91	1	7
VCF0854	MORE TOLERANT OF DIFFERENT MORAL STDS	3.33	2.64	0.70	1	5
VCF0876a	STRENGTH OPIN LAW TO PROTECT GAYS	3.53	2.93	0.60	1	5
VCF0803	LIBERAL-CONSERVATIVE 7PT SCALE	5.26	4.66	0.59	1	7
VCF0806	R POSITION 7PT GOVT HEALTH INSURANCE	4.48	4.28	0.20	1	7
VCF0604	HOW MUCH DOES R TRUST FEDERAL GOVT	2.36	2.55	0.20	1	4
VCF0887	CHILD CARE - FEDERAL SPENDING	1.84	1.65	0.19	1	3
VCF9047	ENVIRONMENT - FEDERAL SPENDING	1.80	1.63	0.17	1	3
VCF9046	FOOD STAMPS SPENDING -FEDERAL SPENDING	2.53	2.38	0.15	1	7
VCF0843	R POSITION 7PT DEFENSE SPENDING	4.55	4.41	0.15	1	7
VCF0890	PUBLIC SCHOOLS - FEDERAL SPENDING	1.55	1.44	0.11	1	3
VCF0809	R POSITION 7PT GOVT GUARANTEED JOBS	5.27	5.17	0.10	1	7
VCF0830	R POSITION 7PT AID TO BLACKS	5.46	5.39	0.07	1	7
VCF9049	SOCIAL SECURITY - FEDERAL SPENDING	1.59	1.59	0.00	1	7

Figure 5.3. Policy Positions of Republicans

more moderate views (i.e., inconsistent with the party core) on these other issues.[12]

It is worth noting that factor analysis and related techniques would confuse the above distinctions. If one runs a factor analysis or principal components analysis, one finds that two dimensions exist in the data: an ideological dimension accounting for most of the issues, and a moral dimension that partially accounts for attitudes on abortion, women, gay rights, and tolerance. This "finding" is obviously misleading, insofar as only the consistent Democrats and Republicans fit nicely into this reduced space.[13] The inconsistent voters, to the extent they are relying upon a reduced choice space, are moving in the *opposite* direction on a substantial subset of issues. For example, a highly educated, proabortion Democrat can be expected to be very liberal on defense spending, tolerance, and so on. But, another Democrat who looks very similar on all demographic measures but happens to be antiabortion is much more moderate than other Democrats on these same issues. For each Democrat, the cluster of related issues can be thought of as moving in an opposite direction conditional upon their position on abortion.

We are thus left with more questions than when we started. Although I chose to focus on abortion, it may well be the case that other "clumps" of interconnected issues exist.[14] How ubiquitous is this phenomena? Is there any way to test for the exact level of nonseparability of this kind (or any other) in survey data?

---

[12] In addition to the demographic controls included in Figures 5.2 and 5.3, I also inspected age cohort, income, region, and several other variables. No substantial differences on any of these variables existed between the groups of interest. Region and income were important to look at, insofar as Southern Democrats and country club Republicans might have explained the differences between groups.

[13] This is reflected in the overall poor fit of the individual issues to the factors, even when one confines the sample to highly educated voters.

[14] There are at least two possible micro-level explanations for clumps/nonseparable issues. First, these dependencies may exist in long-term memory. Imagine, as one example, a budget constraint. One likes more spending on each issue separately, but considered together there is a point at which utility drops off sharply. Second, elite communication may create nonseparabilities. For example, "weakness" on one issue may be used by elites to argue that the candidate is similarly weak on other, related issues. Given the data problems mentioned in this chapter, the best way to distinguish between these explanations would be to generate further logical implications.

Optimization and Preference Complexity

As I have argued, if issues are not independent of other issues or concerns, extracting meaningful information from survey data is a difficult exercise. When preferences are nonseparable, the resultant objective functions[15] make it difficult to interpret survey data; conversely, when preferences are Euclidean, preference data is useful in answering all sorts of questions about the electorate. The goal is to develop an approach that will allow one to discern the underlying level of nonseparability in preference data given its limitations.

Although we have strong reasons from the preceding section on the logical implications of spatial models to suspect that voters have complex preferences, we lack an analytic measure of complexity that could determine whether a particular electorate fell into the simplest case (i.e., separable, Euclidean preferences) or the most complex case (i.e., completely nonseparable preferences).[16] While preferences from 1988 to 2000 seem to be complex, we would like to be able to compare different electorates in different contexts and see how they stack up. What sort of analytic framework would allow us to build such a measure? An example helps to clarify this question.

Example: A "Complex" Objective Function – the Traveling Salesman Problem

The Traveling Salesman Problem (TSP) is a canonical problem in computer science and optimization theory, largely because it is an easily described member of a class of very difficult problems.[17] The setup for

---

[15] The argument presented here is that aggregations of voters are best understood as *objective functions* of varying complexity; if this is so, tools borrowed from optimization theory are appropriate for analyzing different electorates.

[16] In order to discern what makes preferences "complex" or "simple," I relied upon Page's (2000) general framework that differentiates between difficult and complex problems. Qualitatively different aspects of a problem can cause hardships in searching for an outcome. Measures of complexity must be sensitive to the distinct features of a problem that make it "hard" for players. In the case of preferences, separability is the crucial factor in generating complex preferences.

[17] TSP is an NP-complete problem, which means that no polynomial solution exists. That is, as the number of cities increases, the number of steps an algorithm requires to solve the problem increases faster than polynomial time.

the problem is simple: Imagine you are a salesman and have to travel between N cities. Trace the shortest possible path that spans the cities with the constraint that you can only visit each city once. Another way of describing this is to stipulate that your path must be drawn without retracing a route or lifting your pencil from the map.

The difficulty of this problem lies in the fact that each step is contingent upon all prior choices; thus, the problem is highly nonseparable and no clear avenue exists out of this difficulty. In all such problems, it is very easy to get trapped on local optima, and for large N one may miss the global optimum entirely. Imagine the difficulty involved in using a genetic algorithm if all of the genes in each agent were not independent (see Figure 4.1 for an example of how much independence helps us).

It should be noted, however, that the complexity of a particular TSP varies greatly. Imagine, for example, that you are using cities in the Midwestern United States as the basis for your instantiation of the TSP; even with a large number of cities, one immediately intuits that finding a solution will not be very difficult. By contrast, for relatively smaller N, where each element is a location in Manhattan, one apprehends the ugliness of a complex TSP. Thus, even for a problem like TSP, which is known as a class to be generally hard to solve, it is still useful to derive measures which can tell you how difficult a particular member of the class is. That is, when you choose an algorithm to approach a particular TSP, it would be very helpful to know ahead of time whether things were going to be simple or complex.

TSP is a real problem and real people chart routes between cities. Elections represent another problem faced by humans, and like other problems, it is difficult to decide *a priori* how much complexity is present. It may be the case that voters in some countries or time periods have more complex preferences than at other times. If voter preferences are nonseparable, the only justifiable representation of an electorate's preferences would require weak orderings over *all* platforms for *every* voter.[18] If weak orderings were the simplest possible representation of preferences, surveys that asked for ideal points would

---

[18] $\leq$ is a weak ordering on the set of platforms P if three conditions are met: (1) For all α in P, $\alpha \leq \alpha$; (2) If $\alpha \leq \beta$ and $\beta \leq \alpha$ then $\alpha = \beta$; (3) transitivity: If $\alpha \leq \beta$ and $\beta \leq \chi$ then $\alpha \leq \chi$.

not tell us much, as any departure from a voter's ideal would result in completely unpredictable changes in utility.[19]

Alternately, if voters have Euclidean preferences, we could conduct surveys as we do now by recording voter ideal positions across issues. As noted in the introduction to this chapter, spatial models of elections and of electoral bargaining (whether they occur in a legislature or in some other arena) assume that preferences are Euclidean; that is, a Euclidean metric provides easy intuition about the meaning of distance and neighborhoods in the issue space. For example, in an n dimensional issue space if a politician adopts platform $\mathbf{x}$, where $\mathbf{x}$ is a vector of n issue positions, the presence of a Euclidean metric allows one to reason that neighboring platforms are similar to $\mathbf{x}$ in utility. Thus, if $x = (x_1, x_2, \ldots, x_n)$ is replaced by a platform that is some ε different on one policy dimension such that $\mathbf{x}' = (x_1, x_2 \pm \varepsilon, \ldots, x_n)$, we naturally assume that $\mathbf{x}$ and $\mathbf{x}'$ are evaluated almost identically by the voter.

The existence of Euclidean preferences for all relevant actors is more important still for models of political bargaining. As policies are separable by assumption in many models, one may substitute movement on one issue for movement on another; that is, side-payments are usually easy to find. In the general case in which weak orderings describe preferences, however, it is far from clear how bargaining would take place because policies must be evaluated solely as complete platforms (and not as individual, additive parts). Offering to "split the baby" would only sow confusion in such a case.

AN ENCODING FOR PREFERENCE COMPLEXITY

The preceding introduction makes the case for further consideration of the nature of preferences in an electorate. What we lack is a measure that takes current survey data as an input and returns the level of complexity (i.e., nonseparability) that is present in an electorate's

---

[19] For a good overview of this problem, and the ways in which various subfields within economics and political science are damaged by it, see Milyo (2000). As proof that Milyo is not overstating the harm caused by arbitrary limitations on the domain of preferences, consider that several models even assume electorates hold preferences that result in the unlikely existence of a median-in-all-directions. See, for example, Calvert (1985) and McKelvey and Ordeshook (1985a and 1985b). And, for an excellent treatise on preferences and the problem of representation, see Katzner (1970).

preferences. As noted in Chapters 3 and 4, the first step in deriving such a measure is a scheme for encoding preferences. Although there are many such schemes, the encoding settled upon here allows us to leverage existing research in optimization theory and computational modeling.[20] The plan is to build a computational model that will generate lots of different kinds of preferences with tunable levels of nonseparability. This is not different in kind from Monte Carlo experiments, and it will allow us to see if my proposed measure responds correctly to varying levels of complexity in the artificial preference data. The key is to develop a measure that demands no more of the data than what existing political surveys normally provide.

Encoding Preferences

The basic framework for encoding preferences is a fitness (or adaptive) landscape that represents aggregated voter preferences. This encoding is generated as follows:

i. The issue space forms an *adaptive landscape*, of dimensionality $N + 1$ (where the first N dimensions record possible platforms which span all N issues and the extra dimension is a measure of the likelihood of winning the election at that unique platform). One can thus treat adaptive landscapes much like geographical landscapes, where regions of greater height represent policy platforms that will likely be more successful than lower regions.

ii. The difficulty of locating optima on a given landscape can be characterized by measures of *ruggedness* and *slope*. Rugged landscapes have many local optima; alternatively, an example of a simple landscape would be one in which a single peak exists (i.e., 1 optimum). Slope is a measure of the average rate-of-change between any two points on a landscape's surface. A preponderance of voters with Euclidean preferences, for example, would lead to less rugged landscapes than if the electorate were comprised primarily of voters with more complex preferences. Similarly, if voter utility functions decrease gradually as they leave their

---

[20] The work of Kollman, Miller, and Page (1992, 1998) and de Marchi (1999) applies this literature to the problem of elections. Additionally, Bailey (2003) has applied computational methods to the study of campaign finance, Franklin and Rich (n.d.) have built a model that describes party formation, and Taber and Steenbergen (1995) have used computational experiments to analyze different algorithms that describe electoral behavior.

ideal point, landscapes will have smoother slopes than those in which voters have sharply decreasing or uncorrelated utility functions.

iii. Preferences with varying levels of nonseparability will be generated using Kauffman's N-K model (see later).

Given this encoding for the computational model, it is natural to look at existing measures of landscape complexity, and see how these might be applied to the problem of nonseparability in preferences. It is important to remember that any such measure must allow for the use of survey data, even if relying upon this source of data results in a blunter measure.

Kauffman's N-K Model and Complexity Measures for Survey Data

Prior work in population genetics and optimization theory, in particular the work on N-K landscapes of Kauffman (1993), Kauffman and Levin (1987), Kauffman and Weinberger (1989), and Weinberger (1988, 1990), and Page's (n.d.) P-Alpha Model of Rugged Policies, provide analytic frameworks that are enormously useful in approaching the problem of arriving at appropriate measures for electoral complexity. In Kauffman's N-K model, N represents the dimensionality of the fitness landscape (for us, the number of issues present). The parameter K represents the level of constraint (i.e., the level of non-separability) between issues. In the nomenclature provided by the N-K model, K is the number of elements within each subset of related issues.

For example, an electoral landscape with $N = 10$ and $K = 9$ has 10 unique issues, where each issue is constrained by choices on all other issues in a given preference vector. Such levels of high constraint are extraordinarily difficult to search, as choices on positions are not independent, thereby exacerbating the innate combinatorial difficulty of the optimization problem at hand.

Another extreme example would be where $N = 10$ and $K = 0$; in such a landscape, each issue is independent of every other issue, and may be considered separately. Clearly, a homogenous landscape such as this one would allow for easy interpretation of survey data. Note that preferences may be non-Euclidean but still separable.

In the social sciences, nonseparability is most often treated as a complication of the salience matrix in spatial voting models (see Enelow and Hinich and their definition of the A matrix).[21] This theoretical framework is problematic, because nondiagonal elements in a salience matrix only capture *pairwise* nonseparability. N-K models, in contrast, parameterize the level of nonseparability as an integer value that can encompass any possible level of separability among arbitrary subsets of issues (and not simply pairs). Given that no work to date has succeeded in empirically establishing the level of nonseparability present in the preferences of different electorates, it seems vital to have a theoretical framework that generalizes to the full range of possible values.

One can thus use Kauffman's N-K model to generate preferences ranging from very simple, Euclidean preferences to much more complex preferences. Using Kauffman's basic model, I create electorates with different parameter values for N, K, and whether or not the preferences are Euclidean. Given the landscape encoding detailed above, I then generate a landscape that represents the electorate's evaluation for candidates located at every possible platform in the issue space.

To understand the nature of these electorate landscapes, I resorted to full-information measures of landscape complexity. Fortunately, Kauffman has investigated several full-information measures of complexity that can be accommodated to deal with the electoral landscapes generated by my computational model. In addition to the normal measures of mean slope and the number of optima, Kauffman and others have proposed:[22]

> Mean and variance of the fitness of local optima;
> Mean length of an adaptive walk from a random start to an optima;
> The number of improvements possible (i.e., along a gradient) at each point along an adaptive walk;
> The mean basin size of optima;
> The autocorrelation of fitness results during a random walk.

Measures of this kind are essentially *features* (see Chapter 2), which allow us to investigate complex preferences in a parsimonious fashion. In the more specific realm of electorate preferences, one has to

---

[21] The A matrix in Enelow and Hinich can account *only* for pairwise nonseparability with the inclusion of off-diagonal elements. See Lacy (2001b) for a cogent explanation of this.

[22] This list is taken in large part from Kauffman (1993, 55).

remember that the trick is to adapt these measures of complexity to cope with the limitations of survey data, which means we have to focus on a feature space that is measurable given existing data sources.[23] As has been argued throughout this text, choosing the "best" feature space (based upon analytic properties) is not typically a useful enterprise if one cannot measure these features. One has to harmonize analytically justified features with empirically measurable features.

WHEN DATA FAIL YOU, DERIVE A LOGICAL IMPLICATION (AGAIN)

We have come a long way in attempting to derive a measure of preference complexity suitable for survey data, and it is worthwhile to pause for a moment and look back on our steps. First, I demonstrated that the logical implications of spatial models are not maintained when one examines A-NES data. Rather, it seems to be the case that a significant amount of nonseparability exists in the American electorate between 1988 and 2000. Second, I presented a framework for building a computational model of voter preferences based upon Kauffman's N-K model. This model allows us to generate artificial preference data with varying levels of complexity. This is extremely desirable, because we know *everything* about this data and can see whether or not a proposed measure correctly determines the underlying level of preference complexity. Several measures in the optimization literature already accomplish this task; the problem for us is that these measures require much more information than survey data provides. Thus, we have preliminary investigations of real data on the American electorate which suggests that issues are related, and we have a computational model that allows us to generate test beds for new measures. The problem that remains is to create a measure that is parsimonious enough to work with survey data.

---

[23] As noted by Hinich and Munger (1994), the ideal survey would ask respondents to state their opinion on all possible platforms, but this would be quite onerous. There is thus a contrast between the data generated by my computational model (which meets Hinich and Munger's standard of capturing relationships between issues) and real survey data (which only provides respondent ideal points). A good empirical measure of complexity would have to work on both datasets, not just the ideal case.

While it is clear that any possible empirical measure of complexity is partly inadequate given the limitations of survey data, my belief was that one could arrive at a rough approximation that captured the essence of the full-information measures.[24] To construct an empirical measure, consider the measures of ruggedness proposed by Kauffman. All of these measures capture the inherent predictability of a fitness landscape; expressed another way, ideas such as the basin size of an optimum, or the length of an adaptive walk, all point to how smoothly varying a landscape is in any given local neighborhood.

We also saw in the Introduction that this idea of predictability or smoothly varying landscapes has a clear analog to our logical tests of spatial theory. Imagine, for a moment, if voters had completely nonseparable preferences; that is, the only unit of analysis would be complete platforms, and there would be no continuity in policy neighborhoods. What would Figure 5.1 look like? And, more to the point, what would a two- or three-dimensional graph of issue positions measuring the consistency of party affiliation with issue positions look like? It is clear that with maximum preference complexity, voters would be located randomly throughout the issue space and there would be no great propensity for members of the party to cluster together (unless, of course, they had exactly the same platform).

The answer I arrived at thus depends upon deducing a logical implication of the full-information measures along with the preliminary work on the issue of abortion in this chapter. Assume there are N candidates for an office. Using the individual's response to which candidate they prefer, one can divide respondents into N groups, where each group is comprised of respondents who selected a candidate $n \in N$, thus forming a partition on the space of respondents. To construct the measure one would then evaluate the consistency of each subgroup by examining the variance within each subgroup's policy preferences around their preferred candidate's platform. The logical implication is that *variance in preferred policy platforms in each subgroup is a proxy for actual complexity in the electorate.*

Given this implication, the measure of an electorate's complexity is simple, and as we will see, this extraordinarily parsimonious measure (in terms of data requirements) tracks very well with the

---

[24] By "empirical measure" I mean a measure that could be generated using survey data.

full-information measures. The algorithm for constructing this measure can be stated simply:

I. Partition $i \in I$ voters into S disjoint subsets based upon each voter i's choice of candidate.
II. For each subset s_j where $j \in S$, each voter in s_j is represented by a vector $\bar{a}_i$ of policy positions of length N; each component $k \in N$ of this vector has A unique positions. The measure is thus:
$$\mathbf{M}_j = \text{Var}(s_j)$$

This measure, $\mathbf{M}_j$, is broadly applicable to different types of survey data and makes a good deal of intuitive sense. To develop this intuition, consider the two extreme cases. First, imagine that voters have Euclidean preferences. In this case, when one partitions them by their preferred candidate, one will find that voters in each subgroup have very similar preferences. In essence, each candidate has a platform that attracts the "nearest" voters in issue space. Distance obeys our intuition, and voters' will be responsive to side-payments in a bargaining process and local movement in a neighborhood by candidates.

The Euclidean case is illustrated in Figures 5.4 and 5.5. In Figure 5.4, the issue space is one dimensional. With some error, voters more or less vote for the candidate that is closest to their ideal point. Although errors may result (notice the two misclassified voters in these figures), this is the normal result of voter confusion or voter estimates of candidate variance (as detailed in probabilistic voting models). In Figure 5.5, the two-dimensional case is illustrated, and a hyperplane divides the regions favorable to each candidate. In both figures, it is clear that the variance in each subgroup of voters, as constructed using the above measure, will be slight, as voters for a given candidate are constrained within a limited region.

As one would expect, the Euclidean case is simple to analyze and does not require a computational model to generate expectations for

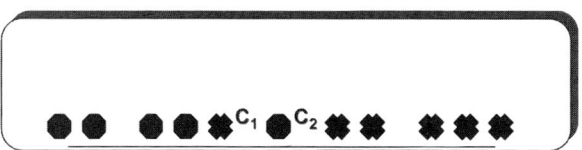

Figure 5.4. One-dimensional Euclidean Preferences

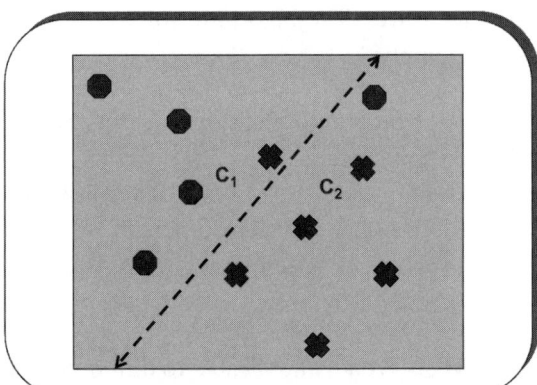

Figure 5.5. Two-dimensional Euclidean Preferences

the above measure M_j. Given that distance in this case is the familiar expression and that μ_{jk} is the mean for subset j on issue k,

$$M_j := \frac{1}{N} \cdot \left[\sum_{i \in s_j} \left[\sum_{k=1}^{N} (a_{ik} - \mu_{jk})^2 \right]^{\frac{1}{2}} \right]$$

It is clear that in the Euclidean case, M_j increases proportionally to the number of issues; thus, it is normalized by N in the equation above. Further, assume that candidates locate near the center of the space as in Figures 5.4 and 5.5. One would then expect that M_j is very small, as Var(•/c) is equal to $(1/c^2)$Var(•). For example, if the separating hyperplane induced by the candidates' locations divides the issue space in half, one would expect that the variance measured by M_j would be one quarter of the value for unconstrained voters.[25]

---

[25] Kauffman derives rough values for various complexity measures in the case in which alleles are normally distributed. In the computational experiments presented here, voters ideal points are distributed uniformly across the issue space to bias *against* finding results consistent with my complexity measure (see the Results section for details on this choice). In the Euclidean case, it is easy to check to see if the experiment yields values consistent with theory. For example, in the case of N = 2 and voter preferences are Euclidean, one can approximate M_j (by using a real distribution instead of a discrete, following Kauffman) by the simple expected value calculation:

$$\text{Var}(D_j) := \iint D_j \frac{1}{(b-a)^2} da_1 da_2$$

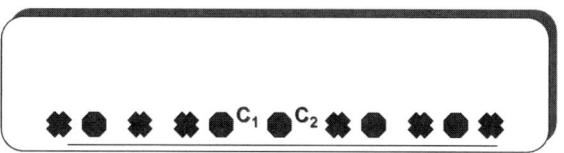

Figure 5.6. Unidimensional Weak Ordering

Next, imagine the most complex case where voters have completely nonseparable preferences represented as weak orderings (i.e., the highly complex case where N = the number of issues and K = N − 1). In this electorate, there is no meaningful concept of a neighborhood in issue space. Simply because a voter's most preferred position, measured as an ideal point on a survey, is (X,Y), there is no relationship whatsoever between the ideal point and surrounding points in the space − the candidate would have to be located exactly on the voter's ideal point to draw any conclusions about the voter's utility. Moving away from (X,Y) by any ε on either issue results in platforms that have completely unrelated utility. In this case, bargaining is nearly impossible and politicians have little latitude to move their platforms predictably during or subsequent to a campaign. The measure detailed here captures this complexity because supporters of a given politician will not have similar ideal points; rather, in the completely nonseparable case their ideal points will seem to be randomly distributed.

This complex case is illustrated in Figures 5.6 and 5.7. As earlier, Figure 5.6 displays a unidimensional issue space, while Figure 5.7

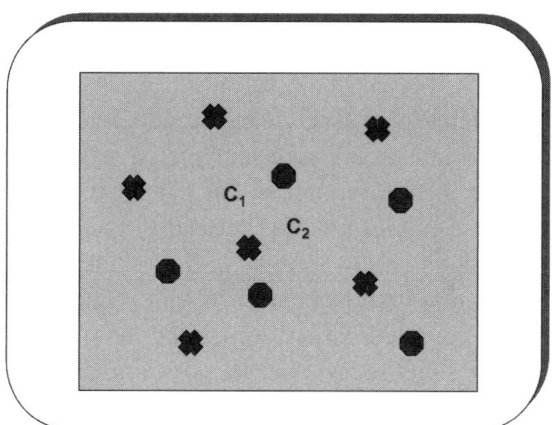

Figure 5.7. N = 2, K = 1 (Weak Ordering)

displays two dimensions. Given that a voter's preferences are described by a weak ordering (i.e., no simpler functional representation exists), it should not be surprising that voters who prefer a given candidate are located apparently randomly throughout the entire issue space. Variance for each subgroup would in these cases be much larger than the Euclidean case. Extending the example, one would expect that for an issue space of identical size, under any set of choices by candidates the value of M_j would be roughly four times that of the Euclidean case.

RESULTS

When evaluating a new empirical measure, such as the one I propose here for preference complexity in an electorate, it is important to see whether or not the empirical measure M_j is consistent with other, full-information measures generated by the computational model. In this case this practice is particularly important, as my complexity measure is designed specifically for use when we have relatively poor information. Surveys that focus solely upon recording a respondent's ideal point make a number of assumptions about the nature of underlying preferences, and this makes any measure that attempts to reconstruct the level of complexity of underlying preferences hazardous.

The computational model I have presented here thus serves two distinct roles. First, it helped me generate intuition about the problem to the point at which I was able to derive a logical implication that led to the creation of the measure M_j. Second, I also can use the full-information measures derived from the computational model's artificial data to verify that M_j really does order electorates from the simple to the complex.

Table 5.1 compares three different measures of complexity. As noted earlier, two of these measures were generated from artificial data and depend upon complete information; one cannot recover them from survey data. These full-information measures – *neighborhood variance* and *adaptive steps* – do, however, have well-understood properties, and to the extent that they correlate with the empirical measure for survey data presented earlier, we can be more confident in the new measure. Neighborhood variance looks at the average amount of change in a neighborhood around a point in the issue space.[26]

---

[26] Neighborhood is defined here as a hamming distance of 1 around a given platform.

Table 5.1. *Computational Results*[1]

	Neighborhood Variance	Adaptive Steps	Variance within Voter Groups (M_j)
Euclidian			
$N = 4, A = 5$	673.61	7.73	1.52
(St. Dev.)	(54.48)	(0.34)	(0.18)
Weak Orderings			
$N = 4, A = 5, K = 0$	519.24	4.09	1.92
(St. Dev.)	(182.31)	(0.95)	(0.14)
$N = 4, A = 5, K = 1$	10404.67	3.33	1.94
(St. Dev.)	(2988.46)	(0.67)	(0.13)
$N = 4, A = 5, K = 3$	6410831	2.14	1.94
(St. Dev.)	(1518946)	(0.25)	(0.10)

[1] Italicized values represent standard deviations for all iterations of a given experiment. In all cases, 100 iterations were performed. Electorates consisted of 1,000 voters with ideal points/weak orderings drawn from uniform distributions. It is important to note that these results hold regardless of the value chosen for A; the table is generated as an example for a single choice of A. Finally, values are normalized for N, the number of issues. Four issues were chosen as a parameter for purposes of illustration; the results are largely invariant under this parameter for $N > 3$.

The intuition behind this measure is that if variance in the neighborhood of a given platform is high, the mean slope of the adaptive landscape is also high – essentially, you have sharp peaks and drastic changes in utility as you take steps around the electoral landscape. When variance is low, you have gently rolling hills, and one platform tends to be evaluated almost the same as other platforms in the neighborhood.

Adaptive steps measures the mean number of steps it is possible to take before getting trapped upon a local optimum.[27] The intuition behind this measure is that if candidates "tweak" platforms by making local improvements, there is a limit to how far they can travel in such a fashion before hitting a local optimum.[28] On smoother, more regular electoral landscapes, one can take more steps, but on more rugged landscapes the risk of being trapped on a local optimum is high at each step.

---

[27] A step is an alteration of an existing platform by randomly changing the value of a single issue in the platform by one unit (i.e., the smallest interval possible).

[28] Most optimization procedures depend upon hillclimbing in some form or another for the systematic aspect of the search, and this measure captures this feature of searches.

As stated earlier, one can only apply these two measures when one has full information about the electorate. In this context, full information means that one has a complete evaluation of every possible platform in the issue space by voters – obviously, existing surveys do not provide this quality of information and my computational model was needed to produce them. The goal is thus to see how full-information measures compare to my more parsimonious measure, which has been designed for real-world surveys that only record ideal points.

As is readily apparent from Table 5.1, both of the full-information measures move in the same direction as preferences become more rugged. In the Euclidean case, neighborhood variance is slight, and the number of adaptive steps is quite large. At the other end of the spectrum, where weak orderings are the only possible representation of preferences (i.e., $K = N - 1$), variance is quite high and the adaptive steps is low.

As one would hope, the complexity measure I propose for survey data is consistent with the full-information measures. In the Euclidean case, in which one would expect supporters of a candidate to "look" much alike, the measure achieves its minimum. In the most complex case, the measure records higher variance, indicating that voters within each subgroup do not have very similar preferences.

Applying the Measure to Survey Data

As noted previously, the goal is simple – find which category of complexity surveys fall into by comparing empirical values for M_j (derived from surveys) with computational results for M_j. Due to widespread use and accessibility, the results presented here utilize A-NES data, the Israeli Election Survey, and a survey designed by Lacy (2001a, 2001b). If, in fact, voter preferences recorded by these surveys are Euclidean, one would expect the complexity measure would match the computational results for Euclidean preferences. Alternately, survey data might betray non-separable preferences.

Table 5.2 displays the results of the survey data from the 1964 and 1980 A-NES, and it is quite clear that American preferences are quite different in the two periods. In 1964, voter preferences are decidedly non-Euclidean, with little difference between the general sample and highly educated voters. The fact that highly educated voters have the

Table 5.2. *Variance for Subgroups of Voters Partitioned by Candidate Choice*[1]

1964	Goldwater	Johnson	Closest Match (M_j)
A = 5 (all)	2.61	2.72	Non-Euclidean (threshold ~1.57)
A = 5 (high education only)	2.27	2.50	Non-Euclidean (threshold ~1.57)
1980	**Reagan**	**Carter**	**Closest Match (M_j)**
A = 7 (all)	2.25	2.40	Non-Euclidean (threshold = ~3.10)
A = 7 (high education only)	1.76	1.74	Non-Euclidean (threshold = ~3.10)
1996 Israeli Study	**Netanyahu**	**Peres**	**Closest Match (M_j)**
A = 4 (all)	1.03	.92	Non-Euclidean (threshold =.~93)

[1] Variance is reported both for the entire electorate (all) and for those with an education of greater than 12 years (high). Two separate issues were used to generate the A = 7 case, and four issues for the A = 4 case. Values for 1992 were tightly clustered and ranged from .95 to 1.16. For 1996, values ranged from .86 to 1.28. In the Israeli case, highly educated voters had almost identical values for M_j.

same value for M_j indicates that genuine complexity (e.g., nonseparability) is responsible, *and not simple randomness*. In 1980, however, preferences are likely Euclidean, especially when one considers that the subset of highly-educated voters has dramatically lower values for M_j than the whole sample. In accord with our intuition about these time periods, Democrats as a group display more complexity on M_j than Republicans in both elections, though less so in 1980.

In addition to the American case, Table 5.2 also shows results for the 1996 Israeli election. Given that results are biased against finding non-Euclidean preferences (see the Appendix on caveats), these results are strong support for the idea that the current Israeli electorate is characterized by nonseparable preferences. Many of the questions on the Israeli survey concerned the peace process along with religious issues, so this finding is in accord with intuition about the Israeli electorate.

A final test of the measure M_j relies upon data collected by Lacy (see 2001a, 2001b for details) in February of 1998. This phone survey used pairs of issue questions along with instruments designed to detect pairwise nonseparability. Questions were asked in a standard branching format, and recorded seven possible values. For example, the environment question Lacy used was:

CLEAN UP ENVIRONMENT: Do you think the amount of money the U.S. spends cleaning up the environment should go up, go down, or remain at current levels?
Follow-up: Go up (down) a lot, somewhat, or a little?

Other seven-valued questions measure attitudes on defense, social spending, education, taxation, welfare, and immigration. For purposes of comparison, it is useful to see if the measure outlined here detects nonseparability across the pairs in this data set, given that Lacy's procedure revealed nonseparability.

As expected, Table 5.3 demonstrates that the measure $\mathbf{M}_j$ also detects the presence of nonseparability across issue pairs for the majority of categories (i.e., Republican or Democrat respondents divided into low and high education groups). Although not all categories register as nonseparable under the measure $\mathbf{M}_j$, these results should be seen as broadly supportive for Lacy's work. Unlike the tests developed by Lacy, $\mathbf{M}_j$ does not explicitly test for question ordering effects; further, the questions used in the survey depend upon relative quantities for a given policy (i.e., more or less), rather than enumerating qualitatively different policy positions. Given these constraints, along with the fact that both low and high education respondents reveal nonseparable preferences, few other interpretations of his data seem likely.

One point raised by the forgoing research deserves clarification. The empirical results presented here detect nonseparable preferences in many different datasets, and one might ask if this is evidence of more voter sophistication than previously thought (Lupia, McCubbins, and Popkin 2000). On the one hand, most survey research, by assuming Euclidean preferences, would "find" that voters are less than perfect citizens, when in fact, the survey design itself was at fault.[29] Voters might simply have more complex preferences than can be

---

[29] This is the argument made by Lacy in the two articles cited earlier.

Table 5.3. *Variance for Issue Pairs Using Data from Lacy (2001a, 2001b)*[1]

Issue Pairs	Lacy% Nonseparable	Republican Value for M_j for Low/High Educations	Democratic Value for M_j for Low/High Educations	Closest Match (M_j)
Environment/ Pollution Regulations	34% or 71%	**2.74**/1.99	**2.55**/2.07	Non-Euclidean (threshold ~2.10)
Income Taxes/Crime Spending	48% or 54%	**2.39**/**2.17**	**2.48**/1.98	Non-Euclidean (threshold ~2.10)
Social Spending/ Defense Spending	28% or 42%	**2.69**/**3.13**	2.11/**2.17**	Non-Euclidean (threshold ~2.15)

[1] Not all issue pairs from Lacy (2001a, 2001b) are included, because the survey questions on Abortion and English Use were measured on different scales, making them unsuitable for use with the measure of non-separability presented here. Two percentage estimates are reported for Lacy; in his work, he measures the direction of the effect (i.e., does Environment occur prior to Pollution, or vice versa?). In the columns for Republican and Democratic respondents, values that indicate nonseparability are boldfaced (i.e., the value is greater than the threshold value indicated in the last column).

recorded with existing surveys, therefore arguing for different sorts of surveys entirely before one can address the question of citizen competence.[30] On the other hand, relatively simple heuristics also might be responsible for nonseparable preferences. For example, if a respondent had some idea that there was a federal budget, preferences on spending policies might be subject to a constraint; that is, once a certain total level of spending was reached, any bundle of policies that when added together resulted in excessive spending would be much less desirable. Other such examples abound, including the constraint on attention found in directional theory (Rabinowitz and MacDonald 1993) and heterogeneous agents (Hong and Page 1998).

---

[30] See Hinich and Munger (1994) on the question of how to design surveys to detect complex preferences.

YET ANOTHER IMPLICATION

Despite the evidence presented above, one could still believe (reasonably) that noise is the culprit, rather than nonseparability. By focusing upon individual issues, I may have inadvertently increased the amount of variance by including issues of little salience to the survey respondents. Or, the problem may be more general. Respondents might not care about any issue, thereby producing the variance measured $\mathbf{M}_j$.

Although I have used the education of respondents to test the hypothesis that noise is responsible, there is a more direct way to examine this question. Using data from the A-NES survey, I performed the following experiment for the 1992, 1996, and 2000 samples:

   I. Run a principal components factor analysis on the most salient/important issue questions on each survey. Not surprisingly, one finds two dimensions. Loosely, one dimension measures economic concerns and the other measures ethical.[31]
   II. Create a space using factor scores where the X axis is the economic dimension and the Y axis is the ethical dimension. Scale each dimension so that positive values equate to conservative positions and negative to liberal positions.

In this space, quadrant 1 (with positive values for X and Y) is where one would expect to find most Republicans. Quadrant 3 (with negative values for X and Y) is where one would expect to find most Democrats.

I am once again interested in looking at inconsistent respondents; that is, how many respondents that are located in quadrants 1 and 3 vote for the wrong party? If one believes that noise is responsible for the findings of this chapter, the implication is clear: Inconsistent respondents should be clustered in only two places. If their issue positions are not well-described by the factor space, they will be located near the origin. This would imply that there is not a great deal of structure to their issue responses and variance is a byproduct of voter inattention or ignorance. Alternately, if the inconsistent voters are cross-pressured

---

[31] For more details, see the author's Web site. Issues were chosen based on their predictive power in standard directional and spatial models. The sample used for the factor analyses was truncated, because most respondents (about two thirds) did not respond to the entire set of issue questions. There are various approaches one might use in interpolating missing values, but this would not affect the results presented here.

(that is, they are conservative on one factor and liberal on the other), they will be located along the X or Y axis within their quadrants and variance indicates ambivalence.

To answer this question, one can either graph the inconsistent voters on a contour map and visually inspect their locations, or one can run a regression where the dependent variable is consistency and the independent variable is distance from the origin.

What is genuinely surprising about this experiment is that not only are inconsistent voters found throughout quadrants 1 and 3, distance has no explanatory power for predicting consistency. Moreover, the number of inconsistent voters is quite large. In 1996, 20 percent are inconsistent and in 1992 and 2000, nearly 30 percent are inconsistent. Keep in mind that the sample used for this experiment is truncated to include only the respondents that answered a large number of issue questions and had structured enough positions to place them in quadrants 1 and 3. Truncating the sample still further to include only those respondents with a college degree or more does not change the results.

One can, of course, still wonder whether nonseparability is the explanation for these results. If noise is ruled out as an alternative explanation, it may be that some other mechanism accounts for the high variance and large numbers of inconsistent voters.[32] Such challenges, however, exemplify the main argument of this book: Specifying competing explanations and testing them against data is the best way to build theory. And when the data are less than perfect, logical implications can serve as excellent substitutes.

FINAL COMMENTS

Models of human decision making underlie almost all research problems in the social sciences. A crucial component of any decision is a set of preferences, and to a large degree, preferences are treated as a matter of assumption, not genuine research. This chapter adds additional

---

[32] Munger (personal communication) suggests that the presence of multiple ideologies may be the actual mechanism. Aldrich (personal communication) suggests that a better way to examine salience would be to leverage the open-ended question on each A-NES that asks which issues are most important to the respondent. Additionally, Aldrich believes that panel data could be helpful in discovering whether changes in issue positions are independent over time.

support to the hypothesis that preferences are worthy of further study. Hopefully, I also have demonstrated that in less than ideal circumstances, it is still possible to test the main implications of a model by deriving a logical implication that matches up with existing data. By calibrating the empirical measure $\mathbf{M}_j$ against the artificial data provided by the computational model and then testing it against a variety of surveys, I was able to add credibility to my hypothesis that electorates contain individuals with nonseparable preferences.

The measure of preference complexity presented here is far from perfect (see the appendix), and throughout I have noted the weaknesses of my own work. Other explanations – for example, elite communication, ignorance, or salience – could account for these results, and nonseparability is not the only source of complexity possible in preferences. The goal of this work, however, is to force researchers to reconsider their models of electoral decision making.

The existing paradigm, which depends upon fitting models ever closer to fixed samples, should be replaced with a new focus on testing the core models against out-of-sample data or with logical implications. Most everyone in the field is guilty of this lapse, and as a result, most models are difficult to compare. Directional theorists should be lauded for producing a number of in-sample comparisons with spatial theory, but, by and large, every voting model has its own empirical referent. In large part, this has prevented other head-to-head comparisons, and has limited the amount of interplay between political psychologists and mathematical modelers. Without agreed-upon dependent variables, this lack of cumulative model building will continue to characterize the field.

Readers may be uncomfortable with the idea that preferences are complex, especially given the modeling difficulties such a position entails. Yet, it seems to me that the best way to counter this work is to directly confront it by building a better model using the same empirical referent.

APPENDIX: CAVEATS, ENDLESS CAVEATS TO THE MEASURE OF PREFERENCE COMPLEXITY

There are six important points to make about the use of complexity measures and survey data. First, in my computational experiment, voter preferences are drawn from uniform distributions. It is quite possible that actual voters are drawn from different distributions. Imagine, for example, that American voters with allegiance to a given party are drawn instead from a truncated normal distribution centered on the candidate and with low variance. If anything, the presence of an alternative distribution would likely decrease the amount of variance reported by my complexity measure, thus pushing the measure to the Euclidean case. The fact that this measure reports substantial variance, despite this, is encouraging.

Of course, this problem can be more extreme insofar as their distribution on ideal points may have little variance, even though their underlying preferences across all policy options are complex. For example, supporters of a candidate may tend to have the same ideal point, particularly on survey questions with little policy granularity; that is, when presented with a four-point policy scale, they may choose the same ideal point simply because of priming, the campaign, and other factors. The measure in no way accounts for this tendency, and to the extent that it exists, my measure of variance in each subset of the partition will be artificially *deflated*. This, in short, is the two-edged nature of a measure designed for existing survey data: It has broad applicability, but is unable to capture some of the nuance one would hope for. The important point, though, is that this measure is conservative, and any findings should be treated with high levels of confidence.

Second, as the number of issues N increases, it is not a straightforward process to normalize the complexity measure $\mathbf{M}_j$. Unlike the continuous case, discrete policy questions and the concomitant discrete platform locations for candidates result in a nonlinear progression of $\mathbf{M}_j$ in N, although it remains monotonic increasing in N. Fortunately, $d(\mathbf{M}_j)/d(N)$ quickly approaches 0 for all values of A; typically, there are only marginal increases in $\mathbf{M}_j$ after 4 or 5 issues. Once again, to bias against finding non-Euclidean preferences, survey data is *always* compared against the limit of $\mathbf{M}_j$. What this means is that even if voter preferences can be represented in fewer dimensions, I nonetheless compare the complexity measure to the limit of $\mathbf{M}_j$.

Third, a related problem concerns the size of the issue space N. As we have seen, normalizing $\mathbf{M}_j$ to account for the size of the issue space is difficult for the Euclidean case, but fortunately $\mathbf{M}_j$ converges to a fixed value quite quickly. Normalizing for N is more difficult, however, when issues are nonseparable (i.e., K > 0), because by definition nonseparability implies that the true complexity of a given set of preferences will only be measured when all relevant issues appear in the survey. Given the paucity of good policy questions on surveys, along with the inconsistency of most surveys in asking any given policy question, one cannot be certain that all relevant policies exist in a single survey. It is thus the case that the level of complexity that is revealed in any given survey may be underestimated, simply because all relevant policy questions were not asked. While this is a nontrivial defect, it is once more the case that this would bias against finding non-Euclidean preferences.

Fourth, it is impossible to distinguish between rational voters with weak orderings for preferences and voters who choose completely at random, with no consistency through time. At root, a weak ordering looks random, insofar as there is no similarity between neighboring platforms. Although it is impossible to discriminate between these two cases using existing survey data, one can offer suggestive evidence by dividing the sample of voters into the lowest and highest educated voters. Table 5.2 reports results for voters with 13 years of education or more and compares this with the total sample. While such a comparison is hardly dispositive, it does appear that education does not result in different results. Thus, the question posed here is important (i.e., we really would like to be able to discriminate with certainty between "random" voters and complex policy voters), but survey limitations prevent us from providing a complete answer.

Fifth, one might argue against the use of the measure $\mathbf{M}_j$ because it fails to distinguish between salient and nonsalient issues. In fact, one might even propose weighting the component issues in the measure by resort to a regression that predicted political choice based upon policy positions (and using the resultant standardized coefficients as weights). Sadly, this puts the cart before the horse, as salience as a concept is only meaningful given separable preferences. As with the other caveats listed here, the presence of nonsalient issues works against any positive findings for the proposed measure to the degree that positions on these issues are correlated with party identification or ideology (Hinich and Munger 1994).

Finally, one will notice in Table 5.1 that values for $\mathbf{M}_j$ flatten dramatically for all non-Euclidean cases. At first blush, this might seem alarming, as there is little ability to discern one value of K from another. While this is a shortcoming, any other result would be more alarming still. By construction, survey data that only records ideal points cannot ever reveal the level of K in non-Euclidean data. To recover the exact value of K from survey data one would have to be able to test the precise nature of dependency between issues; for example, one would have to discriminate between pairwise nonseparability ($K = 1$) and 3-tuples ($K = 2$). Given that this is impossible in survey data, the measure $\mathbf{M}_j$ conforms to what we can reasonably deduce.

It is worth restating that these caveats do not diminish the main contribution of the measure $\mathbf{M}_j$. No measure that relies upon actual survey data would be immune to the forgoing caveats, and, in all cases, I have chosen a course that would mitigate against positive findings of nonseparability.

6

A Short Conclusion

Despite the suspicion that often arises between the methodological camps, it is my belief that most researchers in social science want to move in the same direction. We all have a desire to understand how economic and political actors (ranging from individual voters to crowds to nation states) make decisions. To the extent we understand social science, any of us would be happy to have policy relevance. As noted by Friedman (1953) and Granger (1999), the research community has many shared beliefs – we all, more or less, agree on what "the good" is in terms of outcomes. What we disagree about is methodology, because it is not obvious which approach provides the most leverage in understanding the world. Put another way, while we might all agree on the merits of preventing nuclear warfare, the more salient question is how to discriminate good models and good advice from bad.

Part of the problem is that the social sciences do not have a shared understanding of what constitutes a reasonable question. Too often, asking a good question is confused with providing a good answer. One might want to understand the causes of a particular event (say, World War II), but, without a great deal of care, a few cases do not constitute a coherent problem suitable for research. As I have argued throughout, the main problem that confronts us in research design is the curse of dimensionality. It cannot be ignored, whatever one's methodological orientation. When one resorts to limiting assumptions in game theoretic work, or distributional choices and a functional form in empirical work, one is implicitly making a statement about the parameter space. The curse remains in much the same form in historiography, as every

A Short Conclusion

detail included in a narrative represents a dimension that is used to examine the research question.[1]

Whatever your research question, you thus need to ask whether or not it is possible to distinguish your work from a just-so story. How one deals with the curse of dimensionality is what matters, and as I have argued here, there are three main rules of thumb one should consider.[2] The first rule is to derive a parsimonious feature space/encoding appropriate to the question. This applies with equal force to deductive, statistical, or qualitative modeling. If one refuses to derive a feature space, one is in essence hiding crucial elements of one's work, or worse still, relying upon the software package or some other convention to choose the feature space atheoretically. Adding more details to a model, whether through assumptions, independent variables, historical details, and so on, is of itself never helpful. One needs a framework that allows for *relevant* detail without grossly expanding the size of the parameter space.[3] Deriving a feature space is one way to incorporate details in a theoretically aware process. For example, my efforts in

---

[1] Choosing a level of specificity in an historical narrative is very problematic, if one realizes the nature of parameter spaces. See Lustick (1996) or Goemans (2000) for a restatement of this conceptual problem that relates it to historiographical curve-fitting. Although I do not believe that history (or qualitative work and the examination of small numbers of cases more generally) is a coherent methodology for discovering casual relationships, it can be used to ground assumptions and parameters in the real world. As noted earlier, an excellent example of this practice is found in Rabinowitz, MacDonald, and Listhaug (working paper). One can also look to history as a source for data (for a good example of this practice, see Scruggs and Allen 2004) or for testing logical implications.

[2] An alternative that I do not advocate would be to create only very simple models, thereby avoiding the problems detailed in this book (for a reasoned statement on the virtue of simple models, see Axelrod 1984). At the end of the day, we would like our models to be about *something* important. If our methodologies are not up to the task of addressing the problems we care about, we need to develop better methods. Moreover, simple models are simple because of limiting assumptions, which is one way to hide the curse of dimensionality without eliminating the effects of this curse.

[3] As noted in Chapters 1 and 2, adding independent variables willy-nilly is the most common mistake researchers make in statistical modeling. The analogous problem in qualitative research is the desire for detail. Unless one can justify it, including details of the particular form of government (as one example) in a case study is a waste of time unless one's cases span the possible government types. It is far better to limit oneself to fewer, less granular descriptions of government types; that way, one can span the types with cases.

Chapter 4 are certainly transparent and would be the subject of debate if others were interested in modeling the alliance game. Debating the characteristics of the feature space, rather than comparing incommensurable results, places modeling on a more defensible, empirical footing.

The second rule is to hedge one's bet by resorting to out-of-sample testing. Hopefully, I have presented convincing arguments that evaluating models by examining in-sample comparisons is not possible. That leaves only two options. Either abundant out-of-sample data must be available, or one must derive novel logical implications of a model and see if these implications hold empirically. However assiduous we are in deriving a theoretically justified model, we are always making a hazardous inference. The only way to hedge one's bet is to test inferences against out-of-sample data or logical implications. Without these tests, clever researchers will always succeed in fitting a model to a sample. Their clever graduate students will fit new models to the same sample and claim progress has been made.

It is worth noting the corollary that for out-of-sample testing to work, we all have to focus on the same dependent variables. For example, unless there is some agreement on what constitutes "cooperation" and how to measure it, we will, as a community, derive models that have no common empirical referent. Common measures are thus a prerequisite for progress.

Finally, one should work to develop more complex models that are cumulative in nature. Computational modeling provides at least a promise of more verisimilitude in our models, which raises the ante in interesting ways. By incorporating more elements of the real-world into our models, the odds that one is wrong increase dramatically (and this is a good thing). Moreover, Chapters 4 and 5 demonstrate that the difficulty in incorporating the complex elements of a problem into a model is intimately connected to understanding the phenomenon in question. Complexity always comes at a cost, but wrestling with these issues and building cumulative models seems a better approach than eliminating most issues of interest through limiting assumptions or a fortuitous selection of cases. In short, we should avoid the current practice of creating toy models and letting our analogies from these models to the real world do all the work.

If the goal is to build better models, as it is in most of the physical sciences, I would argue that the social sciences are in need of a paradigm shift. It should be obvious that methods are only useful insofar as they allow us to provide better answers to problems. If it is not obvious that a new estimator or equilibrium concept advances the out-of-sample performance of a particular model, one has to question its relevance. And if a model is so brittle that minor changes to the parameters change the results, this is a cause for concern. Reducing the gap between deductive models and their empirical referents seems to be an acute need in the social sciences, as does building equivalence classes for formal models. Computational modeling provides one avenue toward reaching these goals, and should therefore be seen as a needed complement to existing methodologies.

References

Achen, C. H. 2003. "An agenda for the new political methodology: Microfoundations and art." *Annual Review of Political Science* 5:423–50.
Alchian, Armen. 1950. "Uncertainty, evolution and economic theory." *Journal of Political Economy* 58:211–22.
Aldrich, John. 1995. *Why parties?* Chicago: University of Chicago Press.
Aldrich, John. 1997. "When is it rational to vote?" In *Perspectives on public choice*, ed. Dennis Mueller. New York: Cambridge University Press.
Arrow, K. J. 1963. *Social choice and individual values*. 2nd ed. New York: Wiley.
Arthur, Brian. 1989. "Competing technologies, increasing returns, and lock-in by historical events." *Economic Journal* 99:116–31.
Axelrod, Robert. 1984. *The evolution of cooperation*. New York: Basic Books.
Axelrod, Robert. 1997. "Culture dissemination." *Journal of Conflict Resolution* 41:203–26.
Bailey, Michael. 2003. "The other side of the coin: The hidden benefits of campaign finance." In *Computational models in political economy*, ed. Kollman, Miller, Page. Cambridge, MA: MIT University Press.
Bailey, Michael, and David W. Brady. 1998. "Heterogeneity and representation: The senate and free trade." *American Journal of Political Science* 42:524–44.
Ballard, Dana. 1997. *An introduction to natural computation*. Cambridge, MA: MIT University Press.
Banks, Jeffrey. 2000. "Buying supermajorities in finite legislatures." *American Political Science Review* 94:677–81.
Bates, Robert, Avner Grief, Margaret Levi, Jean-Laurent Rosenthal, and Barry Weingast. 1998. *Analytic narratives*. Princeton, NJ: Princeton University Press.

Beck, Nathaniel, Gary King, and Langche Zeng. 2000. "Improving quantitative studies of international conflict: A conjecture." *American Political Science Review* 94(1):21–36.

Beck, Nathaniel, Gary King, and Langche Zeng. 2004. "Theory and evidence in international conflict: A response to de Marchi, Gelpi, and Grynaviski." *American Political Science Review* 98:379–89.

Bellesiles, Michael. 2000. *Arming America: The origins of a national gun culture.* New York: Soft Skull Press.

Benitez, J. M., J. L. Castro, and Requena. 1997. "Are artificial neural networks black boxes?" *IEEE Transaction on Neural Networks* 8(5):1156–64.

Bennett, D. Scott, and Allan Stam. 2000. "EUGene: A conceptual manual." *International Interactions* 26:179–204.

Berlekamp, Elwyn, John Conway, and Richard Guy. 2001. *Winning ways for your mathematical plays: Volume 1.* Wellesley, MA: A.K. Peters, Ltd.

Bernhardt, M. Daniel, and Daniel E. Ingberman. 1985. "Candidate reputations and the incumbency effect." *Journal of Public Economics* 27:47–67.

Binmore, Kenneth. 1992. *Fun and games: A text on game theory.* New York: D.C. Heath and Co.

Binmore, Kenneth. 1997. "Review of the complexity of cooperation: Agent-based models of competition and collaboration." http://jasss.soc.surrey.ac.uk/1/1/review1.html

Binmore, Kenneth, and Paul Klemperer. 2002. The biggest auction ever: The sale of the British 3G telecom licenses. *Economic Journal* 112:C74–C96.

Bishop, C. M. 1995. *Neural networks for pattern recognition.* Oxford: Oxford University Press.

Black, Duncan. 1958. *The theory of committees and elections.* Repr., Dordrecht, Netherlands: Kluwer Academic, 1987.

Blainey, Geoffrey. 1988. *The causes of war.* 3rd ed. New York: Macmillan.

Boland, Lawrence. 1979. "A critique of Friedman's critics." *Journal of Economic Literature* 17:503–22.

Bremer, Stuart. 1992. "Dangerous dyads: Conditions affecting the likelihood of interstate war, 1816–1965." *Journal of Conflict Resolution* 36(2):309–41.

Brito, Dagobert, and Michael Intriligator. 1985. "Conflict, war, and redistribution." *American Political Science Review* 79:943–57.

Bueno de Mesquita, Bruce, and David Lalman. 1992. *War and reason.* New Haven, CT: Yale University Press.

Bueno de Mesquita, Bruce, and James Morrow. 1999. "Sorting through the wealth of notions." *International Security* 24:56–73.

Buthe, Tim. 2002. "Taking temporality seriously: modeling history and the use of narratives as evidence." *American Political Science Review* 96:481–94.

Calvert, Randall. 1985. "Robustness of the multidimensional voting model." *American Journal of Political Science* 29:69–95.

Camerer, Colin. 2003. *Behavioral game theory: Experiments in strategic interaction.* Princeton, NJ: Princeton University Press.

Canes-Wrone, Brandice, and Scott de Marchi. 2002. "Presidential approval and legislative success" *Journal of Politics* 64:491–509.

Castle, Emery. 1993. "On the communication gap in agricultural economics." *American Journal of Agricultural Economics* 75:84–91.

Cederman, Lars. 1994. "Emergent Polarity: Analyzing State Formation and Power Politics." *International Studies Quarterly* 38:501–33.

Chong, Edwin, and Stanislaw Zak. 1996. *An introduction to optimization.* New York: Wiley Interscience.

Conitzer, Vincent, and Sandholm, Tuomas. 2002. "Complexity results about Nash Equilibria." *SCS Technical Report CMU-CS-02-135.* Pittsburgh: Carnegie Mellon University School of Computer Science.

Conway, John. 1976. *On numbers and games.* New York: Academic Press.

Cox, Gary, and Jonathan Katz. 1996. "Why did the incumbency advantage in U.S. house elections grow?" *American Journal of Political Science* 40:478–97.

Cox, Gary, and Michael Munger. 1989. "Closeness, expenditures, and turnout in the 1982 U.S. House elections." *American Political Science Review* 83:217–31.

Davis, Natalie. 1983. *The return of Martin Guerre.* Cambridge, MA: Harvard University Press.

Davis, Otto, Morris DeGroot, and Melvin Hinich. 1972. "Social preference orderings and majority rule." *Econometrica* 40:147–57.

de Finetti, B. 1974. *Theory of probability: Volume 1.* New York: John Wiley and Sons.

de Marchi, Scott. 1999. "Adaptive Models and Electoral Instability." *Journal of Theoretical Politics* 11:393–419.

de Marchi, Scott, Chris Gelpi, and Jeff Grynaviski. 2004. "Untangling neural networks." *American Political Science Review* 98:371–78.

de Marchi, Scott, and Hein Goemans. 2004. Bargaining and Complex Preferences: Examining the Case of the Israeli Electorate. Duke University Working Paper.

DeGroot, Morris, and Jeff Grynaviski. 2002. *Probability and Statistics.* New York: Addison Wesley.

Delli Carpini, Michael, and Scott Keeter. 1991. "Stability and change in the U.S. public's knowledge of politics." *Public Opinion Quarterly* 27:133–41.

DeLong, E. R., M. D. DeLong, and D. L. Clarke-Pearson. 1988. "Comparing the areas under two or more correlated receiving operator curves: A nonparametric approach." *Biometrics* 44:837–45.

Diamond, Jared. 1997. *Guns, germs, and steel.* New York: W.W. Norton and Company.

Downs, Anthony. 1957. *An economic theory of democracy*. New York: Harper & Row.

Efromovich, Sam. 1999. *Nonparametric curve estimation*. New York: Springer.

Enelow, James, and Melvin Hinich. 1983. "On Plott's pairwise symmetry condition for majority rule equilibrium." *Public Choice* 40:317–21.

Enelow, James, and Melvin Hinich. 1984. *The spatial theory of voting*. New York: Cambridge University Press.

Epstein, Joshua M., and Robert Axtell. 1996. *Growing artificial societies*. Cambridge, MA: MIT University Press.

Fearon, James. 1995. "Rationalist explanations for war." *International Organization* 49:379–414.

Feng-Hsiung, Hsu, Thomas Anantharaman, Murray Campbell, and Andreas Nowatzyk. 1990. "A grandmaster chess machine." *Scientific American* 263:44–50.

Fenno, Richard. 1978. *Home style: house members in their districts*. New York: HarperCollins.

Ferejohn, John. 1986. "Incumbent performance and electoral control." *Public Choice* 50:5–25.

Ferejohn, John. 1993. "The spatial model and elections." In *Information, participation, and choice*, ed. B. Grofman, 107–124. Ann Arbor: University of Michigan Press.

Fiorina, Morris. 1974. *Representation, roll calls, and constituencies*. New York: D.C. Heath.

Fiorina, Morris. 1981. *Retrospective voting in American national elections*. New Haven, CT: Yale University Press.

Fiorina, Morris, and Roger Noll. 1979. "Majority rule models and legislative elections." *The Journal of Politics* 41:1081–1104.

Franklin, Charles, and Mark Rich. n.d. "Emergent formation of political parties." University of Wisconsin Working Paper.

Friedman, Milton. 1953. "The methodology of positive economics." In *Essays in positive economics*, 3–43. Chicago: University of Chicago Press.

Garfinkel, Michelle, and Stergios Skaperdas. 2000. "Conflict without misperceptions or incomplete information." *Journal of Conflict Resolution* 44:793–807.

Gartzke, Erik. 1999. "War is in the error term." *International Organization* 53:567–87.

Gentle, James. 2002. *Elements of computational statistics*. New York: Springer-Verlag.

Gerber, Elisabeth, and Jeffrey Lewis. n.d. "Representing heterogeneous districts." Gerald R. Ford School of Public Policy, University of Michigan Working paper.

Gibbon, Edward. 1776–1788. *The decline and fall of the Roman Empire.* Repr., New York: Everyman's Library, 1993.

Goemans, Hein. 2000. *War and punishment, the causes of war termination and the first world war.* Princeton, NJ: Princeton University Press.

Gonzalez, S. 2000. "Neural networks for macroeconomic forecasting: A complementary approach to linear regression models." Papers Series of Ministere des Finances du Canada 2000–07.

Good, Phillip, and James Hardin. 2003. *Common errors in statistics (and how to avoid them).* New York: Wiley-Interscience.

Granger, Clive. 1999. *Empirical modeling in economics.* New York: Cambridge.

Green, Donald, and Ian Shapiro. 1994. *Pathologies of rational choice theory.* New Haven, CT: Yale University Press.

Greene, William. 1997. *Econometric analysis.* New York: Prentice Hall.

Griffiths, William, Carter Hill, and George Judge. *Learning and practicing econometrics.* New York: Wiley.

Groseclose, Tim, and Jeffrey Milyo. 2004a. "A Test of Media Bias." Working Paper.

Groseclose, Tim, and Jeffrey Milyo. 2004b. "Buying the bums out: What's the dollar value of a seat in Congress?" Working Paper.

Groseclose, Tim, and James Snyder. 2000. "Vote buying, supermajorities, and flooded coalitions." *American Political Science Review* 94:683–84.

Hanley, J. A., and B. J. McNeil. 1982. "The meaning and use of the area under a receiving operator characteristic (ROC) curve." *Radiology* 143:26–36.

Harrell, Frank. 2001. *Regression modeling strategies.* New York: Springer.

Hastie, Trevor, Robert Tibshirani, and Jerome Friedman. 2001. *The elements of statistical learning.* New York: Springer.

Hausman, Daniel, ed. 1984. *The philosophy of economics: An anthology.* 2nd ed. New York: Cambridge University Press.

Hendry, David. 1993. *Econometrics: Methodology.* Oxford: Blackwell.

Hinich, Melvin, and Munger, Michael. 1994. *Ideology and the theory of political choice.* Ann Arbor: University of Michigan Press.

Hinich, Melvin, and Munger, Michael. 1997. *Analytical politics.* New York: Cambridge University Press.

Hirsch, Abraham, and Neil de Marchi. 1984. "Methodology: A comment on Frazer and Boland." *The American Economic Review* 74:782–88.

Holland, John. 1975. *Adaptation in natural and artificial systems.* Ann Arbor: University of Michigan Press.

Holland, John, and John Miller. 1991. "Artificial adaptive agents in economic theory." *The American Economic Review* 81:365–70.

Hong, Lu, and Scott Page. 1998. "Diversity and optimality." Working Paper, Santa Fe Institute.

Isard, Walter, and Charles Anderton. 1999. "Survey of the peace economics literature: Recent key contributions and a comprehensive coverage up to 1992." *Peace Economics, Peace Science and Public Policy* 5:1–93.

Jacobson, Gary. 1996. "House elections in perspective." *Political Science Quarterly* 111:203–23.

Judd, Kenneth. 1998. *Numerical methods in economics.* Cambridge, MA: MIT University Press.

Kahneman, Daniel, and Amos Tversky. 1979. "Prospect theory: An analysis of decision under risk." *Econometrica* 47:263–92.

Katzner, Donald. 1970. *Static demand theory.* New York: Macmillan.

Kauffman, Stuart. 1993. *The origins of order.* New York: Oxford University Press.

Kauffman, Stuart, and Levin, S. 1987. "Towards a general theory of adaptive walks on rugged landscapes." *Journal of Theoretical Biology* 128: 11–45.

Kauffman, Stuart, and Weinberger, E. 1989. "The N-k model of rugged fitness landscapes and its application to maturation of the immune response." *Journal of Theoretical Biology* 141: 211.

Kennedy, Paul. 1987. *The rise and fall of the great powers.* New York: D.C. Heath and Company.

Keynes, John Maynard. 1939. "Professor Tinbergen's method," *Economic Journal* 49:558–68.

King, Gary, Robert Keohane, and Sidney Verba. 1994. *Designing social inquiry.* Princeton, NJ: Princeton University Press.

King, Gary, and Langche Zeng. 2001. "Improving forecasts of state failure." *World Politics* 53:623–658.

Kmenta, Jan. 1997. *Elements of Econometrics.* Ann Arbor: University of Michigan Press.

Kollman, Ken, John Miller, and Scott Page. 1992. "Adaptive parties in spatial elections." *American Political Science Review* 86:929–38.

Kollman, Ken, John Miller, and Scott Page. 1998. "Political parties and electoral landscapes." *British Journal of Political Science* 28:139–58.

Kramer, Gerald. 1973. "On a class of equilibrium conditions for majority rule." *Econometrica* 41:285–97.

Kreps, D., and R. Wilson. 1982. "Reputation and imperfect information." *Journal of Economic Theory* 27:233–79.

Krosnick, Jon, and Matthew Berent. 1993. "Comparisons of party identification and political preferences: The impact of survey question format." *American Journal of Political Science* 37:941–64.

Kuhn, Harold, and Sylvia Nasar, eds. 2002. *The essential John Nash.* Princeton, NJ: Princeton University Press.

Kuklinski, James, Daniel Metlay, and W. Kay. 1982. "Citizen knowledge and choices on the complex issue of nuclear energy." *American Journal of Political Science* 26:615–39.

Lacy, Dean. 2001a. "Nonseparable preferences, measurement error, and unstable survey responses." *Political Analysis* 9(2):1–21.

Lacy, Dean. 2001b. "A Theory of nonseparable preferences in survey responses." *American Journal of Political Science* 45(2):239–58.

Lacy, Dean, and Emerson Niou. 2000. "A Problem with Referenda." *Journal of Theoretical Politics* 12:5–31.

Lave, Charles, and James March. 1975. *An introduction to models in the social sciences*. New York: HarperCollins.

Lupia, Arthur, Matthew D. McCubbins, and Samuel L. Popkin. 2000. *Elements of reason*. New York: Cambridge University Press.

Lustick, Ian S. 1996. "History, historiography, and political science: multiple historical records and the problem of selection bias." *American Political Science Review* 90(3):605–18.

Lustick, Ian S. 1999. "Collective identity." *Journal of artificial societies and social simulation*. http://jasss.soc.surrey.ac.uk/3/1.

Lustick, Ian S., Dan Miodownik, and Roy J. Eidelson. 2004. "Secessionism in multicultural states: Does sharing power prevent or encourage it?" *American Political Science Review* 98(2):209–29.

Mansfield, Edward, and Jack Snyder. 1995. "Democratization and the danger of war." *International Security* 20:5–38.

Maoz, Zeev, and Bruce M. Russett. 1993. "Normative and structural causes of democratic peace." *American Political Science Review* 87(3):624–38.

Masters, Roger. 1988. "Happy warriors: Leaders' facial displays, viewers' emotions, and political support." *American Journal of Political Science* 32:345–68.

McKelvey, Richard, and Peter Ordeshook. 1985a. "Elections with limited information." *Journal of Economic Theory* 36:55–85.

McKelvey, Richard, and Peter Ordeshook. 1985b. "Retrospective voting and elections with limited information." *American Political Science Review*.

McKelvey, Richard. 1976. "General conditions for global intransitivities in formal voting models." *Econometrica* 47:1085–1111.

Miller, John. 1998. "Active Nonlinear Tests (ANTs) of complex simulations models." *Management Science* 44(6):820–30.

Miller, John, and Scott Page. In press. "The Standing Ovation Problem." *Complexity*.

Milyo, Jeffrey. 2000. "Logical deficiencies in spatial models: A constructive critique." *Public Choice* 105:273–89.

Mitchell, Melanie. 1996. *An introduction to genetic algorithms*. Cambridge, MA: MIT University Press.

Morrow, James. 1989. "A twist of truth: A reexamination of the effects of arms races on the occurrence of war." *Journal of Conflict Resolution* 33:500–29.

Mueller, Dennis. 1989. *Public Choice II*. New York: Cambridge University Press.

Mueller, Dennis. 2003. *Public choice III*. New York: Cambridge University Press.

Murphy, Allan H., and Robert L. Winkler. 1992. "Diagnostic verification of probability forecasts." *International Journal of Forecasting* 7:435–55.

Nagel, Ernest. 1961. *The structure of science*. New York: Harcourt, Brace & World, Inc.

Nagel, Ernest. 1963. "Assumptions in economic theory." *The American Economic Review* 53:211–19.

National Science Foundation. 2002. *Empirical implications of theoretical modeling report*. Political Science Program, Directorate For Social, Behavioral, and Economic Sciences.

Niou, Emerson, and Peter Ordeshook. 1991. "Realism vs. neoliberalism: A formulation." *American Journal of Political Science* 35:481–511.

Niou, Emerson, and Peter Ordeshook. 1999. "Return of the Luddites." *International Security* 24:84–96.

Novick, Peter. 1998. *That noble dream: The "objectivity question" and the American historical profession*. New York: Cambridge University Press.

Oneal, John R., and Bruce Russett. 1999. "Assessing the liberal peace with alternative specifications: Trade still reduces conflict." *Journal of Peace Research* 36:423–42.

Osborne, Martin, and Ariel Rubinstein. 1990. *Bargaining and market*. San Diego: Academic Press.

Page, Benjamin. 1977. "Elections and social choice: The state of the evidence." *American Journal of Political Science* 21:639–68.

Page, Scott. 1996. "Two measures of difficulty." *Economic Theory* 8: 321–346.

Page, Scott. n.d. "The p-alpha model of rugged policies." University of Michigan Working Paper.

Papadimitriou, Christos. 1994. *Computational complexity*. New York: Addison-Wesley.

Peltzman, Samuel. 1991. "Review of The Handbook of Industrial Organization." *Journal of Political Economy* 99:201–17.

Plott, Charles. 1967. "A notion of equilibrium and its possibility under majority rule." *American Economic Review* 57:787–806.

Powell, Robert. 1993. "Guns, butter, and anarchy." *American Political Science Review* 87:115–32.

Powell, Robert. 1999. "The modeling enterprise and security studies." *International Security* 24:97–106.

Primo, David, and Jeffrey Milyo. (2004). "Campaign finance and political efficacy: Evidence from the states." University of Rochester Working Paper.

Rabinowitz, George, and Stuart MacDonald. 1989. "A directional theory of issue voting." *American Political Science Review* 83:93–121.

Rabinowitz, George, and Stuart MacDonald. 1993. "Direction and uncertainty in a model of issue voting." *Journal of Theoretical Politics* 5:61–87.

Rabinowitz, George, Stuart MacDonald, and Ola Listhaug. 2004. "Simulating models of issue voting." UNC–Chapel Hill Working Paper.

Ramsay, Kristopher, and Curt Signorino. 2003. "A statistical model of the divide the dollar game." University of Rochester Working Paper.

Rousseau, David, Christopher Gelpi, Dan Reiter, and Paul Huth. 1996. "Assessing the dyadic nature of the democratic peace." *American Political Science Review* 90(3):512–44.

Russell, Stuart, and Peter Norvig. 1995. *Artificial intelligence: A modern approach.* New York: Prentice Hall.

Samuelson, Paul. 1963. "Discussion." *The American Economic Review* 53:227–36.

Schelling, Thomas. 1978. *Micromotives and macrobehavior.* New York: W.W. Norton and Co.

Schofield, Norman. 1984. "Social equilibrium and cycles on compact sets." *Journal of Economic Theory* 33:59–71.

Scott, Paul, and Maria Fasli. 2001. "Benford's Law: An empirical investigation and a novel explanation." *CSM Technical Report* 349.

Scruggs, Lyle, and James Allen. 2004. "Political Partisanship and Welfare State Reform in Advanced Industrial Societies." *American Journal of Political Science* 48:493–512.

Selten, R. 1978. "The Chain-Store Paradox." *Theory and Decision* 9:127–59.

Shapiro, Robert, and Lawrence Jacobs. 1989. "The relationship between public opinion and public policy: A review." In *Political Behavior Annual*, ed. Samuel Long. Boulder, CO: Westview Press.

Signorino, Curtis. 1999. "Strategic interaction and the statistical analysis of international conflict." *American Political Science Review* 93:279–97.

Simon, Herbert. 1963. "Discussion." *The American Economic Review* 53:227–36.

Snyder, Jack. 1991. *Myths of empire: Domestic politics and international ambition.* Ithaca, NY: Cornell University Press.

Spanos, Aris. 1986. *Statistical foundations of econometric modelling.* Cambridge: Cambridge University Press.

Stata Corporation. 2003. *Stata Reference Manual, Release 8.* College Station, TX: Stata Press.

Stokes, Donald. 1963. "Spatial Models of Party Competition." *American Political Science Review* 57:368–77.

Sundaram, Rangarajan. 1996. *A first course in optimization theory.* New York: Cambridge University Press.

Swets, John. 1988. "Measuring the accuracy of diagnostic systems." *Science* 240(4857):1285–94.

Taber, Charles, and Marco Steenbergen. 1995. "Computational experiments in electoral behavior." In *Political judgement: Structure and process*, eds. Milton Lodge and Kathleen McGraw. Ann Arbor: University of Michigan Press.

Taber, Charles, and Richard Timpone. 1996. "Computational modeling." *Sage University Paper Series on Quantitative Applications in the Social Sciences* 07–113.

Taylor, Howard, and Samuel Karlin 1998. *An introduction to stochastic modeling.* New York: Academic Press.

Toynbee, Arnold. 1946. *A study of history.* Oxford: Oxford University Press.

Turk, Matthew, and Alex Pentland. 1991. "Eigenfaces for recognition." *Journal of Cognitive Neuroscience* 3:71–86.

Turner, Henry. 1982. "A review of *The Collapse of the Weimar Republic: Political Economy and Crisis.*" *Political Science Quarterly* 97(4):739–41.

Von Neumann, John, and Oskar Morgenstern. 1944. *Theory of games and economic behavior.* Princeton, NJ: Princeton University Press.

Walt, Stephen. 1999a. "Rigor or rigor mortis?" *International Security* 23:5–48.

Walt, Stephen. 1999b. "A model disagreement." *International Security* 24:115–30.

Wassily, Leontief. 1993. "Can economics be reconstructed as an empirical science?" *American Journal of Agricultural Economics* 75:supplement.

Weinberger, E. 1988. "A more rigorous derivation of some results on rugged fitness landscapes." *Journal of Theoretical Biology* 134:125–29.

Weinberger, E. 1990. "Correlated and uncorrelated fitness landscapes and how to tell the difference." *Biological Cybernetics* 63:325–36.

Whitfield, John. 2003. "Speed of gravity and light equal." *Nature.* http://www.nature.com/nsu/030106/030106-8.html

The William and Mary Quarterly. 2002. *Forum: Historians and Guns.* 59:203–68.

Wilson, Rick, and Catherine Eckel. 1999. "Why fairness?: Facial expressions, evolutionary psychology and the emergence of fairness in simple bargaining games." Invited presentation, Departments of Political Science and Psychology, University of Oregon.

Yates, J. Frank. 1990. *Judgment and decision-making.* New York: Prentice Hall.

Young, Peyton. 2001. *Individual strategy and social structure: An evolutionary theory of institutions.* Princeton, NJ: Princeton University Press.

Zaller, John. 1992. *The nature and origins of mass opinion.* New York: Cambridge University Press.

Index

Abraham, David, xiv
Achen, Christopher, 10
ActiveState Komodo debugging system, 118
Adams, Henry, xiii
Adams, Henry Baxter, xiii
adaptive landscapes, 156
adjacency matrix
algorithms
  genetic, 115–130
  hill-climbing, 130
  machine, 85
alliance games
  agent identification within, 111
  backwards induction in, 121
  Build/Remove phase of, 103
  C (programming) language in component games and, 104, 126
  component utility functions within, 105–109
  as computational models, 102–109, 121
  encoding for, 122–126, 133
  ending condition of, 104
  Fall phase of, 103
  game theory usage for, 110, 126
  genetic algorithms, 130
  idiosyncratic utility functions for, 104, 122
  naïve parameter space in, 121, 125, 128
  normal form matrix in, 125, 126
  optimization theory in, 111, 129–133
  payoff matrix in, 124
  Spring phase of, 103
  stability in, 111
  strategies in, 121, 126
  undirected graphs in
American National Election Survey. *See* A-NES
American Political Science Review, xii, 2, 16, 56
A-NES (American National Election Survey), 147–152, 159
  abortion positions on, 148
  Democratic placement within, 148, 150
  Republican placement within, 148, 151
Arab-Israeli conflict, 58
Arming America: The Origins of a National Gun Culture (Bellesile), xv
artificial intelligence, 83
  Deep Blue as, 83
artificial test sets
  for out-of-sample testing, 55
assumption constraints
  conditions for, 26–27
  in instrumentalism, 24–30
  logical implications of, 29
  parameter space generation from, 29
  rival hypotheses as part of, 26
  technical, 28
  zero turnout in, 26
assumption of unidimensionality
  in conflict initiation model, 92
"assumption spaces"
  disturbance terms for, 29
  in game theory, 29
  IID values in, 29, 30

192   *Index*

"assumption spaces" (*cont.*)
 importance of, 29–30
 MLE generation in, 29
 OLS model and, 29

Beck, Nathaniel, 34
Bellesile, Michael, xv
binary dependent variables
 in mathematical models, 67
Binmore, Ken, 82
Borland Builder series, 119
brittle models, 79, 88–90
 encoding for, 110
 equivalence class theory within, 89
 IPD and, 88
 political economy computational models and, 97

C (programming language), 117
 adjacency matrix in
 in alliance games
 custom data structure in,
Car Talk, 22
Central European History, xiv
chess. *See* machine chess
chi-square test, 71
coding (computational models), 115–121
 Matlab and, 115
 Perl, 113
 programming languages and, 115–117
combinational game theory, 97–98
 computational political economy v., 98
 properties of, 97–98
component games, 107
 alliance games and, 104, 126
 associated utility functions in, 86, 123
 For Better or For Worse game, 106
 Friend and Enemies game, 105
 idiosyncratic utility functions and, 87
 in machine chess, 86–88
 Simple Diplomacy game, 102
 Tough Choices game, 106
computational models, 9
 alliance games as, 102–109
 creation of, 121–129
 defects in, 16–18
 encoding for, 115–121, 128–129
 examples of, 17
 formal theory v., 17
 game theory and, 33
 machine chess as, 98

 for political economy, 96–97
 rules as part of, 9
 state formation investigation as, 97
conflict initiation model
 assumption of unidimensionality as part of, 92
 asymmetric/incomplete information as part of, 93
 empirical estimations for, 89
 Nash equilibrium in, 95
 noncooperative game theory in, 95
 peace dividend as part of, 88
 player limitations as part of, 92
 relevant agent identification as part of, 91
 standard bargaining game in, 90
COW (Correlates of War) project, 56, 57
 alliance portfolio similarity as variable in, 59
 alliance status as variable in, 60
 coding rules within, 62
 contiguous landmass as variable in, 59
 democracy as variable in, 60
 dependent variables for, 57, 59
 distance as variable in, 59
 feature extraction in, 65
 high-risk dyads in, 58, 60
 independent variables for, 61, 66
 military capability asymmetry as variable in, 60
 neural networks in, 56
 out-of-sample sets in, 62
 overfitting in, 62
 peace years as variable for, 60, 61
 power status as variable in, 60
 ROC curves in, 69–70
creative modeling, 38
The Currency Game, 98–102
 bivariate relationships within, 42
 convergence periods within, 99
 DGP in, 41
 in empirical models, 39–43
 multiple regime shifts within, 99
 natural dependent variables in, 40
 path dependent process study in, 99
 penalty terms in, 43
 Perl Code for, 73–74, 77, 98, 100, 120
 Poission model and, 101
 polynomial models in, 42
 programming languages for, 118
 Python Code for, 140–143

"smoothing" in, 43
stochastic terms within, 41
"curse of dimensionality," xvii, xix, 35, 48, 177–178
complex model testing and, 79, 110, 178
mathematical models and, xix–xx
for non-parametric estimation, 47
out-of-sample testing and, 178
parameter spaces and, 43–48
parsimonious features for, 177
research design and, 176–177
in voter preferences, 145

data generating processes. *See* DGP
data mining, 36
data sources
observed, 35–36
Davis, Natalie Zemon, xiii
deductive models
game theory in, 12–13
"state of nature variables" as part of, 8
testing for, 73
Deep Blue, 83
as artificial intelligence, 83
game theory and, 84–86
partial extensive form value generation in, 85
DGP (data generating processes), 3, 23
for The Currency Game, 41
in empirical models, 35, 36
feature sets and, 65
for voter preferences, 145
Dickens, Charles, xvi
dispositive testing, 6
domain-specific knowledge, xviii–xix
in machine chess, 87
for parameter spaces, 51

Eddington, Sir Arthur, 32
EITM ("Empirical Implications of Theoretical Models"), 3
empirical models and, 10–11
goals of, 4
"Empirical Implications of Theoretical Models." *See* EITM
empirical models
for conflict initiation, 89
The Currency Game in, 39–43
DGP in, 35, 36
game structure within, 89–90

ITM and, 10–11
modeling choice as factor in, 43
observed data in, 35–36
overfitting for, 35–38
underfitting in, 39
encoding
for alliance games, 122–126, 133
for brittle models, 110
for computational models, 115–121, 128–129
preference complexity, 156–157
epistemology, 18–24. *See also* instrumentalism
equivalence class theory, 136
within brittle models, 89
for theoretic models, 73
estimable models, 36
Euclidean preferences, 146, 161, 174
one dimension, 161
salience issues for, 149
two dimensional, 162
unidimensional weak ordering, 163
explicit utility functions
in game theory, 80

face recognition, 52
as feature space utility, 51
false correlation
in instrumentalism, 24
feature extraction
explicit, 53
feature spaces and, 52
parameter spaces and, influence on, 51
feature sets, 65
DGP and, 65
feature spaces
data-driven methods for, 51, 52
face recognition and, 51
feature extraction and, 52
in machine chess, 87
in nonparametric estimation, 49–53
principal component analysis for, 52
"process tracing" as part of, 49
"uninformed search methods" for, 52
feed forward neural networks, 64
ROC curves and, 69
Feldman, Gerald, xiv
fitness functions, 131, 134
in genetic algorithms, 133–134
measures of, 134–135
OLS models and, 134

formal theory
  computational models v., 17
  empirical work v., 13
  feature selection as part of, 55
  logical consistency as part of, 13–15
  transparency of, 12

game theory, xvi, xix, 28
  ahistoric assumptions in, 81
  in alliance games, 110, 126
  applications for, 78–79
  "assumption spaces" in, 29
  combinational, 97–98
  computational models and, 33
  in deductive models, 12–13
  Deep Blue and, 84–86
  explicit utility functions in, 80
  games immune from, 83
  instantiation as part of, 80
  machine chess and, applications in, 83, 84, 85
  mathematics v., 5
  Nash equilibrium as part of, 80
  noncooperative, 95
  rationality v., 5, 73, 80–81
  solution concepts as part of, 80
Geertz, Clifford, 49
Gelpi, Christopher, 3, 34
genetic algorithms, 115–130
  crossover in, 131, 132
  fitness functions in, 133–134
  as stochastic method, 130
Graphical User Interface. See GUI
Grynaviski, Jeffrey, 3, 34
GUI (Graphical User Interface)
  in programming languages, 118

Harrod, Jennifer, 149
hill-climbing, 86
  as algorithm, 130
histograms, 63–64
  in MLE model, 63
  in OLS model, 63
  overfitting for, 64
historiography (as discipline), xiii–xv, 176
  alternative approaches to, xiii–xiv
  causality in, xiii
human rationality. See rationality

idiosyncratic utility functions
  in alliance games, 104, 122
  component games and, 87

in machine chess, 84
machine chess and, 126
OLS models and, 86
IID (independent identically distributed) observations, 8
  in "assumption spaces," 29, 30
"Improving Quantitative Studies of International Conflict: A Conjecture" (Beck/King/Zheng), 2
independent identically distributed observations. See IID
"informed search methods"
  "uninformed search methods" v., 52
instantiation
  in game theory, 80
  in programming languages, 124
instrumentalism, 19, 93
  assumption constraints as part of, 24–30
  debates over, 27–28
  false correlation in, 24
  theory development and, 20
IPD (iterated prisoner's dilemma), 30
  brittle models and, 88
  as toy model, xxi
issue space, 173
iterated prisoner's dilemma. See IPD

Java (programming language), 117

Kasparov, Gary, 83
King, Gary, 34
Kolmogorov-Smirnov test
  for ROC curves, 71
Kopeikin, Sergei, 32

logical completeness, 14
logical consistency
  in formal theory, 13–15
logit models
  neural networks v., 65
  ROC curves and, 69

Macchiavelli, Nicolas, xiii
machine algorithms, 85
machine chess, 87
  component games as part of, 86–88
  as computational model, 98
  Deep Blue and, 83
  domain-specific knowledge in, 87
  feature spaces as part of, 87

game theory applications for, 83, 84, 85
idiosyncratic utility functions in, 84, 126
Kasparov, Gary, and, 83
Markov Perfect Equilibrium, 94
mathematical models, 41, 42
  binary dependent variables in, 67
  computational, 9
  COW project as, 56
  "curse of dimensionality" and, xix–xx
  deductive, 8
  empirical, 10–11
  estimable, 36
  evaluation of, 66–72
  logical implications for, 30–32
  logit, 65
  polynomial, 42
  predictive thresholds for, 68
  reasonable loss function for, 66
  ROC curves for, 68
  theoretical, 36
  toy, xxi
mathematics, 5
  game theory v., 5
Matlab, 115
maximum likelihood estimator. *See* MLE
Microsoft Visual Studio, 119
Miller, John, 7
MLE (maximum likelihood estimator) model
  from "assumption spaces," 29
  histograms in, 63
model testing. *See* testing
Monte Carlo experiment, 37
  normals variable in, 37
Munger, Michael, 149

Nash equilibrium
  in conflict initiation model, 95
  in game theory, 80
Nash, John, 82
National Public Radio. *See* NPR
National Science Foundation. *See* NSF
neighborhood estimation
  in parameter spaces, 37, 48
neural networks
  in COW project, 56
  feed forward, 64
  logit models v., 65
N-K models, 157–159, 163
non-Gaussian variables, 66

nonparametric estimation, 45–46, 47–48
  "curse of dimensionality" for, 47
  feature spaces in, 49–53
normal form matrix, 125, 126
normals variable
  in Monte Carlo experiment, 37
Novick, Peter, xiii, xiv
NPR (National Public Radio), 22
NSF (National Science Foundation), 3
"Numerical Recipes" (Press), 117

OLS (ordinary least squares) model
  "assumption spaces" and, 29
  fitness functions and, 134
  histograms in, 63
  idiosyncratic utility functions and, 86
  overfitting and, 38
  parameter spaces and, 44, 46
optimization theory
  in alliance games, 111, 129–133
  genetic algorithms and, 131–132
  TSP and, 153–154
  voter preferences and, 153
ordinary least squares. *See* OLS
out-of-sample testing, 4, 53–56, 73–74, 77
  artificial test sets for, 55
  for COW project, 62
  "curse of dimensionality" and, 178
  model quality as factor for, 54–55
  time series models for, 53
  training sets for, 55
overfitting, 72
  in COW project, 62
  data mining and, 36
  for empirical models, 35–38
  for histograms, 64
  Monte Carlo experiment as, 37
  OLS models and, 38
  Stata function in, 37
  underfitting v., 40

Page, Scott, 7
P-Alpha Model of Rugged Policies, 157
parameter spaces, 40, 72
  from assumption constraints, 29
  "curse of dimensionality" and, 43–48
  domain-specific knowledge for, 51
  feature extraction's influence on, 51
  modeling choice for, 44
  naïve, 121, 125, 128

parameter spaces (*cont.*)
  neighborhood estimation in, 48
  OLS model and, 44, 46
  size of, 44
  for standard bargaining game, 95
payoff matrix, 124
Penrose, Roger, 49
Perl Code (programming language), 113, 118
  for computational models and, 113, 117, 120
  for The Currency Game, 73–74, 77, 98, 100, 120
Poisson model, 45, 101
  The Currency Game and, 101
  properties, 45
political economy computational models, 96–97
  brittle models and, 97
  combinational game theory v., 98
  Markov Perfect Equilibrium within, 94
Political Science Quarterly, xiv
polynomial models, 42
predictive thresholds
  for mathematical model comparisons, 68
preference complexity
  adaptive landscapes for, 156
  encoding, 156–157
  Euclidean preferences and, 161
  issue space in, 173
  measures of, 172
  N-K models for, 157–159
  P-Alpha Model of Rugged Policies, 157
  simple v. complex, 153
  variance in, 160
  for voters, 154–155
preference formation, xviii
Press, William, 117
principal component analysis
  for feature spaces, 52
"process tracing," 49
programming languages (coding), 115–117
  ActiveState Komodo debugging for, 118
  Borland Builder series and, 119
  C, 117
  conditional statements as part of, 116

for The Currency Game, 118
data structures as part of, 116
development environment for, 117–121
GUI as part of, 118
input/output variables in, 116
instantiation in, 124
Java, 117
loops in, 116
Microsoft Visual Studio and, 119
"Numerical Recipes" series, 117
Perl, 117, 118
Python, 117, 118, 120
startup costs for, 119
structs as part of, 124
user-defined functions in, 116
Python (programming language), 117, 118, 120
  for The Currency Game, 140–143

"Rationalist Explanations for War" (Fearon), 90
rationality, 5
  game theory v., 5, 73, 80–81
reasonable loss function
  for mathematical models, 66
  non-Gaussian variables, 66
research design
  "curse of dimensionality" and, 176–177
"resulting convergence"
The Return of Martin Guerre (Davis), xiii
ROC curves
  area under, 70
  chi-square test for, 71
  in COW project, 69–70
  error function of area in, 69
  feed forward neural networks, 69
  Kolmogorov-Smirnov test for, 71
  linear discriminants in, 69
  logit model derivations for, 69
  for mathematical model comparison, 68, 69
  for neural sets, 71

separable/nonseparable preferences, 145, 152, 157, 168
"smoothing," 43
social science theory. *See* formal theory
solution concepts
  in game theory, 80

standard bargaining game
  in conflict initiation model, 90
  parameter space for, 95
Stata function
  for histograms, 63–64
  in overfitting, 37
state formation investigation, 97. *See also*
    political economy computational
    models
statistical methodology
  in social sciences, xvi
stochastic terms
  in The Currency Game, 41
  for genetic algorithms, 130
structs, 124
"Swiss Army Chainsaw," 113. *See also*
    Perl Code

A Tale of Two Cities (Dickens), xvi
technical assumption constraints, 28
testing
  logical implications from, 32
*That Noble Dream: The "Objectivity
    Question" and the American
    Historical Profession* (Novick), xiii
theoretic models, 36. *See also* game
    theory
  equivalency class theory for, 73
theory development
  instrumentalism and, 20
  mapping as part of, 15
theory-driven feature extraction. *See*
    feature extraction

toy models (mathematical), xxi
  IPD, xxi
training sets
  for out-of-sample testing, 55
Traveling Salesman Problem. *See* TSP
TSP (Traveling Salesman Problem),
    153
  optimization theory and, 153–154
Turner, Henry, xiv

underfitting
  in empirical models, 39
  overfitting v., 40
unidimensionality. *See* assumption of
    unidimensionality
"uninformed search methods," 52
  "informed search methods" v., 52

voter preferences
  complexity in, 154–155
  computational results for, 165
  "curse of dimensionality" in, 145
  DGP assumptions for, 145
  optimization theory and, 153
  randomness in, 174
  separable/nonseparable assumptions,
    146, 147, 157
  spatial, 146
  subgroup variances in, 167, 169

zero turnout
  in assumption constraints, 26
Zheng, Langche, 34